8/98

Roger Buckley's book will be essential reading for all those interested in the remarkable history of Hong Kong since 1945 and in its unpredictable future after 1997. In a highly accessible and comprehensive account, the author considers how an obscure British colony on the South China coast emerged from wartime occupation under Imperial Japan to transform itself into an increasingly autonomous and prosperous city-state. He demonstrates how this transformation can only be understood within the context of the extraordinary political, economic and social changes which have taken place over the last fifty years. In conclusion, the author looks into the future of Hong Kong after its handover to China, and suggests how its resilient and resourceful peoples will face the challenges of the post-1997 era.

Hong Kong: the road to 1997

# Hong Kong: the road to 1997

Roger Buckley

*Professor of the History of International Relations*
*International Christian University, Tokyo*

CAMBRIDGE
UNIVERSITY PRESS

PUBLISHED BY THE PRESS SYNDICATE OF THE UNIVERSITY OF CAMBRIDGE
The Pitt Building, Trumpington Street, Cambridge CB2 1RP, United Kingdom

CAMBRIDGE UNIVERSITY PRESS
The Edinburgh Building, Cambridge, CB2 2RU, United Kingdom
40 West 20th Street, New York, NY 10011–4211, USA
10 Stamford Road, Oakleigh, Melbourne 3166, Australia

First published 1997

Printed in the United Kingdom at the University Press, Cambridge

Typeset in 10/12 Plantin

*A catalogue record for this book is available from the British Library*

*Library of Congress Cataloguing in Publication data*
Buckley, Roger, 1944–
Hong Kong: the road to 1997 / Roger Buckley.
 p.  cm.
Includes bibliographical references and index.
ISBN 0 521 47008 0 (hardback). – ISBN 0 521 46979 1 (pbk.)
1. Hong Kong – History.
2. Hong Kong - Politics and government.
3. Hong Kong – Relations – China.
4. China – Relations – Hong Kong.
I. Title.
DS796.H757B83   1997   951.25–dc21   96–37247   CIP

ISBN 0 521 47008 0 hardback
ISBN 0 521 46979 1 paperback

CE

To AB, JB and RFB

In the Far East, the dominant long-term questions concerned the future role and development of a political and military superpower, the People's Republic of China, and an economic superpower, Japan; though for Britain, it was the future of Hong Kong which had to take precedence over everything else.

(Margaret Thatcher, *The Downing Street Years*)

There are trying times ahead.

(Sir Sze-yuen Chung, 21 November 1995)

# Contents

# Preface

It was the standard arrival. Four weeks out from Southampton, the yellow-funnelled P&O liner docked beside the troopships on Kowloon side. The Hong Kong government, whose Marine Department my father was now joining, might have no idea where to house us but it certainly knew its own priorities. Less than twenty-four hours after disembarking, he was back on board *SS Canton* surveying the engine room.

For almost the next half century after going ashore in June 1950 our family would regard the territory as much more than merely a staging point in careers or schooling largely spent elsewhere. My first years there coincided almost to the day with the duration of the Korean war and indeed the first newspaper I can recall reading was the front page of the *South China Morning Post* announcing the downing of yet another MIG-15 in a dogfight over the Korean peninsula. The Hong Kong of my boyhood was a decidely colonial enclave where the few fortunate Europeans and a small number of wealthy Chinese residents existed in a milieu that was remote from the clerks in the counting houses and the absolute poverty of the squatters in their tin shacks on the steep slopes across from our flat in Argyle Street.

Hong Kong in the early 1950s was a highly stratified, grossly unequal and most nervous place thanks to its own past and the international situation. Yet it never thought to disguise or apologize for its behaviour. As a boy it was impossible not to observe the gulf between the colonial civil servants and their deferential Chinese staff; it was equally obvious that the numbers of professional mourners and the cacophony of noise associated with the very public funerals of rich Chinese were on a scale quite beyond the aspirations of the rest of the population. The lavish hospitality at the launch of vessels built in local yards and at the parties given by Chinese businessmen would also long stick in my memory as I faced the inedible gruel of boarding school in the years ahead.

Later, when I started to revisit Hong Kong on a more regular basis from Tokyo, I was immediately confronted with a different territory.

The first disappointment by the late 1970s was urban. My father's white-fronted office, our flat, and the elementary school my brothers and I had attended were all no more. The demolition gang had done for them as the Hong Kong waterfront endured successive reclamation schemes, while Kowloon's valleys were filled in and its hills sliced away for high-rise blocks. The cynics were right – by the time the government and local bodies thought to do anything by way of listing buildings it was all far too late and precious little was left to conserve. Perhaps the best (and worst) illustration of the vandalism was the extraordinary decision to retain only the tall clock tower of what for 60 years had been the terminus for the Kowloon–Canton railway at Tsim Sha Tsui. The tower now stands forlornly on the edge of the cultural centre's acreage of lavatorial tile.

There were major pluses, though, on the balance sheet. The first to assault one after landing at Kai Tak was the new prosperity, evidenced in the huge billboards, the clogged traffic of the streets and the fashionable clothes. Hong Kong was clearly no longer the society of the vast contrasts of my youth; it was richer, its environment was somewhat cleaner, its markets less pungent, and opportunities for educational and cultural pursuits considerably wider. I lectured briefly in the years that followed at various colleges and polytechnics that the governments of the 1950s would have regarded as both expensive and unnecessary. Hong Kong students by the 1980s had a curiosity about Japan and the Asian–Pacific region that my generation ignored by overconcentration on European and north American civilizations. Instead of being taught little or nothing of their own history, school children were now learning how Hong Kong had evolved and listening carefully to what their teachers and friends had to say about the territory's prospects.

Anxiety for the future of Hong Kong was central to public debate throughout my stays in the 1980s and 1990s. The very lengthy period between initial Sino–British negotiations and final reversion of the territory to China had the result, whether deliberately intended or not was unclear, of encouraging a sense of inevitability to the entire process. Most residents, who either could not or would not attempt to leave before 1997, appeared resigned to a fate that had been determined very largely by others in distant capitals. For all the neon, deserved affluence and new social mobility, it was sadly the case that Hong Kong would continue as a dependent territory. It was being shunted against its volition from one form of colonization to another; instead of working its passage to independence, Hong Kong would remain subject to the whim of others.

How Hong Kong picked itself up after the Pacific war, achieved undreamed of riches and finally took the uncomfortable road to 1997 must now be sketched in. What follows is based wherever possible on existing archival sources, supplemented by printed and oral material for the more recent years. Readers should be forewarned, however, that I have unashamedly exploited a host of secondary works in mixing my palette and that the final subjective portrait is intended to be neither a hymn of praise to Hong Kong nor a strident denunciation.

I have extracted from the many important specialist monographs on Hong Kong's political, legal, economic, social and urban scenes only a fraction of their valuable scholarship. In the process aggrieved authors will feel that I have oversimplified their arguments and taken on board merely the cargo that I was searching for. This is doubtless the case but, as anyone who attempts to lecture to university audiences knows only too well, if every statement is first qualified and then refined out of existence, the result is a fast emptying hall. My approach has been to select and synthesize from what is already a large amount of academic baggage in the hope that those curious but not necessarily overfamiliar with events in east Asia may have their appetites whetted.

The starting point for this study was the realization when first looking at documents in the Hong Kong Public Records Office (HKPRO) of how little had been published on the postwar era that utilizes its holdings. Some mornings in the old HKPRO on Murray Road I would find myself virtually the only student who had found his way through the neighbouring vehicular licensing department into the neglected trove. My few co-researchers appeared to be either local journalists on special assignments or overseas visitors hoping for copies of their marriage certificates and service records.

This survey is written for those who may wish to know how an obscure trading post has been transformed through the efforts of its government and peoples into an affluent city-state. It assumes no background knowledge and while quoting liberally from official sources limits academic paraphernalia to a short bibliography and some biographical and statistical data. It begins with an account of the reversion of Hong Kong to British rule in 1945 and concludes with a few estimates on what may or may not transpire after British rule ends in 1997. Historians, however, are neither astrologers nor turf correspondents and should not dabble too deeply into the unknown, if they wish to retain membership of their own trades union. My estimates will appear comic even by the time the manuscript is published.

The American author Washington Irving described in his rambles through early nineteenth-century London how during a languid summer day he stumbled into a 'spacious chamber' full to the ceiling of 'great cases of venerable books'. Here he spied 'many pale, cadaverous personages, poring among mouldy manuscripts' and silently devouring 'with famished voracity' the freshly ordered tomes. 'I had no longer a doubt that I had happened upon a body of magi, deeply engaged in the study of occult sciences', wrote Irving. Moments later the spell was broken when he discovered that he was merely in the reading room of the British Museum. Instead of 'mysterious personages', he now saw 'modern authors' at 'book manufactory'. Observing one flashy writer at work, Irving was intrigued to note how 'dipping into various books, fluttering over the leaves of manuscripts, taking a morsel out of another' the production process moved ahead. Irving about to be forcibly ejected for failing to possess a reader's ticket – correctly regarded the entire operation as the result of a 'pilfering disposition'.

My efforts employ precisely the same 'patchwork' scheme that torpedoed Irving's remaining illusions of authorship. Short of perhaps spending a lifetime working devotedly on the subject, there may be no alternative to the antics that Irving observed in the 1810s. If readers detect echoes of publishers' deadlines in passages they could be correct; the only defence that I can offer is that such conditions mirror their subject. Hong Kong has never forgotten for one moment the economic realities of existence. Its citizens have no difficulty in endorsing statements made in the 1990s by its highest officials that 'the business of Hong Kong is business'. This may explain why the writing of its own history remains very much a minority interest in the territory.

My approach is chronological, without slavishly following earlier conventions. Until recently Hong Kong's past was often defined in terms of the history of successive administrations; governor followed governor with each dignitary automatically earning a self-contained chapter, much as his knighthood came up with the rations. This imperial division certainly simplified the historian's job but, while it made sense in municipal affairs, it has obvious drawbacks when examining international issues, the often frantic economic activity and the social change of recent years.

Throughout the period from 1945 to 1965 I have cited official documents when telling my version of events. Thereafter I have necessarily had to resort to secondary sources and the 'Washington Irving' school of history. The drawbacks are obvious but the prospective reader may care to know that all authors examining British records operate under the same restrictive thirty-year rule. To attempt to make up for the paucity of official material, I have interviewed and corresponded with some of the participants at the heart of recent diplomatic and political developments. There can be no comprehensive history, however, until the more recent British and Hong Kong archives are opened up; access to Chinese records remains improbable.

Hong Kong's postwar half-century is *sui generis*. It begins with its reoccupation by Britain in the summer of 1945, after Japanese control had collapsed following the confusion of the final days of the Pacific war, and ends with the near-completion of arrangements for the territory's reversion to China. In an international era of decolonization and the often precarious emergence of new nation-states, Hong Kong by 1996 remains almost the only significant possession of a wounded European power. While new nations were emerging into poverty, Hong Kong has confounded the critics by first surviving and then hugely expanding as a politically uncertain, but increasingly confident economic giant.

It is a story of impressive material success, social stability and highly cautious constitutional change set against a backcloth of international tension. Hong Kong since 1945 has won very substantial gains on the economic front, while recognizing that its communal well-being has always to reckon with its far stronger neighbour to the north. China and Chinese power simply could not be wished away at any stage of Hong Kong's postwar history. There was never more than the slightest prospect of the territory fitting into the pattern of decolonization that emerged in the 1950s and 1960s for other Asian, African and Caribbean societies administered by London. The process of shedding the skin of colonialism and next experimenting with a usually brief period of self-government before escaping into the joys and pain of full independence was not for Hong Kong. It knew, though some of its peoples preferred to put this unpalatable reality to one side until rather late in the day, that Beijing was destined to be the final arbitrator of Hong Kong's fate. The limitations on Hong Kong's freedom to manoeuvre would certainly vary over the decades as successive governments in China proved either strong or weak but few, at least among those administering Hong Kong and directing its economy, shared many illusions that China would have the last word. The cliché deployed in a thousand editorials that Hong Kong was no more than a borrowed place existing on borrowed time has indeed been confirmed by lengthy Sino–British negotiations since the early 1980s. Hong Kong in the past half-century has moved from reoccupation and recolonization by Britain in 1945 to the often uncomfortable and unwelcome realization that by 1997 it will once again become Chinese territory, though entitled in theory to a fair degree of autonomy in important areas.

This survey traces Hong Kong's journey from its political and economic trials of 1945 to an equally uncertain future after 1997. It is written by an outsider for other outsiders who may be curious to know the outlines of the territory's development over the past half-century, and offers some estimates on what may prove to be Hong Kong's fate in the period after its reversion to China in the summer of 1997.

The popular image of Hong Kong shared by so many in the West today is a ragbag of news on the countdown to 1997 and often anachronistic ideas of the territory as a combined shoppers' paradise and unmitigated sweat shop. Additional snippets of information might encompass the popularity of horse racing, the attractions of Wanchai and the ready availability of unlicensed computer software. Such perceptions, however, certainly do less than adequate justice to a city-state whose *per capita* GDP now exceeds that of Britain, possesses probably the highest ranking in the world for economic freedom and enjoys an impressive degree of social stability.

*Hong Kong: the road to 1997* may perhaps contribute to modifying some existing overseas' opinions. It tackles in the process three huge questions: What are the main features of Hong Kong's remarkable contemporary history? How can these changes be explained? And, lastly, where does Hong Kong go next? In these overambitious tasks I have selected only what appear to me to be the salient events, while neglecting entire topics that have been the subject of individual monographs. The culling has been brutal. I doubt if the general reader will wish to plough through the minutiae of protracted Sino–British diplomacy or requires a constituency-by-constituency analysis of the September 1995 Legislative Council (LegCo) elections, but to cover my bets a short bibliography is provided for those requiring more depth.

I have had in mind two groups of individuals as the potential audience for this survey. First, students at my own university who are required to take courses in contemporary politics, and secondly European business and management trainees who regularly visit Asia from Paris to gain an understanding of the region's recent accomplishments. What follows is intended to provide approximate explanations to their questions. It ought perhaps to be at least part of the historian's job to face the barbs of his colleagues and attempt to exploit the work of specialists for this wider audience. The risks are high but the opportunity to address those who will rarely be members of an advanced seminar has its own challenges and attractions. The survey is very largely a 'top down' account of events espied from Government House and Whitehall. It does not pretend to be a chronicle of the ragged hawkers of my boyhood or the streetsleepers of the 1990s; others will doubtless write what would be the reverse of this administrative history in due course.

The only consolation that may perhaps be offered from this examination of the postwar era is a reminder that while portions of the official record show less self-confidence than many observers may have imagined, Hong Kong has the satisfaction of knowing that its achievements were almost invariably made in the face of a host of very considerable difficulties. The scale of the domestic and external hurdles that were eventually overcome is testimony to the territory's resilience. Many, though not of course, all, crises were faced and met successfully. Any comparison between the supine, newly liberated colony of August 1945 and the affluent but anxious city-state of August 1995 can only be to the credit of the intervening years. Much has gone right. It is, however, apparent from government and private records that this comprehensive improvement in the condition of Hong Kong was neither automatic nor easy. Government House could panic, business houses could go under. Little surely was foreordained and yet the Hong Kong that takes pride in its Victorian ethos is entitled to refer to its successes in terms of that now largely discredited yardstick of the last century – progress.

*Mitaka, January 1996*

# Acknowledgements

I am indebted to my employers, International Christian University, for the grant of sabbatical leave and to the Centre of Asian Studies of the University of Hong Kong for the award of an honorary research fellowship. This study would have been quite impossible but for their generous assistance. I must also thank the staffs of the Public Record Office at Kew, the Hong Kong Public Records Office, the Hong Kong Government Office in London, the Hong Kong Economic and Trade Office in Tokyo, Rhodes House Library (Oxford), the School of Oriental and African Studies (London), the London School of Economics, the library of Hong Kong University and the librarian of International Christian University for permitting the inspection of primary and secondary sources.

Numerous individuals have also contributed greatly to enlarging my understanding of postwar Hong Kong. I am grateful to Dr Alan Birch, Sir Jack Cater, Sir Hugh Cortazzi, Lord Henniker, Ms Coonoor Kripalani-Thadani, Mr David H. T. Lan, Dr Thomas Stanley, Mr Roy Tang, Dr Steve Yui-Sang Tsang, Mr John Walden and Mr Stuart Wolfendale for their reminiscences and views. A number of past and present members of the Hong Kong government and the territory's business houses also corresponded and spoke to me; since their opinions were elicited under Chatham House rules of confidentiality, I can only thank them publicly in this anonymous manner.

The opportunity to research in Hong Kong was greatly aided by Mr Gregory Carley's frequent loan of his flat with the best views of the territory. I must also thank my brothers, John and Richard, for providing me with detailed information on corporate relocations to Bermuda and for showing me Hong Kong, at the risk of courts martial, by land, sea and air.

The text was kindly retyped at speed by my teaching assistant Ms Mikako Yusa; while Ms Marigold Acland and her readers at Cambridge University Press transformed the draft into something more professional. None of the individuals or institutions listed above is responsible for what follows; all errors, omissions and dubious opinions go down on my charge sheet.

# Glossary

| | |
|---|---|
| APEC | Asia–Pacific Economic Cooperation Forum |
| CCP | Chinese Communist Party |
| DAB | Democratic Alliance for the Betterment of Hong Kong |
| ExCo | Executive Council |
| HKPRO | Hong Kong Public Records Office |
| ICAC | Independent Commission Against Corruption |
| KMT | Kuomintang |
| LegCo | Legislative Council |
| MFN | most-favoured-nation |
| NSC | National Security Council |
| OMELCO | Office of the (non-governmental) members of the Executive and Legislative Councils |
| PLA | People's Liberation Army |
| PRC | People's Republic of China |
| SAR | Special Administrative Region of Hong Kong |
| SEZ | Special Economic Zone |
| UNHCR | United Nations High Commissioner for Refugees |
| WTO | World Trade Organization |

*Note*:
The words 'Hong Kong', 'territory' and 'colony' are used interchangeably in the text. When citing nineteenth- and early twentieth-century material the traditional transliteration has been used; thus 'Canton' for what is now normally termed Guangzhou and 'Kwangtung' for the southern province of Guangdong. In the case of names of Hong Kong Chinese, I have attempted to adopt the form that the holders themselves prefer to use.

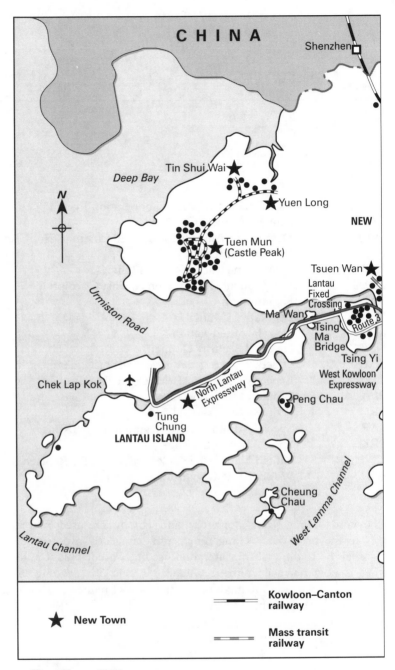

Hong Kong, 1997
Sources: Adapted from material prepared by the Hong Kong
government; *Financial Times*, 4 May 1993.

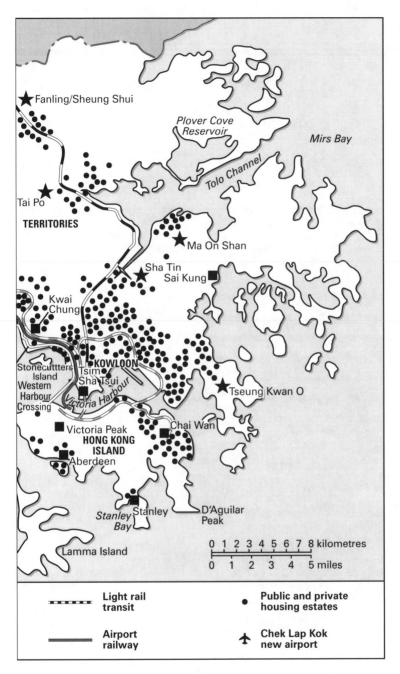

Fanling/Sheung Shui

Plover Cove
Reservoir

Mirs Bay

Tolo Channel

Tai Po

TERRITORIES

Ma On Shan

Sha Tin
Sai Kung

Kwai
Chung

Stonecuttters
Island
Western
Harbour
Crossing

KOWLOON
Tsim
Sha Tsui

Victoria Harbour

Tseung Kwan O

Victoria Peak

Chai Wan

HONG KONG
ISLAND

Aberdeen

Stanley
Bay

Stanley

D'Aguilar
Peak

Lamma Island

0 1 2 3 4 5 6 7 8 kilometres

0 1 2 3 4 5 miles

Light rail
transit

Airport
railway

Public and private
housing estates

Chek Lap Kok
new airport

# Introduction: prewar colony

From its inception Hong Kong has existed on trade, exchange and the provision of financial services. Its Chinese, European and Indian peoples have had little in common beyond a shared respect for making money. Fortune-seekers have been attracted to the territory from the start in the expectation that individual effort might be rewarded and that the authorities would not look too closely at the books. The ethos is unapologetically materialistic. The colony exists to the present on clear mid-Victorian lines. The *North-China Herald*'s economic editor's blunt explanation to his readers in 1864 that the Hongkong and Shanghai Bank's sole 'objective' was 'to make money for the public by making money out of the public' applied throughout the colony. Profit was king and the overscrupulous might find it wiser to take themselves and their consciences to safer havens. The skyline of central Hong Kong in 1896 and 1996 is indicative of where the territory's heart has long been located. It was and remains a business city. It is banks and high-rise offices rather than church spires and towers that crowd the waterfront. The parallel is with the secularism of Tokyo and Singapore rather than the Christianity of Manila and Seoul. Hong Kong's small Anglican cathedral is dwarfed by skyscrapers and overhead road systems.

It was British traders rather than missionaries or marines who invented Hong Kong. A small number of expatriate merchants on the China coast were responsible in the early 1840s for persuading the British government to secure a permanent, safe territorial base close to the Chinese mainland where they would no longer be subject to the irksome restraints on trade that had for so long angered commercial interests. The gaining of the island of Hong Kong was the culmination of a lengthy campaign by British merchants, who had insisted on far greater trading rights than the Chinese authorities had been prepared to grant. The motives of London can hardly be in doubt. Lord Stanley, secretary of state for war and the colonies, told Governor Pottinger in June 1848 that the new Asian possession was founded 'not with a view to colonization, but for diplomatic, commercial and military purposes'. Of

1

this trinity, few questioned that the birth of Hong Kong was over-whelmingly ascribable to economic factors. British merchants wanted unhampered access to the China market and saw in the gaining of Hong Kong the opportunity to best regulate their own affairs and to take aim at China's treasury, largely through the highly lucrative sale of Indian-grown opium.

After tangled, at times farcical, naval and diplomatic action, the Chinese government reluctantly agreed to concede both territorial and commercial rights to Britain, through first the Convention of Chuenpi in January 1841 and then the Treaty of Nanking on 29 August 1842. The process was highly complicated, with both the British and Chinese governments disavowing the Chuenpi convention, though this did not prevent the British occupation of Hong Kong on 26 January 1841. The taking of Hong Kong was the result of firm pressure by British merchant opinion backed up by extensive parliamentary lobbying. The formidable influence of British traders in pressing successive governments in London to acquire a permanent toe-hold off the South China coast was seen from the inception of the new colony. The first stone structure to be erected in Hong Kong was the Jardine Matheson godown. By the end of the 1840s members of the two Scottish trading families would rejoice to learn that 'the nicest houses here' belonged not to the governor or general but to Jardines. It was 'their house' that 'is separate from the others and is situated on a point which overlooks the greater part of the Town, the Rooms here are much larger than in most houses'.

Hong Kong for its first stumbling decades was a raw frontier post uncomfortably positioned between East and West. It was peopled by more than its fair share of racketeers, gamblers, pimps, grog shop-owners, and footloose ex-peasants. Life was nasty, dangerous and confused among Hong Kong's shifting communities. Its merchants, however, felt the place belonged to them as they had pressed the British government to acquire the almost uninhabited small island and they alone had the energy and resources to develop the settlement. Certainly the traders acted as if Hong Kong existed solely for their benefit, prompting them both to publicly denounce officialdom and disparage the Chinese. Yet the early years were difficult, particularly after the initial gold rush flavour had dissolved. The hopes for Hong Kong serving as the focus for vast, almost limitless, trade with southern China and beyond were quickly dashed. Merchants who had salivated over the prospects that the opening of the five treaty ports under the Nanking treaty would bring soon discovered that the truth was more prosaic. The new colony did survive, however, and gradually expanded both to confirm the wisdom of its establishment and to blow away the more inflated froth of its early promoters. It also expanded geographically. The narrow Kowloon peninsula across from Hong Kong island was acquired in 1860 through the Treaty of Peking and the New Territories were incorporated under a 99-year lease in 1898. This added 355 square miles to the area of the colony and required new methods of rural administration for the existing 80,000 Chinese inhabitants.

Hong Kong by the early twentieth century served as an important regional hub for trade between southern China, southeast Asia and across the Pacific to the west coast of the United States. It had periods of considerable prosperity and equally prolonged years of economic recession. The colony certainly grew as an entrepôt but its fate appeared to be dependent on political and economic forces largely beyond its control. It could profit from the trade cycles; it could also gain from the waves of political and social turmoil in China. What it clearly could not do was to stake any viable claim to be in control of its own destiny. Outside forces were invariably stronger than anything the colony could devise; Hong Kong had, in the manner of the proverbial bamboo, to bend with the wind to survive.

Yet some pretence had to be made to disguise military vulnerability. Governor Bowen during the war scare of 1884 that was prompted by the French advance into Indo–China knew only too well that his territory was virtually defenceless. He had warned his masters in the Colonial Office that

if four or five thousand soldiers of any Foreign power were landed at the back of this island they could, of course, march into town (a distance of only four miles) without effective opposition from our small garrison.

Improvements were ordered. The physical presence of the British garrison offered at least some reassurance to residents that the territory would attempt to avoid involvement in regional disputes and that Hong Kong's trade might be protected from pirates or worse through the patrols of its ships on the China station.

The military, however, would always have its share of critics. There were two issues that had their origins in the days of the early encampments. The first sore point was the continued occupation of much commercially attractive land in the heart of Hong Kong by the army and the second was the size of the colony's financial contribution required by London for the upkeep of the garrison.

Over the question of the retention of valuable space in a land-hungry colony the military came off best. Large chunks of central Hong Kong were reserved in the first years for barracks, parade grounds and naval establishments. Movement from the centre was generally resisted by commanding officers, even when alternative sites had been found and the inconvenience to the public of having naval and military accommodation obstructing harbour reclamation schemes readily apparent. The result may have added little to the prestige of the government as complaints continued over the tardiness of rehousing troops and the rationale for a naval dockyard in the middle of town.

Attempts from the 1880s onwards to convert Hong Kong into a colonial fortress in the far east met with predictable opposition from the community's ratepayers. The familiar argument that the British exchequer should pay for the privilege of strengthening the coastal defences of Hong Kong and for the training of local militiamen underlined the orthodox mentality of its businessmen. On the merchants' side, however, it has to be said that the drastic depreciation of the Hong Kong dollar in the late nineteenth century caused through the fall in the value of silver (the metallic standard on the China coast) made the sterling costs for the garrison considerably higher when remitted to London.

Hong Kong's closest and most important linkage was to Canton and its Kwangtung hinterland. It had long been the case, as Governor May remarked in 1912, that the territory was commercially so close to Canton that 'from that aspect the two cities may be considered to be one'. Hong Kong clearly only existed in its first century to serve as the clearing house between what Secretary of State for the Colonies Labouchere in 1856 saw 'as subsidiary to the intercourse between the Chinese and British Empires'. Attention to trade with its neighbour was paramount. Hong Kong's beginnings set the pattern for a century of steady, if generally unspectacular, development.

From the start the aspirations of British merchants frequently clashed with the intentions of the civil and military governments of Hong Kong. What the traders wanted was not necessarily judged to be to the best advantage of the colony. Early governors, almost without exception, were unpopular with the European merchants. Quarrels were commonplace in such a small, insecure, and unhealthy colony. The initial differences centred on the raising of revenue to contribute to the cost of running the new colony. In order that Hong Kong could gradually conform to the colonial standard of attempting to make all territories self-sufficient, it was imperative that the governors devise effective financial measures. This was easier said than done. The merchants were tight-fisted, argumentative and skilled at getting their own way. Instituting a rudimentary system of law and order was for years expensive and feeble rather than cheap and effective, since no one wanted to pay for a competent police force and prison service and the attempts at piecemeal measures failed. Merchant interests seemingly had an answer to each and every scheme put to entice them to contribute to the upkeep of Hong Kong. Government in London was left in little doubt of merchant opinion through memorials that pulled no punches as to what was seen as a farrago of iniquitous rates, government monopolies and unfair levies. Nothing would alter their view that they alone were being asked to finance what was seen by the traders to be the responsibility of the British government and its domestic exchequer.

Chief among initial merchant grievances was the claim that they had moved from Macao to Hong Kong at great expense only to be hoodwinked by Governor Davis over land lease terms. The truth was that many of the original lot purchasers were more intent on speculation than establishing a permanent residence and that without some firm government direction over land the colony would have had little hope of developing beyond its decidedly humble and anarchic beginnings. For years Hong Kong was most unsafe after dark with deserting sailors, Triad gangs and remittance men brazenly ignoring curfews and quite undeterred by the occasional police patrol. In 1847 a parliamentary Select Committee spoke of the colony's 'vagabond and piratical population', yet any prospect of containing the brawls and encouraging a degree of racial tolerance would require the loosening of the commercial houses' purse-strings.

By feuding with successive governors, the merchants demonstrated that there was practically no limit to the narrowness of their vision. Their case was simple: the British parliament and British taxpayer ought to fund the cost of protecting and developing Hong Kong, since it was British trade along the entire China coast that benefited from the colony. Hong Kong served British interests throughout the region and should be funded by Britain rather than the few local merchant firms who happened to be based in the colony. It was, they long maintained, an unfair burden and one made doubly so because the traders had no role in the government of their island. The right to representation in municipal government became the next on their list of rallying cries. It is small wonder that Sir John Davis wrote to Lord Stanley in November 1844 that it was 'much easier to govern the twenty thousand Chinese inhabitants of this Colony, than the few hundreds of English'. Governor Davis' Chinese residents had far fewer hopes of securing relief from local taxation and were hopelessly lost when being tried for alleged offences under English law. The penal code for Chinese residents in the early years of the colony was little short of barbaric; branding and flogging were commonplace measures used as unsuccessful deterrents to curb the crime wave. Efforts to establish a tolerable legal system for Hong Kong were to take many years. The process was hardly helped in the colony's infancy by an extraordinary quarrel between Governor Davis and his Chief Justice that included the charge of drunkenness. The ensuing fracas led to the resignation of the aloof Davis, who left the colony in May 1848 without any of the conventional speeches and congratulatory dinners that officialdom usually endures before departure.

No doubt part of the merchants' cantankerous behaviour towards government can be explained through their general disappointment over the difficulties that the colony experienced in its first years. The sense of frustration that Hong Kong would not immediately provide the kind of returns that many had anticipated all too easily boiled over when faced with demands for greater financial contributions and less irresponsible behaviour. Hong Kong's inability to live up to its El Dorado image left a great number of its trading prospectors deeply wounded. Government House and its occupant served as a convenient symbol of what had gone wrong once the euphoria dissolved. Early photographs of clippers and opium ships nestling next to the newly constructed stone buildings of the waterfront can prove deceptive. The colony did indeed survive and work itself up to something of importance in east Asia but it certainly did not happen overnight. The goldrush failed. Inflated expectations and the greater successes of Shanghai and Singapore landed a goodly number of disgruntled China hands in debt.

Shanghai was Hong Kong's great rival. The two cities both survived by living off their wits and by offering havens of stability as China was convulsed for a century by foreign invasions, civil wars and painful revolution. Shanghai emerged slowly but gradually overtook Hong Kong by the first decades of the twentieth century and proudly boasted that not only was it more prosperous but that it had no time for the restrictive social distinctions of prewar Hong Kong. Hong Kong certainly had little to compare with the skyscrapers on Shanghai's bund or its cosmopolitan population where White Russians and Japanese formed the largest non-Chinese elements. Shanghai, exploiting its bizarre status as an international settlement seemingly in a limbo between a fully-fledged colony and a part of China proper, claimed to run its own affairs in a more representative manner than Hong Kong. It also had the advantage of a fierce, unforgiving, industrial sector, whose cotton mills were a byword for exploitation.

It is ironic that the real winners from the gradual growth of Hong Kong were not the sponsoring European merchants but their Chinese counterparts. Governor Hennessy stated in 1881 that all but one of the eighteen ratepayers then possessing property assessed at over HK$1,000 per quarter were Chinese – the only British firm in the race was Jardine Matheson. This came about for reasons that were very largely beyond the control of the British authorities and merchant houses, assuming that a degree of international stability in the Asian–Pacific region in general and within Hong Kong in particular could be maintained by the imperial power and its coopted clients.

Western attention on the successes the likes of Jardines and the Hongkong and Shanghai Bank has tended to ignore the accomplishments of Chinese firms that also won out in the scramble to acquire new wealth. From the outset the bulk of the population of Hong Kong was Chinese. These new immigrants brought with them sufficient experience, valuable regional contacts and the necessary finance for a fortunate minority to prosper under British civil and military protection. Once the first visible evidence of substantial merchant success was seen in the parading of mistresses, the building of walled mansions, and through munificent contributions to Chinese hospitals and temples, the incentive was there to spur others on to emulate the likes of the Li Sing family and Ko Man Wah.

The early Chinese millionaires had been quick to spy out the commercial advantages afforded by Hong Kong as a useful base from which to serve southeast Asia and the Pacific rim. The colony might have been the creation of British and Parsee merchants but by the turn of the century it was unquestionably dominated by Chinese traders and financiers. It was precisely for this reason that the Colonial Office in London feared that the granting of more than highly limited measures of self-government would lead inexorably to Chinese rule in any system based on rateable property.

The conundrum facing successive governors of Hong Kong was how to run a colony as cheaply as possibly in the interests of rival merchant groupings, who were frequently united only in wanting limited government, while ensuring that understandable dissent from the highly disadvantaged bulk of the working population was contained within manageable channels. The general solution to the Hong Kong problem in its first century from 1841 to 1941 was to pay heed to the financial constraints that money-pinching businessmen of all races welcomed and to avoid granting any substantial measures of home rule that might impair the authority of the civil service to administer the colony as it saw fit. To minimize opposition from Chinese merchant houses and professional organizations, the Hong Kong government gradually instituted both public honours and posts for distinguished leaders of the Chinese communities and made considerable efforts in private to maintain lines of communication with senior Chinese businessmen. At glacial speed the European and Chinese elites began to work at something approaching accord.

The dilemma that many of the local Chinese leaders had to confront during the periodic outbursts of Chinese nationalism directed against British behaviour in interwar China illustrates this commonality of interests. The boycott of British goods and British-owned tram and ferry services in 1925–6 was the most serious of a number of political disputes that left the Chinese merchants caught between support for their own nation and the wish to quickly end disruptions that severely damaged their businesses in Hong Kong. Attempts to act as mediators between the British colonial authorities and Chinese godown coolies and transport workers underlined the awkward unspoken reality that the merchant elite and the Hong Kong government needed each other, particularly during periods of danger.

Hong Kong on the eve of the Second World War presented a dismal advertisement for European colonialism. The sad state of the colony can be glimpsed from the government's own reportage where portions of the statistical information make for damning reading. The authorities admitted that in the case of infant mortality the rate among young Chinese was nearly six times the corresponding rate among non-Chinese infants. Equally, the same report for 1939 noted how

an overcrowded labour market reducing possible earnings, taken in conjunction with increased rents and a general rise in the cost of living amounting to about 45 percent since the outbreak of the European War, has had an adverse effect on the general standard of nutrition.

Average wages were pitifully small (day labourers could expect a maximum of 80 cents a day) and made the existence of most Chinese perilous in the extreme. The only weak defence of Hong Kong's standing by 1941 was that conditions in southern China were worse, thanks to the Japanese advance and the depreciation of the currency. The influx of refugees from the region into Hong Kong proved, as in the past, that the colony acted as a barometer for conditions in its hinterland. Yet thousands of these newly arrived immigrants from China would shortly be leaving with equal speed in the next few years as the expectation that Imperial Japan might be deterred from attacking Hong Kong was seen to be another of the many regional illusions shared by the West in the Pacific.

Sino–Japanese hostilities, as the Hong Kong government was obliged to admit, were damaging the territory long before the eventual military invasion of December 1941. Trade was off, the influx of refugees brought epidemics and panic buying of scarce commodities, and the government ran budgetary deficits in both 1938 and 1939. Among its domestic problems that were briefly reported but evident to all residents was the practice of dumping in the streets those who had died from infectious diseases and the 'enormous illicit traffic in opium and heroin pills', which the government conceded amounted to 'wholesale addiction'. Since it alone sold opium through licensed shops at a profit, the authorities could do little but look the other way when reviewing the anti-social results of its drug monopoly.

Hong Kong in December 1941 was a decidedly unequal, intolerant territory. Opportunities to acquire wealth and thereby display its fruits through conspicuous consumption clearly still existed and conditions in southern China were sufficiently dire to encourage yet more migrants to take their chance, but for the overwhelming majority of Hong Kong's residents there was a great deal of pain and very limited pleasure. Some of the issues facing the territory would have required an imaginative political and financial response that would not be forthcoming for at least another generation, yet it is striking to see how little was even attempted. The University of Hong Kong only had 507 regular students in 1939, while at the bottom of the pile many received only the most rudimentary of primary education before being thrown onto a highly competitive labour market. The fact in 1939 that serious overcrowding of the hospitals in Hong Kong continued throughout the year and that the death toll from beri-beri, cholera and dysentery fever was so high suggests that the authorities were on occasion virtually powerless to do much beyond containing some of the worst issues of public health and hygiene. No one in government was able to offer anything but a casual guess even as to the size of the colony's population. Waves of refugees made the tasks of the authorities enormously difficult but official statements to the effect that it was 'impossible to exercise effective control over emigration and immigration' surely worsened the situation. Hong Kong by 1941 had become the victim of its history. Its past determination to act both as a free port and a free territory no longer provided the regional advantages of the past.

Hong Kong was ill-prepared to face what was to be the greatest challenge in its entire history. The colony had existed for a century without inspiring any particular loyalties among its peoples. The European administrative, mercantile and military elements had traditionally been birds of passage. Their numbers were extraordinary few when compared with Chinese residents – in 1939 there were only 566 registered non-Chinese births against a Chinese total of 46,675 and the government statisticians knew that the actual figure of Chinese births was itself greatly understated. Hong Kong certainly had some Chinese, Anglo–Chinese, Parsee, Indian and Portuguese families who could proudly trace their ancestry back to the beginnings of the colony but such historical links to Hong Kong were rare. Most residents had been born elsewhere and regarded the colony as no more than a transitory home. British officials and Chinese rickshaw-pullers shared a common interest in earning what they could from the place and then debunking. Dreams of retirement invariably centred on getting away from the overcrowded, humid colony; most British bureaucrats and bankers had no intention of spending more than a portion of their careers in Hong Kong. Equally those immigrants from southern China who survived the pace and were fortunate enough to be able to save something from their paltry wages longed to return to their ancestors' village in Kwangtung or up the coast to Swatow and Amoy. Not many succeeded but the lure of Hong Kong to the hungry and ambitious alike ensured that the colony was the main beneficiary in this intensely competitive maelstrom.

Prewar Hong Kong had not moved far from the political and economic ideology of its Victorian youth. The government's efforts to recognize and then undertake a wider round of responsibilities was still very much in its infancy in 1941. The influx of perhaps 650,000 immigrants from southern China in the late 1930s had almost over-whelmed its rudimentary public services without, however, spurring the administration forward into fashioning a more modern bureaucracy. The limits to its creativity are perhaps best typified by the establishment of the Urban Council in 1935. Yet even this body, concerned as it was with the provision of elementary sanitation, rat-catching and public bath-houses, possessed only advisory powers and had only the most superficial of suffrages for an elected minority of its members. The brief report of the chairman of the Urban Council for 1939 – the last year before the Japanese occupation for which detailed government material is available – offers depressing reading. Hong Kong clearly was far from ready to make any but token attempts to cope with its expanding population and the grim urban environment in which the great majority of its residents had to make a living. Factory legislation and town planning were only in their infancy in the late 1930s; the colony clearly remained sceptical of introducing major reforms that would require developing a greatly expanded revenue base drawn from its more affluent sector.

This weak sense of civic awareness would continue through the critical days of the Japanese invasion and the long years of occupation and postwar reconstruction. Hong Kong was indeed slow to accept that its successful elements of whatever racial background had a responsibility to assist those less fortunate than themselves through social services requiring substantial public expenditure. Certainly there were long-established philanthropic ventures to which many leaders of Chinese groups took pride in making significant financial contributions, but the scale of the problems and the demographic realities could hardly be met by such charities alone. Only when the administration gave a belated lead would the territory gradually shift its attitudes and slowly accept that uncoordinated ad hoc mixtures of public and private efforts were hardly a substitute for government initiatives framed around professional staff enjoying adequate compensation and equipped to carry through long-term programmes. Medical services, public education, and social welfare schemes can only be described as rudimentary before the 1960s and undoubtedly reflect the community's preference for individual, family and clan efforts rather than comprehensive arrangements of incalculable cost and consequence. It went against the Hong Kong grain to reckon with programmes that might eventually become universal, particularly when the British bureaucracy efficiently took care of its own and the more prosperous Chinese families also made their private arrangements.

The lack of significant communal loyalties to Hong Kong during its first century, and indeed beyond, was hardly ameliorated by the system of government that existed up to 1941. The colony was run by a British-appointed governor, who supervised an administration and acted in cooperation with hand-picked Executive and Legislative Councils. The system was in reality somewhat more flexible and had necessarily to take into account the views of leading European and Chinese individuals and interests, but the formal structure permitted the accretion of a great range of powers in the hands of a very few individuals, who were rarely answerable to the wider community. It was a political system that had worked unchallenged in the prewar years, although newspapers in the aftermath of the Pacific War would speak scathingly of its inadequacies, not least because it collapsed during its most testing days. Events of December 1941 revealed only too starkly how weak the *ancien régime* had become. It failed to serve as a focus for Chinese sympathies when the enemy was at the gate and neither its civilian nor military branches were able to organize effective resistance to Imperial Japan.

Partly because of financial constraints during the 1930s that were the consequence of the colony's declining trade position, the Hong Kong government had rarely provided more than a limited range of public services to its residents. Equally, Chinese representation on government bodies was extraordinarily limited. Sir Chouson Chow was appointed the first Chinese member of the Executive Council in July 1926, while the less important Legislative Council continued to have a cast-iron non-elected British majority designed to do the bidding of the governor of the day. The constitutional arrangements that evolved in Hong Kong during its first century were plainly undemocratic. The system of retaining most powers in the hands of the governor and his bureaucracy was designed to avoid the granting of more than limited status to the very small minority of British residents in Hong Kong and likewise to prevent the Chinese ratepayers from exercising the potential power that their greater numbers and financial strength would suggest. Any serious attempt at introducing representative government in the period from the 1880s onward would logically have resulted in the more affluent Chinese residents gaining the whip hand. This the Colonial Office was not prepared to countenance; nor equally would it permit a minuscule British electorate to run the show. Instead, as Secretary of State for the Colonies Joseph Chamberlain ruled in denying British petitioners who were pressing for municipal reform in May 1896, 'Hong Kong is to remain a Crown Colony'. So it would remain for much of the next century. It was an artificial, if subtle, method of restraining British merchant claims for the right to have a major voice in what many saw as 'their' colony and blunting Chinese assertions for advancement. The government was to continue to act as umpire between rival racial and commercial interests, while gradually coopting wider elements inside the administrative circle.

Yet the process of assimilation had not been strenuously implemented by 1941. While the government had some informal ties to the base of Hong Kong's social structure by encouraging local community work in the ever-spreading urban areas and through the more conservative and still rural New Territories, the results were far from outstanding. If leading Chinese merchants were prepared to support the charitable Tung Wah Board and cooperate with the British bureaucracy so much the better, but the system was hardly any more representational in 1941 that it had been half a century earlier. Authority clearly continued to reside in the governor and his officials. Most Chinese of any political persuasion required of their prewar colonial overlords only two things: residents wanted the government to do as little as possible to impede their opportunities for private financial gain and to adequately defend the borders of Hong Kong. The extended economic tensions of the 1930s and then the long-predicted invasion of the colony in December 1941 gave the lie to British power. In the circumstances it is hardly surprising that the battle for Hong Kong should have been fought out between the two largest rival imperialist nations in the AsianPacific region with the unfortunate Chinese residents acting largely as bystanders in the short, unequal struggle.

Britain's loss of Hong Kong was inevitable, given the global strategic factors that were in play and the unfortunate conditions that had existed within the colony over many years. Hong Kong's government and the cabinet in London must share responsibility for the disasters of 1941. The colony was ill-prepared both within and without to offer effective resistance to Imperial Japan. The internal problems of the colony were long-standing and yet had remained largely unrectified for many years. At the core of the issue was the inability of successive administrations to begin to win over what a later great power in southeast Asia would term the hearts and minds of those it claimed to be protecting. The reality was that Hong Kong Chinese residents felt little or no active loyalty to British rule; many saw themselves as merely temporary migrants in what was assumed to be a safe haven, or at least a less dangerous foreign enclave, on the South China coast. The Hong Kong authorities had judged themselves largely powerless to stem this tide of refugees and equally had felt unable to do much for their welfare once the new arrivals were ensconced in Hong Kong. Even wealthier long-established Chinese merchant families possessing British nationality would shortly be seen to have a decidedly weak attachment to the Crown. The limited role of the colonial state and the tendency towards racial and social exclusivity further discouraged the development of a wider, more harmonious sense of community. Hong Kong in 1941 was divided into a set of Chinese, European and Indian groupings that had little in common.

Once Hong Kong was invaded, the colonial government reaped the whirlwind. The lack of trust between races left few Chinese willing or able to assist in the defence of the territory. The British military quickly found itself unable to draw on the community for emergency assistance and indeed had actively discouraged any such preparations in the prewar period. It was seen as solely the task of the imperial forces to defend Hong Kong; everybody else got in the way. This psychology of mistrust of the Chinese residents was immediately repaid in kind. All too late in the day the Hong Kong police discovered the extent of fifth column cells and the ability of criminal elements to determine the outcome on the streets. The fact that Japanese agents had been able to make such easy inroads into Hong Kong was a further indication of the superficial nature of British authority; underneath, the roots were rotten.

The defence of Hong Kong was also made worse by the quality of its leaders. The traditions of the colonial service had long insisted that its members should be rotated periodically around the globe. While this encouraged innovation on occasion and discouraged peculation, it had its drawbacks as well. Colonial governors might find themselves shunted between continents. Sir Henry Blake, for example, served successively as governor of the Bahamas, Newfoundland and Jamaica before being appointed to Hong Kong in 1898 and later still gaining the Ceylon prize prior to eventual retirement. The governor at the outbreak of the Pacific war, Sir Mark Young, had earlier been posted to Sierra Leone, Palestine, Barbados and Tanganyika. Young had the misfortune to arrive in Hong Kong only in September 1941 to replace Sir Geoffrey Northcote, who had served most of his career in west Africa. Young was too raw to be able to enforce much in the way of change, while Major-General Christopher Maltby was equally new to his post as commander of British forces in the colony. Both Young and Maltby had to make the best they could of their inheritance at a time when Britain remained uncertain as to Japan's intentions in the Pacific and feared having to fight on additional fronts. In any fully global war that could see Germany, Italy and Japan in active cooperation there would be few resources left for Hong Kong.

Neither Young nor Maltby was given the time to attempt to improve either the administrative or military deficiencies of Hong Kong. Yet with the cards they were dealt there was not a great deal that could be effectively done if Tokyo chose to attack British, American and Dutch possessions in the Asian–Pacific region. Even if more had been attempted to enlist the support of Chinese residents in Hong Kong and there had been greater cooperation between rival civil and military agencies, the deficiencies remain striking. Major-General Maltby had too few troops and Governor Young was in charge of a badly demoralized colony. There was still a degree of outward self-confidence in the last months of 1941 but evidence such as the shipping out of expatriate families to Australia, revelations of serious instances of official corruption and the massed departure of Chinese refugees suggest that all was indeed not well.

The long-discussed invasion and capture of Hong Kong was quickly done. Japanese forces, battle-hardy from campaigning in China, could not be denied their prize for long. Major-General Maltby's defence of the colony was based first on holding the hills around Kowloon against Lieutenant-General Sakai's forces and then, after the unexpectedly quick loss of the mainland, through organizing a final stand on the island itself. The Hong Kong garrison, comprising a mixed bag of regulars, volunteers and paper shufflers, mustered little more then 10,600 men and it was apparent from the outset that some units were unfit for the demanding task of resisting the determined, frontal Japanese assaults. Winston Churchill and the war cabinet in London might urge resistance to the last but the situation on the ground was hopeless once Kowloon had been lost. There could have been fiercer counter-attacks, but the need to throw inexperienced troops into the fray was questionable.

Maltby never had a chance. His forces were asked to defend too large an area with too few units and with almost no aerial or naval support. Better training and tactics could have done little but delay the inevitable, particularly when rumours of reinforcements from both China and Singapore were shown to be illusory. The fighting left the colony facing acute food shortages and exposed the crowded tenements of central Hong Kong to uncontested bombardment by Japanese guns. Governor Young had initially rejected offers of negotiated surrender but the consequences if he had continued to refuse to capitulate would have been mayhem for all remaining peoples in Hong Kong. Sir Mark Young then became the first governor to surrender British territory since the loss of the American colonies a century and a half earlier.

'The defences of this colony were on a limited scale, with the object of denying the harbour to an enemy rather than retaining the harbour for the use of our fleet', Maltby wrote at the beginning of his later despatch on operations in Hong Kong during December 1941. The problems that he faced in the winter months prior to the Japanese invasion made it almost certain that the outcome could not be in doubt since, as he acknowledged in his published report, 'I and my forces may have been a hostage to fortune'. The only consolation that Maltby could claim was that his attempted defence of Hong Kong tied down some Imperial Japanese soldiery that might otherwise had been diverted to more vital strategic tasks. His assertion that 'we gambled and lost, but it was a worthwhile gamble' is hard to accept, however, given the colony's unpreparedness and the rapidity with which Japan attacked and conquered the territory.

Hong Kong's disadvantages and Japanese strengths combined to produce a quick victory that led to a lengthy occupation. It was a humiliating defeat for London. After a hundred years of British rule the colony was in Japanese hands with its former military and civilian masters now held captive in POW and internment camps. To make the transfer of power doubly obvious to all residents who remained in Hong Kong, the Japanese authorities seized and then rebuilt Government House.

Maltby's *post mortem* on the capture of Hong Kong illustrates that the prewar attitudes of European administrators and commanders contributed enormously to their own downfall. The Hong Kong government was not prepared to put its civil defence plans into operation until the governor was satisfied that war was imminent, the number of Chinese in uniform was far too few, the colony was riddled with fifth columnists and Maltby freely admitted that he had fully shared the common prejudices of his generation in seriously underestimating the military prowess of his Asian adversary. He noted that Japanese intelligence was excellent and that fast nightwork by infantry in 'rubber soled boots' quickly cut the defending British forces into two, while seemingly disregarding casualties. What particularly surprised the British command was the 'efficiency of the enemy air force', whereby 'their opening attack on Kai Tak aerodrome by low level attack down to sixty feet was carried out with skill and marked boldness'. He wrote after the event that 'my general impression at the time was that either the Japanese pilots had reached a surprisingly high standard of training, or that German pilots were leading their flights'.

Virtually everything that the British, American, French and Dutch military mind in the AsianPacific region had been led to believe about the Imperial Japanese forces was proved wrong, almost literally overnight. It was a salutary lesson. Instead of imagining that Japanese tactics were conventional, its armaments poor and victories earned on the continent against Chinese scratch units had been 'flattering as there had never been real opposition', the West suddenly discovered that what was happening in Manchuria could be replicated in Malaya and Mandalay.

British military deficiencies in troop strength and experience – green Canadian troops had the bad luck to arrive in Hong Kong only in mid-November and were under fire long before they could be expected to do themselves justice – plus the near-total absence of naval and air power left the defence of Hong Kong in a hopeless position. The quick Japanese capture of the high ground overlooking Kowloon and Hong Kong island proved decisive. Lack of ammunition, the isolation of uncoordinated British units, shortages of water and heavy artillery and the distinct possibility of 'severe retaliation' on the territory's civilian population led to surrender. On Christmas Day 1941, as Maltby recalled afterwards,

At 1515 hours I advised H.E. The Governor and Commander in chief that no further useful military resistance was possible and I then ordered all Commanding Officers to break off the fighting and to capitulate to the nearest Japanese Commander, as and when the enemy advanced and opportunity offered.

After Hong Kong had surrendered on Christmas Day 1941, it was placed under immediate military occupation. The next three and half years were at best highly unpleasant and at worse subject to barbarism and cannibalism. Life was tightly controlled and Hong Kong was run exclusively for the benefit of its new rulers. Evidence of the general condition of Hong Kong has always been crudely (but correctly) seen in its population statistics: during the three years and eight months of Japanese rule it has been estimated that the number of residents shrank from 1,600,000 to less than 600,000. Those who could escape did so; those who remained and would not cooperate faced the inevitable consequences. It was by any standards the blackest period in Hong Kong's history.

# 1    Reoccupation: postwar comeback, 1945–7

[The p]opulation in general seems glad to see us back and [a] harbour
filled with British warships gives obvious pleasure but we must bring
much more than ability to maintain order if our welcome is to endure.
Difficult times lie ahead.

(Rear-Admiral Cecil Harcourt to Chiefs of Staff, 18 September 1945)

in these democratic days it is an essential function of the ruler to
educate the ruled to a sense of their civic duties.

(Sir Robert Kotewall to Brigadier MacDougall, Hong Kong, 25 April 1946)

There was nothing very glorious about the British reoccupation of Hong
Kong in August 1945. It was the product of both quick thinking and
good fortune as action took place simultaneously on domestic and Allied
fronts in the scramble for succession to defeated Imperial Japan. The
internal situation was the result of prompt action by Colonial Secretary
Franklin Gimson and a small number of British internees in asserting
control over the territory once news of the Japanese surrender had
percolated through to the beleaguered camps. The international situation, however, was still highly confused when British naval units arrived
off Hong Kong to support Gimson's claims, while diplomats in
Washington, London and Chungking continued to fight their battles
over who should be permitted control of the disputed territory.

To back up Gimson's bid to be in charge of Hong Kong it was vital
that sufficient British military force be on hand as quickly as possible.
Here luck favoured the Royal Navy. Admiral Fraser had been told on 13
August that the retaking of Hong Kong would have the highest priority
once Imperial Japan had formally surrendered, though the Chinese
government was insisting that it alone had title to Hong Kong. The
interval between Japan's agreement to capitulate and the final signing of
the surrender documents in Tokyo Bay on 2 September permitted a
small British light cruiser task force under Rear-Admiral Cecil Harcourt
to be detached from the British Pacific Fleet with orders to steam
immediately for the territory. General MacArthur's ruling that no Allied
theatre commanders were to jump the gun and institute local surrender

ceremonies did not prevent British forces from reoccupying Hong Kong and, in effect, demonstrating that possession is invariably nine-tenths of the law. China's claims to Hong Kong, reinforced in the view of Chiang Kai-shek by the fact that he alone was entitled to administer the surrender of all Japanese forces within the China theatre, came to naught through Chiang's unwillingness to press China's claims. To have persisted in so doing would have risked losing the good will of the United States at a time when the entire future of China was in doubt. Chiang's position was also weakened by the differences in outlook between President Truman and his predecessor with regard to European colonialism in Asia. Franklin Roosevelt's sympathies for China, at least when that nation was still fighting Imperial Japan, were not fully shared by Truman and this factor certainly aided the British push to retake Hong Kong. Truman informed newly elected Prime Minister Clement Attlee that the US government had no objection to a British commander accepting the surrender of Japanese forces in Hong Kong, provided there was adequate military coordination with China.

The initial messages from Hong Kong to London were encouraging. Gimson's first reports, after being sent by messenger for transmission from the British consulate in Macao, announced that he had

sufficient staff to set up civil service administration immediately, including patrol of New Territories for a short period without outside assistance. I am taking oath as officer administering the government.

The arrival of the British naval task force under Admiral Harcourt continued this relatively smooth process. Harcourt informed the Admiralty that the 'situation remains quiet, although Jap executioner who fell into Chinese hands came to an untimely end'. He worked methodically forward; first clearing the harbour and then edging on from the island of Hong Kong. Harcourt reported back to London that the docks were quickly occupied and

by 1600 hours 4th September I intend to take over maintenance of law and order for city of Kowloon. On 5th September Japanese will be disarmed including officers' swords. Swords of Jap General and admiral will be surrendered to me personally when surrender terms are signed. It will not be possible to put Japs into prisoners' cage until our own prisoners can be embarked in Empress of Australia.

Harcourt continued confidently 'after that there will remain some 2,500 Japs in New Territory [sic] who will have to be rounded up'.

The returning British military had to face two immediate problems. The first issue was to determine who would run Hong Kong and the second was to reckon how this unenviable task could be accomplished.

The surprising answer to both questions was through a small number of British officials in conjunction with local Japanese surrendered personnel. Britain got Hong Kong back because its POWs and internees were there on the spot; it was able to keep it going in the first tense weeks through using whoever and whatever could be dragooned into service. The reoccupation of Hong Kong was an Anglo–Japanese affair. It required both the efforts of civil servants and Imperial Japanese soldiers; overnight prison camp guards became allies of their former captives. The arrival of Rear-Admiral Harcourt's task force off Hong Kong then served as a necessary demonstration of military strength to support the embryonic 'Ex-Internees Administration' being organized by Franklin Gimson.

The relative success made of regaining control of Hong Kong had immediate international consequences. It contradicted much of the wartime debate in Allied chanceries and academic gatherings on the probable future of what was widely seen to be an anachronism on the edge of China; it spat in the face of the new tidal wave of anti-colonialism. It confirmed, however, the remarks of Winston Churchill to General Hurley, the US ambassador to China in April 1945. After one meeting with the ambassador Churchill had minuted:

General Hurley seemed to wish to confine the conversation to Civil banalities. I took him up with violence about Hong Kong and said that never would we yield an inch of the territory that was under the British Flag. As for the leased territory, in connection with the water supply, that did not come up till 1998 or thereabouts. In the meanwhile we would set up distilling machinery which would give us all the water we wanted and more. The General-Ambassador accepted this without further demur.

Harcourt's decisiveness quickly paid off. (His labours would be recognized later by the naming after him of the main road that runs astride the naval base in the centre of the city.) His strategy towards the Japanese forces was 'to sail straight in despite the mine risk' and 'to keep them on the go so that they never had time to take breath'. This worked once it became apparent that there would be no formal bargaining between the two sides.

His first priority was to secure the territory. Japanese documents suggest that the Japanese side had drawn up a considerable list of concessions in return for their 'cooperation'. Japan's 'proposals' were extensive, detailed and based on the expectation that 'fair and just treatment will be given towards the Japanese on the part of the British'. The Japanese military pledged their assistance in providing for 'the public peace and order' and then followed this up with an extraordinarily lengthy set of conditions indicative of the thoroughness of Imperial staff work even at the moment of collapse. These included permission to carry both side arms and ceremonial swords, payment for labour detachments and swift repatriation.

The British negotiators, not surprisingly, found much of this approach unacceptable in theory but had in reality to agree to portions never-theless. Since Churchill and Attlee had both wanted to see the earliest possible British presence in the region this required that Japanese troops be extensively mobilized as peacekeepers over southeast Asia and Hong Kong. There was no alternative in the face of the herculean tasks that had to be tackled immediately. The feeding alone of thousands, indeed millions, of residents of southeast Asia was merely one of the challenges that Admiral Louis Mountbatten had to solve in his huge regional theatre of operations.

Hong Kong was more fortunate than other parts in the region. By 11 November Harcourt could report to Secretary of State for the Colonies George Hall that the reoccupation was progressing 'much better than was ever expected or hoped'. He told London that essential services such as the trams were now running and that '[t]he next great step forward in rehabilitating Hong Kong lies with the supply machinery backing us from the outside', though until then the colony would have to face 'bare larders, empty godowns and [a] harbour full of men-of-war instead of merchantmen'. Harcourt advocated the early reopening of Hong Kong to trade since the territory was 'ripe for it'. He concluded by sensing 'without doubt' that 'Hong Kong's future looks bright, and that the number of those who advocate its return to China daily grows less', though adding a rider that 'our every action is carefully scrutinized and we need to maintain a high standard in all respects to keep the position that we have so far attained'.

Japanese forces were put to work as gendamerie, hospital orderlies and labourers. Harcourt noted that the new POWs

not only kept their camps well disciplined and in extremely good order, but hundreds of them are employed on working parties clearing up the mess, improving the aerodrome, etc. and they all work extremely well. We have been careful to keep them clear of Chinese labour so that we cannot be accused of employing the Japanese and thus taking the bread out of the mouths of Chinese coolies.

Organizing the reconstruction work was the responsibility of Harcourt and a handful of civil affairs officers under David MacDougall, who had arrived from London to gradually take over from Gimson's exhausted team. It was an exhilarating and frantic period. As one senior figure explained proudly in mid-October to his superior in the Colonial Office:

'The pace of the work here continues killing.' (Perhaps the only advantage of working these 15-hour days was that it precluded lengthy reporting to London, in the initial weeks at least.) MacDougall appears to have worked well with Harcourt and the military under General Festing; he also acted quickly to refashion Hong Kong's approaches to China. MacDougall, who had served in Hong Kong prewar, argued to the Colonial Office that a fresh strategy was badly needed in which there ought to be greater recognition of China's changing circumstances. MacDougall noted sarcastically that:

So many people come so many hundreds of miles on triple A priority to tell me that a new China has been born, and that Hong Kong is, as it were, no longer an island. Everyone seems now to say and to think what would have been usefully said and thought any time from 1937 to 1941. But this is late 1945 and the situation has changed. Then China needed friends: now she has more candidates for friendship than she knows what to do with. Our cards now in Hong Kong are the same as they always were – courtesy, efficiency and usefulness – but some of these chaps would have you fawning all over the Chinese.

MacDougall then went to the heart of his programme for a reconstructed Hong Kong by demonstrating its value to China without any excessive flummery. 'The Chinese', he maintained,

are like any other people, and within limits they will like us only insofar as we are useful – and that can be very, very useful indeed. The sooner we realize this and work at the job the better. The lighter forms of the gesture and protestation of friendship are a prewar luxury. The 1941 technique no longer serves.

For MacDougall a revived Hong Kong capable of acting as the hub of the region could pay sizeable dividends for both sides but this was little more than a rare profession of faith in the autumn of 1945.

Everything, of course, remained contingent on getting Hong Kong back on its feet and working as closely as possible with the Chinese authorities. MacDougall's thoughts on a suitable Sino–Hong Kong relationship were followed in the next paragraph of his report by action in the more mundane world of Rent Restriction Proclamations and Vegetable Marketing Schemes; state intervention within Hong Kong and the winning overseas of firewood from Borneo, coal from Shanghai and peanut oil from wherever it appeared on the Asian market had to have priority if the colony was to have any chance of a future.

Certainly Harcourt and MacDougall knew that there could be no favourable heritage from the Japanese interregnum. The Japanese legacy to the returning British was merely a cowed population, a bare cupboard and a deserted harbour. Indeed, perhaps, the only enduring tangible legacy of the Imperial occupation had been the rebuilding by the

Japanese military of Government House. Once the Japanese war memorial had been blown up it was to be virtually all that remained physically of the war years. (Legend has it that the first British officers to reuse its billiard table were less than amused to discover that their Japanese counterparts had sawn off portions of the table legs and shortened all cues.)

Recovery progressed far quicker than the wartime planners back at the Colonial Office in Whitehall had predicted. Certainly there were occasional signs of desperation, as when officials in Hong Kong would report in late November 1945 that 'we are hopelessly short of transport', and MacDougall had had to inform his superior in London that 'we have taken large chances and used much bluff' on issues as diverse as price controls, and over restarting industrial production and fisheries. Equally, it was evident that MacDougall and his men were grossly overworked but they had earned the satisfaction of seeing significant improvement in Hong Kong's well-being almost immediately. Harcourt as early as 18 September informed London that the colony was 'quiet', although the fact that he had ordered 'strong patrols' out on the streets made it difficult to gauge accurately the state of public opinion. Still he reported confidently in his next sentence to the Admiralty that the 'population estimated soon to reach one million is relatively healthy and adequately clothed'. Fortunately, Hong Kong had escaped destruction on anything remotely comparable to the scale of Tokyo or Dresden, and experienced remarkably little overall damage. British estimates put the average at approximately 15 per cent of housing stock, thanks to a 'combination of bombing, fire and looting'. This last factor paralleled the scenes of December 1941 when looters had made off with whatever they could grab from godowns and smashed shop windows.

The initial picture was of British improvisation being matched by a generally cool response from Hong Kong residents. The Admiralty was told in no uncertain terms that reinforcements were 'most urgently required' if Harcourt and MacDougall were to go much beyond the maintenance of civil order and the provision of essential services. Staff in Hong Kong calculated that 'there are four times as many Chinese flags as British displayed in the city' and warned that '[d]ifficult times lie ahead'. Yet, by the beginning of November 1945, Harcourt was able to write at length to Colonial Secretary Hall on the satisfactory progress made in reoccupying and revitalizing Hong Kong. The pressganged Japanese were 'entirely docile'.

The rapid and relatively easy switch to civilian from military control in Hong Kong indicates the general state of affairs within the colony. By mid-October MacDougall, the chief civil affairs officer, was made

answerable to the Colonial Office for non-military matters. The relationship between the services and civil affairs administration worked well, as
MacDougall was relieved to report. He told his superiors in Whitehall
that Harcourt

takes the possibly optimistic view that I was sent out because I knew the job and
the Colony, and he shows every disposition to accept my advice on all save
service matters.

Although the formal handover to total civilian control had to wait until
Sir Mark Young's return to his post on 1 May 1946 it was apparent long
before then that Hong Kong was already set on making its presence felt
as a stable, economic force in the region. The garrisoning of Hong Kong
by No. 3 Commando Brigade increasingly shifted from its earlier
internal security mission.

The three key figures in the successful reoccupation of Hong Kong
were Gimson, Harcourt and MacDougall. Together they secured the
territory and began the process of putting it back on its feet. All played
necessary roles but in terms of Hong Kong's long-term future it was
MacDougall who deserves to be singled out for particular praise.
MacDougall's job as chief civil affairs officer required both careful
attention to his immediate instructions to ensure the 'maintenance of
law and order and prevention of disease and unrest' and a lengthy
agenda for reconstruction and reorganization. Initial British governmental thinking for Hong Kong appears to have reckoned with
substantial changes to the prewar structure, including administrative
and educational reforms, but the lack of personnel in the first months
after repossession inevitably encouraged an ad hoc approach by the
government. The Whitehall committee working on the transition from
military to civil government for Hong Kong was reminded on 2 January
1946 that the Civil Affairs Administration was still highly dependent on
'military personnel, civilian ex internees and public utility companies'
employees (also ex internees)' for policing, supplies and essential
services. The difficulty of gaining adequate staff persisted, admittedly
in a less severe form, to impair the prospects for any radical
remodelling of the territory. It would prove almost impossible to
encourage already overstretched staff to reckon with anything but the
immediate day-to-day issues in the months and indeed the first years
following reoccupation.

The War Office in London, for example, was informed in August
1947 that in the financial area

our difficulties here have been acute; there is a serious lack of experienced staff
and we are inundated with preoccupation and occupation claims of all kinds. On

top of all this we have had to introduce a system of income tax and negotiations with the Chinese Government over a financial agreement have made heavy demands on my time, often amounting to seven hours a day.

Hong Kong's Accountant General had noted in 1945 that 'numerous advances (loans) were made in the early months to provide firms with dollar currency and to get such currency into circulation', yet even in May 1951 these financial ramifications were still being tackled by the territory's bureaucracy.

The major question of the first months of reoccupation was hardly the painless switch to non-military government but rather the nature of the new postwar civil administration. It was an issue that had long preoccupied officials but one on which there were shortly to be initiatives and disappointments as a semblance of normality emerged. Few would have cared to predict that despite the election of a new Labour government in Britain and extensive talk of Asian decolonization so little progress would be made over reforming Hong Kong. Indeed, the political situation by 1951 was to be almost identical with 1941. Despite Hong Kong's humiliating surrender, its lengthy Japanese occupation and a series of postwar constitutional schemes, the much-heralded reform programme was a dismal failure.

Why so little emerged from a host of policy proposals has to be answered. The first place to look for clues to the imbroglio is London. It was civil servants in Whitehall who initiated the discussion of constitutional reform for Hong Kong and it was in these same corridors that decisions were taken later to postpone indefinitely anything but superficial change to the status quo. Interdepartmental committees were formed to consider Hong Kong's future long before the defeat of Imperial Japan. Much of their work assumed that a high degree of reform was required both to assuage those overseas who castigated British colonialism and because Hong Kong deserved better than a return to the narrow prewar pattern of administration. Not all officials assumed, however, that Hong Kong would automatically revert to Britain. The War Cabinet's far eastern economic subcommittee, for example, was told in May 1945 that '[f]rom the economic point of view, unless the Chinese Government acquiesced in the continuance of British possession of the Colony, it would not be worth very much to us'. Certainly these tended to be the opinions of members of the Foreign Office rather than the Colonial Office but the anxieties of British trading interests persisted, suggesting that awareness of American and Chinese hostility left the position decidedly confused. Even the guidance for the Colonial Office representative at the San Francisco Conference of 1945 recalled that 'we have indicated our readiness to discuss the future of the New Territories, with the Chinese after the war', though quickly cautioning that 'any adjustment' would only be possible through later joint discussion.

The imprecision of British official thinking on Hong Kong ensured that those on the spot after reoccupation would not be overburdened with directives and could contribute to the making of fresh policies. The disadvantage was that time was lost and the opportunity for new initiatives disappeared. Talk on a 'proposed new constitution' progressed without much sense of urgency and was almost certainly weakened further by the cordial attitude of the Truman administration in accepting that Hong Kong's future rested with Britain. Without the spur of international comment it became increasingly tempting to tackle the question of Hong Kong's political reform on an ad hoc basis. Minimalism won.

Initially there were expectations of radical change. The English-language press maintained in December 1945 that 'Hong Kong will not meekly acquiesce in an attempted resuscitation of the worn out government machine which let us down so badly in 1941'. But it did and the territory would have to wait until 1992 before a serious reform programme was announced. The suggestion that the Japanese occupation led to any very vigorous alteration in the status quo is difficult to sustain; Chinese voices within Hong Kong gained in strength only over time.

The changes contemplated by British officials centred merely on widening the franchise and either enlarging the existing political institutions or creating new bodies equipped initially to tackle the dry issues of local government. For any of these plans to work there would have to be, of course, a fresh appreciation among returning British subjects that change in racial attitudes was vital. This was soon shown to be an unwarranted assumption. The initial secret draft of the civil affairs policy directives for Hong Kong began its Chinese policy statement by announcing that '[t]here should be no discrimination, statutory or otherwise on racial grounds'. Twelve months later Colonial Office minutes from May 1945 warned frankly that prewar 'with a population of 96% Chinese and only 4% non-Chinese the problem of racial discrimination was always the main concern of the Government'. Privilege could all too easily go to 'the latest arrived shop-assistant at Lane Crawford's (provided his skin was white) which would be denied to a Chinese millionaire or even a returned graduate of Oxford'. The almost blanket denial of Chinese residency on the Peak before 1945 accurately symbolized this colour bar. Public opinion polls conducted by

English-language newspapers in the months after reoccupation make it apparent that there had been no immediate conversion among Hong Kong's European residents. Few were eager to consider any political reforms that might weaken the grip of the British administration. This near-monopoly on power was hardly to be diluted in the ensuing three decades.

From the spring of 1944 the Colonial Office's thinking had been in the direction of reestablishing the familiar pattern of government through Executive and Legislative Councils. Yet it also saw the necessity of 'including representatives of the chief local communities and interests' and by the time Japan surrendered had reached the stage of pressing at least for municipal reform. This in itself was hardly a major breakthrough but it could in theory have been the starting point for later, more radical, political change in the colony. Discussion, unfortunately, progressed far too slowly. It may have been that some delay was necessary in order to sound out local opinion and kindle public debate over the appropriateness of London's initiative, but valuable time was lost. Only after Sir Mark Young returned as governor, despite concern that his health had not fully recovered from wartime imprisonment, did serious soundings get underway. Young's dispatch to Colonial Secretary Creech Jones of 22 October 1946 heralds the first, however belated, attempts by some within the Hong Kong government to offer at least a sketch map of constitutional change.

It was a decidedly modest beginning. The 'Young Plan' was no more than an attempt to square the circle of British intransigence within Hong Kong, international concern over a thoroughly undisguised colonial structure and the 'decided lack of enthusiasm for any constitutional changes' discerned by Young among Hong Kong's peoples. It proposed a new Municipal Council, drawing its responsibilities initially from the existing Urban Council, with councillors elected in equal numbers from among Chinese, non-Chinese and professional associations. Young's tentative proposals intended that 'a considerable transfer of powers should be aimed at and secondly that the transference should be effected gradually'. Certainly Young's prose suggested no urgency. His un-doubted diligence was unmatched by the slightest hint of excitement or even sense of civic occasion. The whole exercise was guaranteed to raise only cautious expectations; it was hardly a new deal for Hong Kong.

Yet even the gradualism set out in the Young Plan was rejected by the British authorities in Hong Kong and London. Any explanation for this disappointment must account for the change of heart in the Colonial Office and events on the ground within Hong Kong. Young himself felt in October 1946 that the hesitant reaction within the colony was attributable 'in part to apathy and in part to apprehension'. The novelty of the exercise and concern over possible infiltration of Kuomintang elements into the proposed municipality certainly played their part in sabotaging the business but Young's entire approach needs to be questioned. His public broadcast of 22 August 1946 provides clues aplenty that the attempt to get constitutional reform off the ground was likely to fail. His lack of dynamism would not normally have mattered so much in a conventional colonial administrator, but Hong Kong had reason to hold higher hopes of its returning governor.

The broadcast was both too detailed and too dull to inspire any but the most gifted specialist in local government, thereby automatically excluding virtually the entire population of Hong Kong and closing the debate almost before it had begun. If the subject of political reform could only be described in terms of public health, education and the licensing of vehicles, then few should have been particularly surprised by the outcome. When this was compounded by adding that a government commission might have to be convened first to decide which municipal services should be incorporated and how they then would be financed, the outcome was hardly in doubt.

Interest within Hong Kong, however, certainly existed over constitutional reform. Perhaps the lengthiest private submission to the governor was received from Sir Robert Kotewall, who submitted a confidential memorandum in April 1946 that refuted the conventional wisdom that all the Chinese residents of Hong Kong expected from their rulers was 'peace, security, and a minimum of interference with the pursuits of their livelihood'. Kotewall, drawing on his long experience both in and out of government, maintained that a small, articulate minority of the Chinese population 'will not only make its voice heard but heeded'. He argued that membership of the Legislative Council ought to be substantially revised to favour the Chinese community, though he quickly conceded that the 'problem of the election of Chinese candidates is beset with pitfalls'. While rejecting universal suffrage, Kotewall suggested 'some system of "electoral colleges"' based on wards or districts, patterned on existing street committees could, if suitably modified, give the territory 'a healthily large suffrage for participation in the work of the legislature and of the Municipal Council'.

Kotewall was certainly no radical but he did press for a series of changes that cumulatively would make for a different Hong Kong. His advocacy of an unofficial majority in the legislature able to outvote government officials, the suggestion that a new Municipal Council should replace the moribund Urban Council and his wish for a stronger Secretariat for Chinese Affairs, handling what he saw to be closer and more important ties with China, were all serious proposals that he hoped the new governor would consider. The fact that Sir Mark Young returned Kotewall's carefully composed seventeen-page confidential memorandum to MacDougall within a day of having received it was hardly a good omen for reform.

The Colonial Office was also at fault in not making up its collective mind on the issue sooner and for leaving Young with too broad a mandate. The governor was roughly treated both by officials and by his minister. He was faced with periods of indecision from Whitehall and even at one stage in 1946 asked by Colonial Secretary Creech Jones to recast his entire scheme. Young's humiliations continued in the refusal of his superiors to publish his proposals on his return to Britain. It was, officialdom maintained, impossible to concede his point until after more studies had been completed, but since the governor was largely carrying out London's instructions he had reason indeed to feel let down. Changes to departmental personnel within the Colonial Office also brought in those less sympathetic to political reform in Hong Kong, to the extent that at times it looked as if the Young Plan was being seen as Young's alone rather than the collective wisdom of both wartime planners and those advising the Labour government from the summer of 1945 onwards.

Creech Jones' original instructions to Governor Young were never carried out. The hope of the secretary of state for the colonies that Sir Mark Young in March 1946 should be aware of 'the necessity for a liberal constitution and his meeting every section of the community and trying to break down social distrust' had dissolved by the summer of 1947. By this date Creech Jones could only write that

the essential thing now is to get the thing moving and experience will indicate any defects and popular agitation will bring to light any shortcomings or need for more liberal provision.

Yet a scheme to institute such slight changes to municipal government was a decidedly modest outcome to wartime and postwar hopes; the Young Plan was hardly testimony that a Labour government might congratulate itself on. In July 1947 Creech Jones was reduced to minuting to his divided staff that it had 'obviously been hard to reconcile all the differences of views', but since 'constitutions are always open to amendment in the light of experience and a start should be made with no further loss of time, I feel we must go ahead on this basis'.

Once in retirement it may well have been galling for Creech Jones to read in the memoirs of his more prominent cabinet colleagues of their successes and to note how colonial issues were rarely given more than a brief mention. He may indeed have been, as the *New Statesman* charitably suggested in December 1963, 'the man responsible above all others for giving the modern Labour Party a colonial conscience', but his authority over matters involving Hong Kong appears to have been largely constrained by officials in both Whitehall and the territory. Certainly parliamentary interest was slender and the fact that Creech Jones merely devoted one sentence to Hong Kong in a lengthy statement to the Commons in July 1947 strongly suggests that the Colonial Office and its appointee in Government House could conduct business largely free of close scrutiny from above and without. The territory's hopes of self-development, however, would next be restricted by regional troubles that threatened to cancel out the promising initial efforts of the reconstruction period.

# 2    Consolidation: the Grantham years, 1947–58

Until conditions change, we intend to remain in Hong Kong.
(Foreign Secretary Ernest Bevin to Secretary of State Dean Acheson,
13 September 1949)

Hong Kong is Different.
(Sir Alexander Grantham, *Corona*, January 1959)

Once Sir Alexander Grantham was appointed as Young's successor the writing was on the wall for Hong Kong's 'New Deal'. Grantham, an old Hong Kong hand who had first arrived in the colony as a cadet in 1922, was chosen with the full knowledge that he wanted as little as possible to do with constitutional change. He had made his views plain in correspondence and meetings with officials in London prior to the formal announcement of his posting. Grantham, who would later claim in public that 'the problem in Hong Kong is different from that in other colonies, for Hong Kong can never become independent', wanted no truck with the Young Plan. The new governor, knowing his territory from interwar experience, was adamant that it was best to let sleeping dogs lie. He saw his task as largely to continue with the reconstruction of Hong Kong and to provide an efficient and inexpensive administration that would take all necessary political decisions to further these economic and social ends. Grantham ran a benevolent despotism, while keeping a careful eye on the changing Chinese scene across the border.

In the short and medium term he was entitled to his opinions. Writing in retirement he felt justified in claiming he had carried out the correct policies for a city-state that was still very largely 'politically apathetic'. Governor Grantham represented continuity and the scrapping of the Harcourt–Young schemes that left the colony in the late 1940s approximately where it had been politically when Grantham had last seen Hong Kong in 1935. The old guard was able indeed to fight off those who sensed the need for, at the very least, a modification of the prewar pattern of government. Hong Kong quickly became Grantham's bailiwick. He identified his task as to provide the 'individual liberty and freedom' that kept up what he called 'the humming activity of the Colony'.

If Grantham stubbornly resisted the political agenda inherited from his predecessor he had no qualms about continuing with existing economic policies that had produced results in the brief yet important Harcourt–Young era. The new governor might note in crossing the harbour at his welcoming ceremonies in July 1947 that 'instead of being crowded and noisy with ships from all over the world and smart passenger liners, now only a few battered freighters in war-time paint were to be seen', but this ignores the desolation of two years earlier and the prospects for improvement that were by then encouragingly underway. Instead of the uncharted wrecks and mines of 1945, the harbour, by the time of Grantham's arrival, was already handling considerable cargo and its administrators and agents were endeavouring to keep turnaround times to a minimum. Reputations were being remade.

Equally, it was not taking Hong Kong's traders and manufacturers long to put their businesses back on the map. Hong Kong's early recovery would lead to claims by the spring of 1947 that the territory had made 'the biggest post-war rehabilitation of any place in the Far East between Ceylon and Tokyo'. Statistics suggest that trade was about to exceed its prewar levels by this period and that recovery, though admittedly perhaps precarious, might be sustainable. The greater the improvement in what was initially a subsistence level standard of living and the demonstrable success of the British administration in assisting reconstruction, the greater the confidence of many Hong Kong residents in the government. Political dividends might accrue from economic success.

Results were aided by a more interventionist approach by the authorities. Those who fondly imagine that Hong Kong's prosperity was created solely by its entrepreneurs and flexible labour markets may be unaware of how important the role of the government could be during the immediate postwar period. Food, fuel and housing were its first concern. Strict measures were introduced to ration rice, though by ending immigration controls at the Chinese border Harcourt employed a different ploy to secure extra food supplies. In fact neither the rice schemes nor the anticipated imports from Canton achieved more than a very approximate success. The Hong Kong government never had sufficient staff to properly police the rice shops and, as Harcourt dryly pointed out to the Colonial Office, the swap of people for food was another mismatch. He noted that '[i]n effect we cancelled restrictions we could not enforce and Canton offered food she does not possess'.

Temporary trade controls were imposed following reoccupation. It was necessary both to restrict exports of newsprint, metals, foodstuffs and all cotton yarns and to license the import of manufactured goods and raw materials. This never seriously interfered with blackmarke-teering or the barter trades but it was draconian by prewar Hong Kong standards. Yet the government was clearly playing a larger role in economic matters. This did not damage the local economy, as monthly trade reports by the end of December 1947 indicate that the annual import and export totals were 'easily a record in the history of the Colony' and that, since prices were falling, 'the gains are, indeed, spectacular'.

It was a period of ration cards and housing shortages for even the more fortunate, while squatters in tin shacks on Kowloon's bare hillsides were left to their own devices quite beyond hope of government assistance. Fishermen and farmers might be encouraged to join new marketing and educational schemes but newly arrived refugees from China's civil wars could expect little in the way of charity. Getting a poorly paid job and then gradually improving one's lot was seen as the way ahead. The Hong Kong government certainly adopted new economic and financial responsibilities after 1945 but it was always cautious during the years of austerity to maintain a limited state. Budgets ought to balance and civil servants should keep clear of backstreet factories. When the secretary of state for the colonies was asked a parliamentary question in December 1960 on 'what minimum wage regulations are in force in Hong Kong?', the full reply from Ian Macleod was merely 'none'.

The Hong Kong government had acted quickly, however, in the autumn of 1945 to cope with the territory's sorry financial situation. The question of how to deal with all the Japanese military currency in circulation had to be tackled immediately if the public was to regain confidence and small businesses could start trading once again. The Military Administration ruled that what its officers termed worthless Japanese 'banana currency' should be scrapped and supplies of Hongkong and Shanghai Bank notes (along with those of the two other designated banks) were rushed in as replacement. Those Hong Kong citizens who held on to their Japanese military currency would continue to campaign over the next half century for decent compensation, feeling that neither the British nor Japanese sides had done enough to assist.

Trade patterns changed after 1945 as Hong Kong was able to rise on the tide of international reconstruction. The first issue, however, was with the colony's neighbour. Relations with China suffered inevitably from the chaos of the civil war where, as consular reports from Canton noted monotonously month after month, scores of bodies would be found dead on the streets from starvation every morning and power blackouts were the norm. Unemployment, rampant inflation and banditry further weakened the Chinese economy and inevitably left Hong Kong increasingly obliged to look elsewhere if it wanted to ensure its own recovery.

By the end of 1947 the Hong Kong departments were regretting

the decline throughout the year of trade with China, which can be traced to the runaway inflation prevailing in that country, the stringent restrictions imposed on imports and the fictitious official rates of exchange which have tended to drive exports into illicit channels.

Although China was still Hong Kong's largest trade partner, the statistics show that Malaya now ranked second and that, to the surprise of nearly everyone, Hong Kong's links to Japan were expanding, thanks to the initiative of the colony's traders, government officials and the encouragement of General MacArthur's staff in Tokyo.

Much improvisation and the ability of bankers and clients alike to react quickly to differing circumstances certainly helped get Hong Kong back on its feet. The government too played its part by reckoning astutely where it should help and where it was best to keep out. Most departments were small and kept that way even when persuasive submissions for engaging extra staff were filed. Only gradually, for example, did the scene recorded in November 1945 of 'a six foot excise officer, perched on the back of a bicycle being pedalled along the street by a Chinese coolie' give way to a motorized revenue service. Equally it took the disastrous Christmas Day 1953 fire at Shek Kip Mei to galvanize Governor Grantham's administration to adopt more strenuous rehousing measures. It was then quickly seen by the bureaucracy as essential to accelerate squatter programmes that by the end of the decade would lead to multi-million dollar urban renewal schemes. In this instance, as Grantham cabled to the secretary of state for the colonies on 29 December 1953 'speed is politically of the essence' and the governor reacted commendably. Grantham could lead when he wanted to.

Whether the government should have intervened more actively in the first postwar years was frequently debated against the background of new state powers in Britain and elsewhere. Generally the authorities held that their action would be largely ineffective unless backed up by a far larger civil service that the community would accept. Officialdom disliked the very obvious price gauging that shortages inevitably encouraged and yet knew, as the government price controller admitted in January 1951, that an activist system would be met by 'widespread attempts at evasion and obstruction on the part of local merchants'. The financial secretary had been advised from 1949 that the issues were highly complex and would require, in the case of price controls for pharmaceuticals, 'Gestapo powers' to root out the culprits.

Contributing to Grantham's wish to leave the Young Plan on the shelf was the attitude of the Executive and Legislative Council memberships. The prewar pattern of close associations and private meetings between these individuals and the governor now reasserted itself, allowing the new governor to hear at first hand the objections of the Unofficial Councillors to any proposed new body that would inevitably over time assume political and financial responsibilities that presently rested securely in their grasp. A confident Grantham could therefore stall outrageously over his instructions to introduce draft legislation to establish the proposed municipal schemes and had the satisfaction of learning that Whitehall itself was now beginning to discover sound reasons of its own for ignoring the Young Plan. The fact that by 1948 Creech Jones was himself increasingly preoccupied with the Palestine question also helped derail the prospects for political reform. The longer the delays in gaining action in both Hong Kong and at the London end, the less the likelihood that Governor Grantham would ever have to put through constitutional changes that he had long held to be against the best interests of his colony.

Grantham's approach to political change rarely wavered. He did everything within his considerable power to prevent constitutional debate. When, for example, members of the Reform Club continued to lobby for both legislative and economic improvement in July 1950 Grantham's officials gave its chairman the cold shoulder. The governor, well aware that the Reform Club was a pressure group composed largely of moderate business interests led by Brook Bernacchi that cut across racial lines, worked hard to reduce its voice. Only at the end of May 1952 did he permit elections to the relatively powerless Urban Council on a highly restricted franchise and with only one polling station open for an electorate of nearly 10,000 Hong Kong citizens. The results on a low turnout were then seized upon by those in the Legislative Council as evidence of continuing political apathy of the colony and proved, retrospectively, to signal the end rather than the intended beginning of political reform in the lengthy Grantham era and indeed beyond.

Final conclusive evidence that Governor Grantham had indeed carried the day was clear when Alan Lennox-Boyd visited Hong Kong in the summer of 1955. The secretary of state for the colonies made it apparent in broadcasts and discussions that there was to be no change in

Hong Kong's political status. The Conservative government wanted to leave Hong Kong well alone and was relieved to discover that it had responsibility for one territory at least that was not striving for self-government and could be trusted to remain absent from the front pages of British newspapers, unlike areas such as Cyprus and Kenya. Prosperity rather than political reform was seen to be Hong Kong's goal in the 1950s. The extension of Sir Alexander Grantham's term as governor for a further period of two years to 1957 signalled the cabinet's general satisfaction with his stewardship.

Throughout this long period, relations with China were, as always, critical to Hong Kong's fate. Governor Grantham invariably insisted that 'it is foreign policy and not Colonial policy, e.g. the development toward dominion status or internal self-government, that is basic to everything in Hong Kong'. He inherited the problem of dealing with one uncertain Chinese government and finally left Hong Kong after some success in mending fences with its successor.

Even after decisions had been taken at the highest Allied level in the summer of 1945 to coordinate the surrender process it had been far from certain how Anglo–Chinese relations would evolve on the ground. Clearly the South Chinese military authorities had large forces at their disposal in the region surrounding Hong Kong and Harcourt reported to his superiors that the atmosphere was tense. Efforts to appear conciliatory once again in possession of the territory only added insult to injury in some Chinese eyes. Yet in a press interview on 28 September 1945 Marshal Pan Hwa-kuo had noted that the Chinese delegation to the surrender ceremonies in Hong Kong had cooperated with the British authorities. Pan explained that the 'British wished to retake Hong Kong as it was snatched from their hands by the Japanese'. He stressed that since

Britain and China are Allied nations, arrangements were consequently made that Governor [*sic*] Harcourt represented Commander Chiang Kai-shek to accept the surrender of [the] Hong Kong enemy in exactly the same way as General MacArthur acted as a representative for Allies other than America to conduct the Surrender Ceremony at Tokyo.

In answer to questions on the extent of Sino–British negotiations over ensuring the handover of Japanese munitions and resources Pan again stressed the joint work underway. Intelligence reports confirm that Hong Kong was indeed seen as useful to China in providing port and transit facilities for the Chinese 8th Army and that possible incidents were kept to a minimum. Permitting Chinese naval craft to use the harbour and instructing RAF planes to spray DDT as part of an anti-cholera campaign over Canton were additional British gestures that did no harm. Formal contact with South China followed quickly. General Festing and Governor Young visited Canton in the summer of 1946 and Young paid a further, brief farewell tour in May of the next year. This occasion provoked Young into a rare outburst of anger at the inadequacies of postwar Britain in being unable to provide the insignia with which to decorate General Chang Fa-kuei. (The day was saved by Young borrowing the CBE belonging to Arthur Morse, the manager of the Hongkong and Shanghai Bank.)

As Hong Kong demonstrated what Whitehall in December 1946 had described as its 'recuperative capacity', Governor Grantham was able to spend more time cultivating ties with not only South China but indeed the entire Asian region. It could only work to further Hong Kong interests and the frequent overseas forays by Grantham did indeed, as a member of his colonial secretariat put it in July 1947, 'serve as a useful antidote to those inclined to accuse Hong Kong of insularity'. Between the summer of 1947 and the winter of 1949 Grantham had paid three visits to China as well as addressing conferences in Singapore and seeing General MacArthur in Tokyo.

British and Chinese reporting on Governor Grantham's handling of ties with China suggests that considerable improvement was being made by the time of Grantham's visit to Nanking in October 1947 but that thereafter the internal situation prevented close contacts at the highest level. Chiang Kai-shek's suggestion in conversation with Grantham that he might himself visit Hong Kong during a future tour of his southern regions never materialized. It is, however, an indication of cordiality that suggests that portions of the bitterness of 1945 had been discarded.

More local questions involving officials in Canton and Hong Kong were the subject of continual discussion. Police officers and political advisors from both sides of the border had to deal with the handing over of suspected wartime collaborators, constant smuggling, the presence of Chinese communists in Hong Kong and the potentially volatile question of KMT behaviour in the territory. For Governor Young it had been concern over what may have been an exaggerated threat of possible subversion by KMT elements in the territory that had provoked him to make haste slowly over his initial constitutional proposals. Certainly, the strength of KMT sympathizers in labour organizations and among business groups could never be ignored by the Hong Kong government and incidents, such as Chinese demonstrations over the Kowloon Walled City, did indeed occur. In the case of the Walled City, itself a warren of disputed jurisdiction between Britain and China since the nineteenth century, Dr T.V. Soong, the governor of Kwangtung, told

Grantham that he regarded the affair as a nonsense. Soong was reported as saying 'he could not understand why so much fuss was being made about such a miserable mound of rubble'.

When Sino–British relations were reasonably cordial it was possible, as General Festing had been able to claim during a press interview with the *Canton Daily Sun* in May 1946, to regard Hong Kong and its neighbour as 'largely complementary'. In the language of scores of goodwill visits and hospitable receptions, 'the closer the liaison between the two cities becomes, the closer obviously will be their mutual benefit'. But it was rarely as simple as the bromides might suggest; press campaigns could easily be orchestrated to talk up an anti-British line and the necessary provocations were frequently at hand. If it was not the unanswerable issue of the return of the territory to Chinese hands, it could equally well be the misbehaviour of the authorities in planning a new airport or the temporary suppression of a pro-Nanking journal. The attention, however, that the British officials in Hong Kong gave to Chinese affairs probably helped prevent any fatal rift in the years between reoccupation and the proclamation of the People's Republic of China (PRC) in October 1949. The Chinese government representative in the colony and his KMT staff were given every possible courtesy from the provision of scarce accommodation to suitable transport and by all accounts T.W. Kwok, in return, was conciliatory and had no wish to entangle relations.

Hong Kong only became a prominent cabinet issue when seemingly threatened by the imminent birth of the PRC in 1949 and the outbreak of the Korean war in the following June. It had been apparent long before 1949 that the KMT was in difficulties but commentators were cautious about assessing the prospects of any final communist victory in the Chinese civil war. It was not until the spring of 1948 that the Central Committee of the Chinese Communist Party (CCP) was prepared to predict victory in three years' time, though by the autumn of the same year it was clear that the KMT's support was crumbling both through the loss of key cities and mass desertions and in November Mao Zedong felt sufficiently confident to boast that 'only another year or so may be needed to overthrow [the KMT] completely'.

Certainly by the summer of 1949 it was a major concern of the British government to consider the future of Hong Kong in the light of the forthcoming Communist domination of the subcontinent. This involved a new attention to Hong Kong's defences and required the sounding out of the United States over what it might be prepared to do in the case of an emergency. For some it looked as if the territory was as ill-equipped in 1949 as it had been in 1941 when it faced and failed to meet the challenge from Imperial Japan. Foreign Secretary Bevin spoke with Secretary of State Acheson on the subject in June. The American response, as reported by Bevin, was to reckon that the new Chinese government would

in due course demand the retrocession of Hong Kong or at any rate the surrender of the New Territories. If we refused they would probably apply an economic boycott or blockade and create the greatest possible amount of disturbance by infiltration.

The Truman administration, however, posed a series of questions to the foreign secretary, including what the British might do 'if the Communists used all measures short of armed attack' and how the United Nations could be of assistance in a forum where Beijing was unlikely to be a member, to which plainly there were no easy answers. The optimistic reply by Bevin in September left much to fate, since it was hardly the case that 'the authorities in Hong Kong were now confident of their ability to face armed aggression, economic blockade or subversive activities from within'. Three days later Bevin met the Portuguese defence minister in Washington only to inform him flatly that it was unlikely that Britain could do anything to help protect Macao. The assurance that Bevin gave that the new Chinese regime would leave both colonial enclaves well alone in order to concentrate on national reconstruction can hardly have been much consolation to Lisbon.

Yet to its Allies the cabinet held fast to the view that Hong Kong in all probability would not face invasion. The objective was to stand firm and convey the impression to all parties that there would be no retreat. The first community that required persuasion was Hong Kong itself. British forces garrisoning the territory were themselves sceptical of their role. The colonial secretariat in Hong Kong informed London in July 1949 that

[w]e find that many of the rank and file of the armed Forces here, and quite a number of the officers, are completely ignorant about Hong Kong and its raison d'être and therefore some are saying that there is no good reason for them being here.

With the Chinese civil war nearing its climax and the prospect of border clashes having to be considered officials attempted to answer the question 'Why Hong Kong?'. Their response was far from reassuring. The troops were instructed that they were 'policemen of the Empire', who by their presence served to protect a superb Oriental shop-window for British goods'. To these roles the anonymous authors added the reminder that 'the city which our countrymen raised from the barren rock now commercially dominates the Far East'. Prose and sentiment of this calibre provided easy meat for Fleet Street. The *Manchester Guardian* pointed out in August that 'the soldier will ask himself why he should sweat for the taipan on the Peak' and suggested that it was hardly export promotion but the need to demonstrate Britain's anti-Communist resolve that best explained why the Hong Kong garrison was important. Reference in the Commons to Hong Kong becoming the Berlin (or sometimes the Gibraltar) of Asia quickly turned the phrase into a cliché. Reinforcements were sent; encouraging noises made to all in the territory. Support from the United States and the Commonwealth was generally forthcoming, though Secretary Acheson's public statements denying any American defence commitment to Hong Kong contrasted sharply with the more encouraging private conversations he was holding simultaneously with the British government and its Foreign Office staff.

Hong Kong's future was obviously linked to the decisions of the new Chinese government. In order both to protect the territory and to safeguard British investments in China proper the cabinet quickly opted to recognize the PRC as the sovereign government of the subcontinent. The decision of 6 December 1950 was taken after considerable division within the Attlee administration and in the face of disagreements among Allies and Commonwealth members. It was a highly controversial act that, unfortunately for the Labour government, achieved fewer of its purposes than its advocates had intended. It did not result in any immediate response from Beijing beyond the opening of negotiations by officials from the two governments. There were simply too many recent unsolved Anglo–Chinese issues for a smooth beginning, these disagreements including questions that had a direct bearing on Hong Kong.

One particularly sensitive question concerned the rightful ownership of aircraft held at Kai Tak airport. The dispute centred over whether the civil planes, formerly owned by the KMT and then sold to General Chennault of wartime 'flying tigers' fame, should be handed over to the PRC as the government of China and heir to Nationalist-owned property. The issue came before the Supreme Court in Hong Kong where the ruling in favour of Beijing in February 1950 was then appealed. This led the PRC to issue a note in mid-May that was highly critical of the manner in which the Hong Kong authorities had handled the whole affair. What some persisted as seeing as a relatively trivial dispute was regarded by the PRC's Zhou Enlai as a political test case, where 'such a sacred property right of the Central People's government should be respected by the Hong Kong government'.

The fact that Britain and Hong Kong should also be embroiled simultaneously in difficulties with the retreating Nationalists only added to the near-impossibility of making policies that could be accepted by the major parties. The KMT might bomb British shipping and blockade Chinese ports, feeling thoroughly disgruntled by the withdrawal of British recognition, while the new Chinese government moved only slowly to accept diplomatic relations, and this at no more that the sub-ambassadorial level. Little went right for London; cabinet hopes were largely unrealized. Its efforts were partly rebuffed by the PRC and Britain's allies refused to join the recognition process.

For Hong Kong, however, it was a different tale. The colony was not subject either to direct military attack or any sustained campaign of internal subversion in the period immediately after the PRC came to power. The British government might be in near-total disagreement with the United States over the question of diplomatic recognition of what the tabloids termed 'red' China and in the debate over the PRC's admittance to the United Nations, while still failing to gain much from moving closer to Beijing, but at least its position in Hong Kong appeared relatively satisfactory. This was an important consolation. It obviously reassured the peoples of Hong Kong, it was a relief to British commercial interests in east Asia and it defused what would have a serious domestic political crisis.

Yet this lack of direct Chinese involvement in Hong Kong after the establishment of the PRC was followed in June 1950 by the outbreak of the Korean war. Once again Hong Kong felt threatened; once again its fate depended on international forces about which it could do precious little. There was no way of knowing how the new Chinese government would react, particularly when its People's Liberation Army (PLA) intervened in the Korean fighting as the forces under General MacArthur massed near the Manchurian border. Concentrated attacks by the PLA on UN positions in mid-October 1950 heralded yet more fears in Hong Kong.

Attention on Korea, however, made the immediate threat to Hong Kong less rather than more probable. Indeed evidence suggests that consideration of Hong Kong's fate was never among the immediate priorities of the new regime. Press reports from official sources in September 1949 entitled 'foreign Aggressors must not be allowed to annex Chinese territory' refer specifically to the liberation of 'all Chinese territory including Tibet, Sinkiang, Hainan and Formosa'. Coping with these areas, even after Taiwan had been excluded following President Truman's despatch of the US Seventh Fleet to the straits to block the PRC from invading the last remaining KMT redoubt, was more than enough for the PLA, while it was simultaneously fighting a bitter war in

Korea and coping with counter-revolutionaries. It was the imminent danger of encirclement that Beijing's leaders saw in the intervention of the United States in Korea and the Taiwan straits that posed a new challenge to the integrity of China. Under such circumstances policy with regard to Hong Kong's future would have to wait.

Attlee was concerned not to permit the despatch of British troops from Hong Kong as reinforcements to the Korean peninsula until he had received assurances from his defence staff that there were no foreseeable risks to the colony. China might have 5 million men under arms but the vast scale of its casualties during the war and the difficulties of attempting to create the conditions for modernization when foreign trade at least with the West was largely prohibited through an American-led embargo left Hong Kong in a more fortunate position than perhaps it deserved.

The colony's fate rested on the manner in which its government and traders reacted to the economic restrictions imposed on the PRC. It had been the view of the British before the October 1949 revolution that Hong Kong's future 'might depend on whether the Communists found the existence of a well-organized, well-run British port convenient for their trade with the outside world'. Foreign Secretary Bevin's blustering insistence to Dean Acheson that London could defend Hong Kong had, even before the outbreak of the Korean war, the additional complication of having to cope with the United States' insistence that there be controls on trade with the PRC. It soon emerged that American economic pressure might be almost as great a problem to the Hong Kong authorities as the political and military threats from across the border. Hong Kong might be ground to powder between the two antagonists.

Hong Kong, however, had to attempt had to get along with both Washington and Beijing. The territory, as the Foreign Office's paper on China noted in January 1949, 'would be living on the edge of a volcano' once communism triumphed in the subcontinent. Equally, Hong Kong could hardly ignore the United States' refusal to either recognize the PRC or trade openly with it. Major Anglo–American differences over the recognition of China were bad enough but to fail to agree on the extent of Western trade with the PRC could only extend the present embarrassments into the indefinite future. It could also cripple the territory.

Much of the Anglo–American debate took place at the highest political level, with the Foreign Office usually representing the government in its dealings with a disappointed United States. While the Truman administration ultimately had to accept that Britain was acting out of consideration for the security of Hong Kong and to protect its financial and commercial interests in China and beyond, it rarely disguised its feelings. At an absolute minimum State Department officials proposed that recognition should only be considered after there was clear evidence that the new Chinese regime intended to fulfil its international treaty obligations. As the Chatham House *Survey of World Affairs* for 1949–50 footnoted: 'In American eyes recognition involved an element of approbation. British diplomatic tradition based recognition purely on facts.' The behaviour of the Chinese government in unilaterally taking over British properties in Beijing and Shanghai, however, left many observers noting how little the cabinet had gained from recognition – beyond a serious fracture with the United States that worsened further with disagreements on the conduct of the Korean war.

The United States' imposition of an economic blockage on the PRC threatened the welfare of Hong Kong. While accepting the need for an embargo on strategic goods, Secretary Bevin was reluctant to go the whole hog and impose a total ban on trade between British territories and the PRC. The objections of traders were to be expected but others also complained that American export control lists with regard to Beijing were more comprehensive than the trade prohibition counterpart for the Soviet Union. There was also the very real concern that any British challenge to the Chinese government could lead to the suspension of food exports to a Hong Kong faced with feeding yet more new refugees every day and the even greater risk of possible Chinese military action.

Hong Kong and China did maintain trading links during the Korean war. Some of this activity was illegal, some was questionable and a further portion was licit. All of it, however, enraged members of Congress sympathetic towards the KMT and those facing reelection during an unpopular war, who felt Hong Kong was gaining unfairly from the carnage in Korea. The British government also faced its own periods of embarrassment in the Commons when explaining its trade policies towards the PRC. Ministers were obliged to make statements that only reinforced the dilemma of turning a blind eye to Hong Kong's trade, while having almost simultaneously to announce UN casualty figures. Statements by the president of the board of trade appeared to deny virtually all exports of strategic products but still argued that: 'We considered that it would reduce the chances of reaching a reasonable settlement if we were to stop all trade.' Yet after additional measures were approved by the United Nations in May 1951 the cabinet was obliged to introduce more stringent measures with regard to Hong Kong's trade with the PRC. Sir Hartley Shawcross announced that as of 25 June 1951 there would be licence controls on all exports from Britain to China and Hong Kong and that similar restrictions would apply to

Hong Kong's dealings with China. While still insisting that Britain would not impose a total ban on trade (strategic goods excepted) the action did play its part in preventing a more serious rift with the Congress, where legislation was amended to permit greater presidential discretion over determining whether foreign governments should be penalized for what was seen as trading with the enemy.

The Truman administration had little sympathy for Hong Kong's plight; it regarded the territory as acting against the interests of the United States and the United Nations in failing to prevent trading with the PRC. While not wishing to see Hong Kong swallowed up by Beijing, the American government felt that its contribution to aiding the territory in the event of a full-scale emergency would be primarily in the form of 'furnishing relief assistance'. Only 'in the light of our own military commitments and capabilities at that time' would the president in late August 1950 consider anything more concrete. His National Security Council reckoned that the Communists could best employ 'disorder, subversion, and sabotage' against Hong Kong since, as the NSC authors pithily noted, 'these could in all probability eventually achieve the objective without military intervention'.

The State Department officials in east Asia had long stressed that any effective trade embargo on the PRC would require full British cooperation. The American consul general in Shanghai in February 1949 had warned his superiors that British agreement 'would have to include Hong Kong' and feared that traders would acquire invoices in Hong Kong that might circumvent American controls. (It would not be too difficult to falsify documentation to make it appear that goods for export to the West had originated in the colony rather than being merely offloaded there for transshipment.) Undoubtedly Hong Kong interests gained from the desperate need of the PRC to acquire a range of imports and exports during the Korean fighting. The extent, however, of the colony's involvement is not easily discovered, since obviously barter trade and smuggling can only be very approximately estimated.

It was apparent from the summer of 1950 that supervision of Hong Kong exports to Communist China required British compliance and that unless this was forthcoming there would remain no prospect of controlling the China trade. Press reports in Hong Kong on the opportunities that the war was bringing to the territory paralleled the reputed comments of Prime Minister Shigeru Yoshida in Tokyo that the Korean conflict was a 'gift of the gods' that had seemingly made possible the miraculous improvement in the Japanese economy. Millions of dollars flowed into Hong Kong from a variety of dubious Chinese sources. Fortunes could be made literally overnight. The risks were enormous but the profits equally large for those who could acquire the war materiel and successfully deliver it to Chinese agents across the border.

There were indeed lengthy Anglo–American negotiations on what specific products ought to be controlled and how the regulatory process should be carried out. Agreement in principle was easy to achieve but getting the highly detailed strategic lists upheld was an entirely different matter. US officials had warned in the summer of 1949 that Hong Kong sources were providing what was regarded as information of 'doubtful accuracy and value'. The American press also feared that British commercial interests would inevitably offer resistance to American-led schemes and that the manufacture of a 'common front' between London and its Allies would be far from easy.

The debate on trade embargoes against the PRC continued throughout the Korean war and beyond. Britain's governments in the 1950s did not wish to antagonize the PRC but could not easily persuade Washington to withdraw its trade embargo. Changes came gradually and reluctantly. It was only possible for President Eisenhower to eliminate what was termed the 'China differential' in 1958 after the British conservative government had broken ranks with the United States and announced that it would no longer accept a more stringent trade boycott for China trade than that required for the West's dealings with the Soviet Union. The president, who had previously been boxed in by congressional opponents, followed up the British initiative by supporting the Macmillan cabinet's decision. Joint talks between the multinational Allied consultative group led eventually to the abolition of the China differential.

Hong Kong's pivotal role in any attempt to impose sanctions on the PRC was apparent to all before Mao Zedong gained power. American consular officials in China stressed to the State Department that essential imports such as oil and rubber were flowing to Communist areas and by April 1949 there were American predictions that previous British 'acquiescence in [the] use [of] Hong Kong as [a] Communist trading centre' might be modified. Such hopes never materialized. Secretary Acheson's concerns of May 1949 that possible American controls 'could be subverted via Brit[ish] channels' quickly proved to be the case. The American consul in Shanghai warned in July 1949 that British officials in China prior to the Communist takeover were reluctant to accept the

need for realistic rational export controls at Hong Kong, a problem which will become pressing once Communists take Canton. Until British agree to some effective supervision over Hong Kong exports to Communist China, western powers will obviously lack essential economic leverage for dealing with Communists on important problems. Unaware [of] any satisfactory substitute for export controls at Hong Kong.

It was not, however, only Britain that appeared to be dragging its feet. General MacArthur's staff in Tokyo were equally eager to maintain substantial trading links with any new Chinese regime in 1949, since north China was traditionally an important source of soy beans and the costs could be offset by the sale of Japanese steel products. While such arrangements might be acceptable, the question of strategic exports was far more serious and the diplomatic manoeuvring more difficult. It was for Hong Kong a period of tension with major strains on the economic and social structure through the influx of large numbers of immigrants from across the border. Government statistics estimated the total population of the territory in April 1950 at 2,360,000 people, which represented the highest figure in its history. After a further year of population growth, immigration controls had to be imposed to deter still more refugees from arriving from China.

Those in the United States who (rightly) complained of British laxity over the trade embargo might have recalled that it was American-made military equipment with which the KMT frequently inflicted damage on foreign shipping. When British merchantmen attempted to visit Chinese ports, they faced attack from both Chinese Nationalists and Communists. This risk of bombardment from rival Chinese forces was not, however, as perilous as the surprise attack on *HMS Amethyst* up the Yangtze in April 1949 when severe casualties were inflicted on both British and PLA forces. The political consequences of this bitter incident resulted in the cabinet ordering immediate military reinforcements to Hong Kong and saw Sino–British relations registering a further setback.

Conversations between Secretary Morrison and US Ambassador Gifford in London indicate the difficulties that persisted throughout the coming to power of the CCP and the subsequent Korean war period. Ambassador Gifford warned the secretary of state in May 1951 that the issue of Hong Kong's trade with the PRC was proving a 'difficult and embarrassing question'. He noted that elements of American public opinion seemed to think that important strategic war materials were going to China from Hong Kong and requested Morrison to publish information on whether 'goods of military value were going from Hong Kong to China'. Gifford carefully stated that it was 'his impression that the volume and importance of these goods had been much exaggerated' but cautioned that there remained 'a very strong wave of anti-British feeling in the United States at the moment, whipped up by the reports they were hearing about Hong Kong'. Lack of a united Anglo–American front over the recognition of the PRC, disagreements over appropriate strategy for the conduct of the war in Korea, and a view that London and Hong Kong were continually uncooperative over restricting the transshipment of raw materials and strategic goods to the PRC led to a lengthy period of tension. It was during this period of very considerable strain that President Truman noted, when being briefed on preparations of a draft peace treaty for occupied Japan, that it was encouraging to learn of at least one Asian issue where there was general agreement between Washington and London.

Governor Grantham might joke in retrospect that '[i]t was not, however, the intention of the American authorities to strangle Hong Kong and Macao, although sometimes it almost seemed so!' but the situation was far from amusing in the early 1950s. Grantham points out in his memoirs that 'Hong Kong had always lived by entrepot trade . . . Stop that flow, and Hong Kong would die'. There was undoubtedly a danger of the American embargoes doing precisely that, though attributing responsibility for the difficult position Hong Kong found itself in during the Korean war is a harder task. Grantham concedes that the United States was correct to complain of laxities over smuggling and trade evasions in the first months of the anti-PRC campaign, but the governor could also note that the American consulate's clandestine and propaganda activities in Hong Kong left something to be desired.

The attempted solution to the danger of what Grantham admitted later might have proved to be 'the economic ruin of the Colony' was diversification away from being exclusively a trading territory to one that could begin the process of industrialization, albeit under highly inauspicious circumstances. Those somewhat jaded audiences who have become used to hearing repeatedly of Hong Kong's economic dynamism may have forgotten the unpleasant realities of the early 1950s. The departmental records for the Colony's trade in 1951 and 1952 make for sober reading. Total trade for the whole of 1952 was reported by the department of commerce and industry to be significantly less than in the previous year. Imports for 1952 were valued at $3,779.5 million (down 22.4 per cent on the 1951 figures) and exports at $2,899.0 million (down by 34.6 per cent). The difficulties persisted even after the signing of the Korean armistice in 1953. Indeed, the anonymous author of the departmental statistics for 1953 could only report that

[t]he best that can be said for 1953 is that it was no better and only very slightly worse than 1952. After a promising start which gave every indication that the year would be favourable, trade in terms of value slumped badly during the summer and though there was a small recovery in the autumn it was still running at a much lower rate than 1952.

Against this gloomy picture there were 'a few bright spots, notably increased exports of Hong Kong manufactured goods' and the commerce and industry department held that perhaps an estimated 30 per cent of Hong Kong's total exports might be reasonably classified as being in this broad category. When, however, the types of production that the territory was capable of developing are examined it becomes apparent that the territory was only at a very early stage of industrialization. New developments at the end of 1953, for example, consisted largely of light engineering, enamelling, and above all textile manufacturing, though the government's own commentator warned that the 'knitting mills in Hong Kong are mainly using obsolete machines'.

Under the difficult circumstances of trade restrictions and regional conflict it is doubtful whether Governor Grantham's later claim that this proved to be the saving of Hong Kong can be left unchallenged. Certainly local 'resilience and resourcefulness' got industry going but even the governor in retirement had to admit that industrialization was a slow and painful process and that only '[g]radually things picked up until a reasonable degree of prosperity had returned'. It was more a case of desperation than careful planning. The historian of the Hongkong and Shanghai Bank's postwar rise noted that its chief manager Arthur Morse in the autumn of 1945 'was anxious to restore Hong Kong as a viable, profitable, entrepot economy – his focus was on public utilities, the port, and docks'. It was circumstances rather more than conscious planning that dictated the gradual shift away from the profitable and familiar to the hazardous and new.

Certainly the industrial sector grew at an impressive rate throughout the 1950s and 1960s. Scores of new factories were built by former Shanghai entrepreneurs using local labour and finance. The textile goods in the first years inevitably were cheaply made and exported largely to Asian and African developing countries. However, as the mills and their workforces became increasingly sophisticated and turned out finer clothes, the criticisms of Lancashire became louder, echoing very much the comments that had been made both before the Second World War and again afterwards with regard to undercutting and unfair competition from Japan. Yet Governor Grantham's remarks that '[b]asically the trouble is that the Hong Kong operative works harder than his English counterpart, and the Hong Kong mill-owner uses his plant more intensively' did little to encourage much sympathy for the colony's plight.

An illustration of the successes of the burgeoning textile industry was the expansion in banking conducted initially in corrugated-iron sub-branches in tandem with the new backstreet mills. The Hongkong and

Shanghai Bank, for example, opened its small Mongkok branch office in 1948, only to have to rebuild in 1954 in the shape of a modern, eight-storey building better equipped to cope with the crush of business. The fact that the Hongkong and Shanghai Bank would have 48 branches and subbranches throughout the territory by 1966 is testimony indeed to the impact of industrialization on the community. Banks granted substantial advances for new factory schemes and then saw, if they were lucky, a double return in the shape of loan repayments and the opening of new mills where managerial skills were able to ride the tide of global demand for reasonably priced textile and consumer products. For the first postwar generation the image of Hong Kong held by those in Europe and Japan remained stubbornly fixed on cheap shirts and plastic flowers.

By the end of the 1950s the economy of Hong Kong had improved. The success of the territory in its drive towards industrialization is best seen in the reaction of other nations to Hong Kong's exporting prowess. The commerce and industry department reports for December 1959 speak of 'the problem of Hong Kong garment exports to the United States of America' and the requirement to license certain types of textiles before shipment to Britain could be arranged. The territory's Textiles Negotiating Committee had voluntarily accepted the need for quotas on cotton exports in order to contain the concerns of mill-owners and their workforces overseas. Hong Kong government officials, who had generally rejected excessive intervention in the economic realm, were now obliged to carefully monitor textile trade. In April 1953 Governor Grantham had cabled triumphantly to Colonial Secretary Oliver Lyttelton 'All Price Controls have now been removed'; his successor Sir Robert Black had been forced to promote 'the Exportation of Cotton Manufactures (Prohibition) Regulations, 1959' to assuage public opinion overseas. There were clearly limits to laissez-faire, with the colony's officials having to mediate between ambitious exporters and aggrieved Lancastrians.

New trade patterns had to be found if Hong Kong was to survive in the early 1950s. Alternative outlets to the semi-blocked China connection were urgently required in order to help alleviate what, in the short term at least, was certain to be a period of rough weather. The most obvious method to improve Hong Kong's predicament was to search for opportunities elsewhere in the region. Particular attention was placed on Japan and Indonesia. Links to Japan predated the Korean war and provide an illustration of the 'quiet' trade diplomacy of the Hong Kong government during an era when public hostility towards Tokyo was understandably pronounced. The authorities in the territory needed no reminding of how their fellow residents felt on the subject of postwar

Japan. Indeed the British Foreign Office felt (largely mistakenly) that the experiences of former internees had prejudiced their thinking, though even before the Japanese peace treaty had been signed the official Hong Kong view was that 'the time has come to suppress personal feelings'.

In February 1952 Foreign Secretary Eden pressed Secretary of State Dean Acheson to 'modify their trade embargo policy in the interests of the colony'. Eden agreed that 'there might be justifiable complaints on both sides' but warned that Hong Kong faced a 'serious risk of unemployment and of growing Communism in the Colony'. Acheson appeared sympathetic but Eden knew that American press publicity over the carriage of strategic goods in Panamanian registered ships was damaging to the British case. An American administration fighting an unpopular war in Korea could hardly accept what the draft British cabinet paper on the China question bluntly termed the fact that 'We cannot live without trade'. It was, of course, exactly the language that Hong Kong enjoyed hearing but it could not be translated into action in the early 1950s.

Government action towards defeated Japan avoided vindictive behaviour. By 1946 a small Hong Kong unit had begun operating within the British mission in Tokyo to develop trade links; initially this had to be on a government-to-government basis but with the hope that a gradual relaxation of controls by MacArthur's staff would lead to private business opportunities. Relations between the American officials and Hong Kong were amicable from the start and the territory gained a sizeable number of concessions from the arrangement, including priority shipments of coal, that led to the government's representative in Tokyo claiming that the growth of trade by 1950 between the territory and Japan had been nothing short of 'phenomenal'. Hong Kong officials were able to build on their cordial relations with MacArthur's GHQ and Japanese economic bureaucrats to the extent that, as the territory's representative in Tokyo reported in June 1952, both the US military staff and Japanese officials 'have been, and still are, eager to put trade our way'. But for governmental restrictions there is every indication that the early postwar trade between Hong Kong and Japan would have been even more extensive. Statistics drawn from the Hong Kong annual report for 1952 confirm the unquestioned importance of the two-way trade. Japan's exports to the territory slightly exceeded those of the United Kingdom's and at over $HK482,000,000 comprised 12.8 per cent of the Colony's total. The major items imported from Japan were described as 'fish, fruits and vegetables, textiles, manufactures of non-metallic minerals and metals and metal manufactures'.

Linked to the encouragement of trading ties was a skilful approach to mending political fences with Japan. The Hong Kong government moved as fast as it dared in restoring consular representation and residential rights for Japanese citizens within the territory. It was certainly not all plain sailing, however, as Governor Grantham made clear when he informed the secretary of state for colonies in April 1948 that

> in the interests of Hong Kong business firms I am opposed to their re-establishment of Japanese representatives here. It would not result in larger volumes of Japanese exports and imports flowing through Hong Kong nor would their admission be favourably regarded by the Chinese. If China were to agree to admit Japanese businessmen [the] argument for Hong Kong following suit would be stronger.

Yet such arguments were quickly jettisoned as the international debate over possible peace terms for Japan grew. By 1951 it was obvious that Japan would soon have a free hand once again and that with other nations proving eager to court Japan it made for good politics to endorse this trend. The anti-Japanese mood of many within Hong Kong and concern over local unemployment could no longer prevent a more generous public stance. In government circles, however, the necessity of establishing cordial relations with occupied Japan certainly predates the formal announcements of a new relationship with Tokyo. Governor Grantham, for example, had replied to questions from Whitehall on the possible allocation of Japanese reparations to the territory in December 1947 that what Hong Kong hoped to see was the '[e]arly rehabilitation of Japan', since without economic recovery there could obviously be neither the prospect of gaining compensation for wartime damage nor improved trade opportunities. Hong Kong government officials based in Tokyo scrambled to devise schemes that placed traditionally free-wheeling firms within the circumscribed world of military bureaucracy and currency controls. In attempting to allocate foreign exchange and deal with firms impatient to trade with Japan the acting director of supplies, trade and industry acknowledged in correspondence with the secretary of the Hong Kong General Chamber of Commerce in March 1949 that '[i]t is, of course, impossible to satisfy everybody, especially when allocations must necessarily be made on a fairly arbitrary basis'. It is perhaps not surprising that Hong Kong should have gained preferential treatment in Tokyo, though under the difficult economic circumstances the government had to maintain a waiting list of firms hoping to gain the chance of trading with Japan.

Initially Japanese trade officials were permitted to visit Hong Kong and then with the advent of the San Francisco peace settlements a more formal relationship was confirmed. In the 1950s Japanese companies and their employees were granted working visas and as the scale of their operations increased the restrictions on numbers were lifted. The peoples of Hong Kong, however, retained understandable bitterness towards Japan and it would be poor history to imagine that the wartime horrors were instantly blotted out simply because the two governments were able to cooperate effectively in the economic field.

What perhaps made the greatest contribution to the improvement in relations was the rapid growth of the Japanese economy from the mid-1950s onward, which ensured that Japan and Hong Kong escaped the polarization and economic competition of the past. Once Japan began to witness high-speed growth it permitted a much greater complementarity to the economic relationship. Hong Kong's performance was patently not in the same league as that of Japan after its reconstruction had been completed. This led to a situation whereby Hong Kong again needed Japan in a manner, of course, that would never be reciprocated. Government statistics confirm how vital the Japanese market quickly proved to be for the territory.

Government attitudes towards Japan were certainly well in advance of public opinion and clearly the initiatives of the authorities in widening links with Japan had to be undertaken with discretion. In 1953 the Hong Kong government banned even a Japanese circus from entering the territory and refused to permit football matches between Hong Kong and Japan out of concern for possible demonstrations. Yet when it came to considering the technological and managerial advantages that territory might gain from encouraging Japanese investment there was, argued the director of commerce and industry in November 1960, a need for Japanese 'quality standards, marketing techniques, [and] organization methods'. It was a thesis that Britain would find itself having to accept a generation later.

Grantham did his best to reassure Hong Kong as it faced multiple external and internal uncertainties in the 1950s. But he knew only too well that his colony was vulnerable once the PRC had established itself in power and that 'if any provocative acts against China had their origin in Hong Kong, Hong Kong would be the first to suffer from Chinese retaliation'. The territory was indeed an uneasy place during the Korean War. American citizens were advised by their government to leave, and some American enterprises, including the Chase Bank, did so, much to the chagrin of the governor. Equally, some of those European residents who had been interned during the Pacific war were fearful that they might face a similar ordeal a second time. Even more relevant for the stability of the territory was the obvious concern of the many thousands of its Chinese residents, the most recent arrivals of whom had managed to escape to Hong Kong precisely in order to avoid communism.

The weaknesses of Hong Kong's position in the years between the outbreak of the Korean war and the eventual relaxation of Allied trade sanctions on China did not, however, destroy its self-confidence. The territory had its share of war scares with their uncomfortable memories of an earlier era but this did not prevent the Grantham administration from demonstrating that it was generally both competent and able to maintain order. Under these circumstances the newly arrived Chinese peoples of the territory got on with the formidable task of conquering their poverty.

# 3    Growth: the 1960s

We did very well this year, because business was so good and there was
so much money about.
(Radio broadcast on Hong Kong's budget by Financial Secretary
A.G. Clarke, 1 March 1961)

Those who sneer at Chinese millionaires making profits in our Colony
would do well to remember that without their capital Hong Kong's
industrialisation would have been sadly held back.
(President of the Board of Trade F.J. Erroll, April 1962)

The economic successes of early postwar Hong Kong were quickly
recognized both within the territory and overseas. This prompted its
government to make a series of frank statements that both praised the
business community and acknowledged that the colonial administration
was caught between remaining on the sidelines and employing portions
of its new funds for greater social investment.

After a decade as financial secretary A.G. Clarke made his final speech
on 1 March 1961, predicting that his

successor will make exactly the same mistake that I have always made. He will
underestimate revenue. He will underestimate his revenue, because, like me, like
many others, he will never be able to comprehend how new and successful
industries can be created overnight out of nothing, in face of every possible
handicap; how new trade can suddenly start up in some way that has never been
thought of before; he, like me, will never be able to comprehend how on earth
our enterprising, ingenious, hardworking people can ever manage to accomplish
so much with so little.

The retiring financial secretary's words of praise for local entrepreneurs were well chosen and recognized that their efforts had contributed
in no small way to the funding of the improvements introduced in the
late 1950s. Clarke explained that government expenditure

has to keep on going up because you are asking for so many things; and you are
quite right to ask for them. We are trying to meet your wishes. We are spending
hundreds of millions to provide you with more water; we are building hospitals
and clinics to provide you with more medical care; we are building schools to

provide education for your children; we are spending millions to rehouse our squatters, and we propose to spend more millions to rehouse those unfortunates who are living in condemned buildings in the slums.

Sounding like a British politician on the hustings, the financial secretary explained that '[w]e want to get on with all this if we possibly can', particularly because 'during the year we have been having a boom such as Hong Kong has never experienced'. To reinforce his record Clarke told his radio audience that 'the Hong Kong dollar is the most trusted currency in the East, and we want it to stay that way', adding for good measure that the territory had 'very small public debt' and generally achieved a surplus of revenue over expenditure. Despite the financial secretary's assertion on 'the general unpredicability of events in this place', the Hong Kong government felt entitled to grant itself the good housekeeping award for frugality and success at balancing its books.

The difficulties that it might face in the future, however, were not inconsiderable, given that although the public was anxious for a greater range of public services there remained no very clear channel whereby these demands might be voiced. Clarke in his farewell radio address could only suggest that

if you feel that you belong to this place, if you take a real interest in Hong Kong, . . . study what you read in the paper tomorrow [on the budget] in the light of what I have told you, and . . . let your views be known; whether you agree, or whether you think we are on the wrong lines.

Yet evidence was already emerging of the changes to Hong Kong. One symbol of the government's gradual awakening to the need for greater expenditure could be seen shortly in the formal opening of City Hall in March 1962. As a building it had little of the beauty or dignity of its Victorian predecessor but it did serve as a symbol of increased official attention to the wider interests of the communities of Hong Kong. At the mundane level of the inner city tenement dweller, however, what mattered far more than the general state of the economy or new civic architecture was the desperate housing situation. Hong Kong might be getting richer but this did not appear to be either reducing the gross inequalities of income or making much impact on the still squalid urban environment.

The starting point for government discussion on Hong Kong's immense urban challenge was the enormous expansion of the territory's population in the immediate postwar period. The statistics may have been rough and ready during these years but the message of extra-ordinary growth was obvious. In the autumn of 1945 Hong Kong's population was only approximately 600,000 but within fifteen years, thanks to the huge influx of refugees escaping communism, it had long exceeded its prewar peak and reached 4 million. How to house, feed and provide at least rudimentary public services was vital for maintaining the stability and prosperity of the colony. It was perhaps the greatest challenge faced by its first postwar generation of bureaucrats, engineers and developers. One important method exhaustively followed to rehouse the citizens of Hong Kong was through an ambitious series of new towns. Indeed one authority has argued that this considerable accomplishment has rarely attracted the overseas attention that it deserves, stressing that the creation of 'homes for three and one half million people over three decades at a cost of some HK$78 billion is a major public investment by any standards' and that the successes and failures of these projects tell us a great deal about both the governmental policies and social patterns of Hong Kong.

The initial attempts to grapple with the problems of postwar urban areas were less than successful. Ambitious proposals in 1948 from Sir Patrick Abercrombie, the doyen of city planners, for urban renewal were not followed up, as Governor Grantham admitted to the Colonial Office. He and his advisors felt that the scale of Abercrombie's housing reforms was too large, given the financial situation facing the territory as it coped with piecemeal reconstruction. The temptation for most of the government was to rely on prewar efforts to cope and to let the familiar Public Works Department meet the challenge created by population growth, squatting and a rapacious demand for urban space to build houses and factories. Yet existing prewar facilities simply could no longer withstand the pressures of thousands of new residents. The situation was graphically explained by the professor of geography of Hong Kong University:

holdings have been reduced into smaller and smaller interior units. Floors have been partitioned off into cubicles and sublet by the principal tenant; the cubicles themselves have been further subdivided into bedspaces; in extreme cases bedspaces have been occupied on a shift system by three different sets of inhabitants. Roofs, cellars and lofts have been let and, before strict official control was instituted, the population still spilled over on to the pavements.

Hong Kong had begun to look like Calcutta.

The territory exhibited a paradox. Hong Kong might be booming but its peoples still faced the problems of crowded streets, uncomfortable housing, limited choices of education and an economic system obsessed with short-term gain. The largest change in the lives of many people in Hong Kong by the 1960s was undoubtedly in the area of city planning. This took the form of slow recognition by the government that urban congestion might best be alleviated by the construction of new towns. The huge programme was intended to be the venue where Hong Kong's 'solutions to the dual problem of residential congestion and industrial land shortages were formulated and tested'. The debating point for all subsequent planning was widespread recognition that simply to reuse the existing urban zones more efficiently and with a modicum of respect for the environment would never prove satisfactory. The government instead had to identify and then plan for large-scale development on new sites; only in this way would there be some prospect of having the luxury of starting afresh away from the older tenements and the newer temporary sheds.

What may be less well known is that from its inception the new town movement was closely linked with Hong Kong's industrialization schemes. While the creation of stark apartment complexes housing thousands of people has deservedly been noted, attention has rarely been placed on the determination to encourage entrepreneurs to purchase land from the government for factory usage. In this manner it was hoped that the living and working areas for many recently moved residents in the new towns might be in close proximity. This was a highly pragmatic means of coupling both the need to clear squatter areas and encourage the new settlements to become productive commercial and industrial sites. Anything that made good business sense was seen as deserving of a try.

The initial new towns were reflective of the rough and ready approaches of an earlier Hong Kong. Students of the postwar 'urban programme' even doubt whether the term can be accurately applied to the first experiments at Kwun Tong in eastern Kowloon. Perhaps it was only too typical of the government's modest beginnings that the site selected had originally been the municipal rubbish dump and that there were some expectations at least that the new settlement would eventually turn a profit for the government. True to form, the industrialization plans went ahead far more smoothly than the rehousing arrangements, where the stipulated requirement of new factory owners to contribute to the housing of their own employees was frequently disregarded. The government, virtually by default in this instance, had then to step in to promote the accommodation and services that private enterprise tended to neglect.

It was from these somewhat inauspicious beginnings that Hong Kong's self-styled 'experiment in the production of wholly new townships' stumbled out of the starting stalls. Since the whole concept was relatively novel for Hong Kong and the pressures that the government found itself facing were quite without precedent, it is hardly surprising that it took time for the schemes to get into their stride. Kwun Tong, for example, was described by one official as late as 1970 as having serious deficiencies, since the 'basic community facilities which decide the quality of life in any community, have generally not been provided at even a minimal rate'. The local city district officer warned that 'this situation could result in serious social upheavals in a young community which is becoming better educated and better paid month by month'. Government deficiencies in the provision of hospital beds, secondary schools and hectares of open space for what had by then become home to over 500,000 people were public knowledge but it took at least another decade before much was finally done to rectify the situation. A scathing commentary in the meantime had been published by Y.K. Chan that noted the

high degree of overcrowding, lack of environmental beauty, recreation and entertainment facilities, the problem of traffic congestion, shortage of spaces for commercial/business undertakings, all these problems reflect that an urban district is neither sufficiently nor well planned.

Kwun Tong, in other words, looked all too obviously like the old familiar confusion and cacophony it was intended to do away with and only marginally resembled the brave new world of the city beautiful movement.

In Hong Kong's partial defence it could at least be said that a start had been made; indeed in the two important areas of rehousing a very considerable number of squatter families and persuading industrialists to set up factories in the new town some successes were clearly evident. Urban geographers now began to refer to 'the Kwun Tong model' and to gingerly draw lessons from its example. As the author Roger Bristow would later note, there was recognition by the end of the 1950s that 'new-town building in Hong Kong had become an accepted and major part of the government's public works programme'.

What followed was no straight linear pattern but a gradual switch to more intensive and careful rebuilding with associated industrial opportunities being offered through government land sales in areas linked to new housing areas. This factor was increasingly important as the demography of Hong Kong altered from the 1960s to the 1970s with more teenagers seeking to enter the labour market and new industrial land needing to be found to cope with this reality. Employment opportunities in the vicinity of the new towns therefore made good sense, assuming the land supplies could be secured and industrialists could be persuaded to relocate in the zones provided.

In both instances the successes outweigh the failures when the new towns are put on the historian's scales. Certainly the government can stand accused of a great deal of 'ad hoccery' but the tendency to assume that this was a fault peculiar to the postwar administrations of Hong Kong needs to be strongly resisted. There were financial constraints and policy changes that resulted in far from consistent planning decisions, yet that has only to be expected in any political system that remains subject to even a degree of public accountability and pluralism. To point the finger at the territory's officials for 'the fact that the nature and form of the Hong Kong new towns are born out of short-term thinking and policy-making with limited horizons' is to underestimate the considerable accomplishments. The charge that the new towns 'are creations with major long-term consequences' but 'formative decisions have proceeded on an incremental, pragmatic basis, as with much else in Hong Kong planning' risks neglecting the tasks that faced and indeed continue to confront those attempting to grapple with human and financial questions that can at best be contained rather than solved. The limited size and the inhospitable topography of Hong Kong as an entity when unfortunately combined with an extremely high population density are important mitigating factors that should not be overlooked by any jury called upon to hear the charges against the urban planners.

It took decades and an entirely new approach to government spending before it became possible for the Hong Kong government to boast in its annual review for 1991 that '[f]irm plans have been made to ensure that, by the turn of the century, all Hong Kong people who need homes should be adequately housed'. To recall the desperate situation in the early 1950s and contrast it with the confident assertions of the 1990s is to note the distance that has been covered and to appreciate the irony of the present authorities being able to complete the redevelopment of the oldest housing blocks that dated back to the infancy of public estate building. Hong Kong's new towns have now come full circle. The experience gained has led to better designs, an easing of the tight space restrictions and a great deal of experience of value for improving urban planning throughout the territory; developing new towns has helped raise the admittedly low environmental standards elsewhere in Hong Kong and provided a core of information of use to the wider Asian region.

By the early 1960s change was afoot over the sensitive question of whether a master plan was required within which future urban development could be more effectively placed. Officials urged the government to order a 'regional land use plan for the Colony' supported by the necessary associated staff. Later experts on Hong Kong's new towns had already approved the start for the Kwai Chung and Tsuen Wan urban programmes, while the frequently voiced criticism that insufficient funding was being made available also tarnishes the reputation of the territory.

Tsuen Wan – also known more excitedly as Gin Drinkers' Bay in English – began life as a factory site before the Pacific war but its rapid development from the 1960s rested on the reclamation of its bay area. This was achieved by simply slicing off the adjacent hillsides and using the land-fill to provide the foundations for industrial and residential zones. The result was again a messy compromise with differences emerging over population densities and doubts over whether the provision of shops and schools was adequate for the huge influx of over 400,000 residents by the 1970s. Difficulties over building the necessary communication facilities for what was to be an important container port were compounded by the delays in getting drainage and secondary roads constructed. Some indication of the problems facing the planners is the description in 1971 by the senior planning officer for the Hong Kong government on how land had to be found for 'service reservoirs, sewage treatment works, bus termini, ferry concourses, schools, car parks, hospitals, clinics and police stations' in the Kwai Chung–Tsuen Wan areas with a protective green belt hopefully enveloping the entire new town.

Clearer evidence that the Hong Kong authorities were committed to the provision of new satellite towns in at least semi-rural areas beyond the major population centres was next seen at Sha Tin. At stake was what the director of public works called in August 1962 the 'answer to the question of where to go after Kwai Chung/Tsuen Wan'. The result was both development westwards to Tuen Mun (Castle Peak) and north-wards to the low-lying, marshy edges of Sha Tin. These proposals were followed up with decentralization policies by the government, linked to new official bodies to oversee the ambitious guidelines and stricter housing standards. For the first time in its postwar history the territory now possessed highly detailed documentation and regulations, which were published in 1969 as the Colony Outline Plan. The massive evidence on population estimates, industrial forecasts and proposed transportation schemes supplied for the plan rightly suggests the professionalism by then fully at work among the territory's planning staff.

Sha Tin came next. The scale and novelty of its development stands in contrast to the more pedestrian earlier urban projects. It was to be one of only two schemes that have been defined as being prepared from 'mostly virgin sites as theoretically independent, self-contained, ba-lanced settlements'. There had been a series of proposals for Sha Tin in earlier years but reclamation and transport decisions in the 1960s led to final approval for plans to house approximately a million people in largely low-cost public housing. The expectation was that new estuary land would be provided for 'residential and industrial development within the framework of a balanced land-use pattern which will allow people to live within a reasonable distance of their place of work'. Initially at least it was assumed that many of the jobs would be in the light industrial field since there would obviously be no easy access to container port facilities.

The rival to Sha Tin was the proposal to develop in the more westerly coastal areas of Tuen Mun. Indeed some in government felt strongly that a better case could be made for the latter, since costs were reckoned to be less than half those likely to be incurred on Sha Tin. As the senior planning officer put it diplomatically in 1971, the 'arguments for and against developing either Castle Peak or Sha Tin or both have been going back and forth for a number of years'. He then noted in the best bureaucratic tradition that, 'in fact funds have been voted for the first stages in the development of both towns, and at Castle Peak 54 acres had already been reclaimed by March 1970'. As in all major planning exercises in Hong Kong, a great deal of revision to population density proposals and the redesigning of railway and power supplies was made in the development of Castle Peak. At times the history of the new town appears to be little more than a succession of planning amendments with switches in the public housing requirements and a series of extensions to the outline plans. The statement by the Tuen Mun New Town Development Office in 1982 that '[n]ew problems, opportunities and needs are regularly being identified in Tuen Mun and as a result, New Town planning proposals have had to be applied in a reasonably flexible manner' was doubtless the case. This, the document continued, 'required that planners, deal with, and make decisions regarding, a number of important planning matters on an incremental basis – as a result they are sufficiently flexible to adapt to any new or changing circumstances'.

Later new towns inevitably reflected changes to the objectives of the Hong Kong government, considerable experience gained from earlier urban planning and the greater expectations of the territory's peoples. What appears remarkable to most outsiders is the general acceptance, probably without much overt enthusiasm, of high-rise housing in very dense clusters and at least the creation of some civic awareness. Portions of this are surely a reflection of the unpleasant environments from which many of the first-generation occupants were drawn and the obvious pragmatism which led residents to recall what their unluckier relatives and friends still had to endure. Yet it was all too obvious that many of the blocks were sited very close to each other and equally that the landscaping of the surrounding areas was often limited. The absence of much attention to the physical landscape before the mid-1970s was a disappointment but one that was partly rectified in later projects that incorporated village structures at, for example, Fanling/Sheung Shui near the border with the PRC, though there remained public concern over the incorporation of additional portions of the New Territories within the planners' orbit.

Definite evidence of how literally millions of people have reacted to Hong Kong's new town development is surprisingly hard to discover. Some material is available for the layman but any conclusions ought to be decidedly cautious. The suggestion that traditional intense village patterns of China led the first generation of apartment dwellers to feel reasonably comfortable is often noted but whether

Hong Kong can therefore be put forward as a particular example of the generalization that successful urban design must understand, make use of, and be formulated for the 'user culture' of its potential inhabitants

is not easily demonstrated. The transportation drawbacks whereby many high-rise blocks are held captive to a maze of clogged roads and the very high density of closely built monotonous structures may have been unavoidable but this is hardly a cause for celebration. To the outsider there appears a degree of sterility to some of the architecture and the overall planning.

While parts of the government were concentrating on the immense housing problems of Hong Kong, others in the administration had to reckon with fierce economic and political challenges from overseas. The importance of the textiles industry to postwar Hong Kong needs no underlining. Its success, as D.R. Holmes, the government's director of commerce and industry noted in 1965, was a 'spectacular' achievement, given that it reversed much of the economic history of the territory's past century. There are indeed grounds for accepting at least some of the official rhetoric and reckoning that 'an economic miracle' has been worked under hostile conditions. Yet, in a passage of considerably greater caution, there were caveats buried away in the fine print. Holmes concluded his survey by stressing that future prosperity 'depends largely on developments which will take place outside Hong Kong and over which Hong Kong will have little or no control'. Faced with Western textile restrictions first by Britain and then through further international agreements (the Geneva Accords), the warning was spelled out that greater illiberalism in global trade and the advent of newer competitors with lower costs could yet jeopardize recent gains.

The pessimists have been proved wrong in the three decades since the government voiced fears for the well-being of the textiles industry. Growth since the 1960s has largely followed the lines of official and private predictions that enhancement of the manufacturing standards of cotton products would have to be steadily improved for the territory to flourish. Over time the label 'made in Hong Kong' changed from meaning shoddy produce to recognition of high-quality consumer goods. As one official report wryly commented when noting the restrictive foreign measures imposed on Hong Kong cotton piece goods in the 1960s: 'This is usually the price of success.'

At a time of uncertainty in the 1950s it was the textile-owners and operatives who unaided created the territory's infant manufacturing base and gave a relieved government cause for celebration. The extent to which the authorities saw the burgeoning textile mills as playing a vital part of the development of the entire community can be sensed from commentary in 1965 that

even a small percentage expansion in this key industry in the years ahead would constitute a substantial and valuable contribution to the solution of the economic and social problems with which Hong Kong is beset.

Clearly, if the textile sector was itself subject to mighty pressures, the Hong Kong government was even more at the mercy of its most important industry. The vulnerability of the administration could hardly have been stated more bluntly: either Hong Kong's textile bosses had to deliver or the already fragile workings of the territory would be put instantly at risk. The government was dependent on its experienced ex-Shanghai entrepreneurs and a workforce that accepted a three-shift system to keep the textile industry buoyant. In the two decades from the early 1950s to 1970s the colony literally rested on the shoulders of this one sector.

The successes of the textile industry were critical for the evolution of the territory. The government did what it could to encourage training and technological innovation but beyond such pleadings and pressing its trading partners to refrain from overprotectionist measures it was left on the sidelines. It knew that 'even a minor recession in the cotton textile field could have a most serious effect on Hong Kong's prosperity generally and on the employment situation', yet it was virtually power-less to do much beyond tamper at the edges of any problem. By its own calculations 17 per cent of the total working population were directly dependent on this one industry in 1964 and it reckoned that as many as 625,000 residents of the territory were supported by the textile industry either directly or indirectly.

The responsibilities of the textile industry deserve considerable attention in any history of postwar Hong Kong; indeed it is difficult to imagine how the territory could have survived but for the exporting zeal of the mill-owners. Beginning with antiquated machinery and an uncertain market, the refugee managers acted boldly. By as early as 1959 all the territory's cotton woven exports to Britain were subject to a restraint agreement, which was quickly followed by longer-term arrangements for the period 1963–5 that anticipated no growth beyond an annual ceiling of 185 million square yards on all woven cotton products. Lancashire's insistence on limits to Hong Kong's expansion was a precedent that led quickly to international pacts throughout the 1960s. The Hong Kong government could only note in its own publications that even after the lengthy initial agreement had been faithfully adhered to, the prospect was for yet more international negotiations and ceilings. Its main fear was that instead of utilizing the interval as a breathing space for rethinking and readjustment, the developed world's textile lobby would still remain far from satisfied. Temporary measures could quickly become permanent restraints.

The best illustration of Hong Kong's progress towards industrialization was the reaction of other textile powers to the territory's exporting prowess. By the late 1950s the evidence was clear that Britain and the United States urgently needed to persuade Hong Kong to reduce what was seen by their own domestic industries as an onslaught that threatened to submerge the West. The call for voluntary restraint left the Hong Kong authorities caught between attempting to support its own nascent industry and the strenuous calls of other textile nations for an end to what one US trade envoy in 1959 described as 'a flood of cheap textile imports from Hong Kong'. The United States wanted the government of Hong Kong 'to police . . . a control system' that would limit the export of certain categories of textiles. Hong Kong was warned that 'the case of Hong Kong garments was so serious that Congressional action early in the next session was certain' and

if Hong Kong continued to abuse its privileges in the US market and did not refrain from damaging its best customer by 'disorderly marketing', it would almost certainly lose the greater part of that market in the near future.

The situation by February 1960 was sufficiently serious for the Colony's Department of Commerce and Industry to urge voluntary restraint on its textile industry, even though Hong Kong's mill-owners and trade unionists were deeply divided over the wisdom of such a policy and it went against the commercial creed of the territory. The realities were grim. If Hong Kong accepted a voluntary quota scheme it knew full well that any such precedent could be employed again and again, if the occasion so warranted, yet the truth was that 'Hong Kong believes in free trade, but unfortunately it is about the only place left in the world which does'. The government had to admit that '[n]o country, not even the UK, is likely to concede to Hong Kong industry the right to sell to it on an unlimited basis'.

It was the job of the Hong Kong authorities to cobble together an agreement that might satisfy the protectionist voices behind the Eisenhower and Kennedy administrations, while permitting the territory as many opportunities as possible to continue with expanding its first industrial sector. Unpopularity for Hong Kong's officials was thereby guaranteed, though the lack of a political system with elected representatives probably made it easier to take unpleasant decisions and escape excessive public censure.

The problem was essentially created by the rapidity of Hong Kong's successes in exporting to Britain and the United States. The breakaway Hong Kong Garment Manufacturers (for the USA) Association admitted as much in a memorandum of December 1959 but hoped also that the American side would note the difficulties that the territory faced. The Association argued that

[s]ince 1945 the Colony has struggled, virtually unaided, to earn the basic necessities of life for its people in exceptionally unfavourable circumstances which include the influx of countless refugees.

Yet this hope that other nations would behave sympathetically towards Hong Kong was already put in doubt by the uncomfortable reality that the British government was itself urging restraint on the territory. Pressure from Lancashire, which had been a major factor behind the difficulties in gaining parliamentary support for the Japanese peace settlement in the early 1950s, was now being directed at Hong Kong. Washington could hardly not be interested in gaining similar safeguards, particularly as it had been successful in persuading Tokyo to accept 'voluntary' quotas in 1957.

These international forces were in the end far too great for the Hong Kong government to combat. The British ambassador in Washington warned the Foreign Office in May 1961 that the 'threat' to Hong Kong could only be removed by agreeing to an immediate 'temporary quota scheme'. Worse from Hong Kong's point of view was the greater public attention placed on the deteriorating prospects for the American textile industry once President Kennedy assumed office. Governor Black's position was inevitably weak when he attempted to mitigate the pain. In the division of labour his officials had to work with local industrialists, while the British government handled the negotiations with the United States. Black's fears of 'very severe unemployment in the garment industry' were based on rumours that the American side proposed to recommend substantial reductions.

The announcement by President Kennedy on 2 May 1961 that he was summoning an international conference to settle textile trade disputes brought Hong Kong into the limelight. The president directed the Department of State to organize an early meeting of the principal textile exporting and importing countries, that would 'seek an international understanding which will provide a basis for trade that will avoid undue disruption of established industries'. Kennedy's seven-point programme was clearly intended to find means of relief for Southern textile states in the light of 'rapid technological change, shifts in consumer preference, and increasing international competition'. The president's belief was that aid for American textile groups could be met, 'while at the same time recognizing the national interest in expansion of world trade and the successful development of less-developed nations'. This last hope was never particularly large, given the political forces that had pressed Eisenhower and Kennedy to damp down Asian competition.

The British government was equally suspicious of Hong Kong's emergence as an important textile manufacturer. The territory's Commerce and Industry Department, obliged to persuade local groups to swallow some form of restrictive scheme, knew by 1960 that

Hong Kong industry has been making serious inroads into the home markets of UK and USA industries as well as their overseas markets, and that these industries will not stand aside and allow themselves to be strangled to death.

The screams of Hong Kong manufacturers, unionists and chambers of commerce were in vain. The government realized that the 'alternative to voluntary restraint by Hong Kong industry is compulsory restriction by the Government in the country of the affected industry'.

What had next to be carefully negotiated was the degree of maximum restraint that Hong Kong would accept. The process began against a groundswell of considerable hostility within the United States. Its textile industry had lobbied hard and successfully to gain the ear of first the Congress and now the White House; it was also helped by sections of the press. UPI in New York quoted one textile-owner as describing the territory as 'a sort of cancer on the world's textile and garment industry. So we think Washington should take drastic measures against it'. Statistics that alleged the discrepancy in wage levels between the American worker and his Hong Kong counterpart to be as high as US$1 versus US10 cents were circulated. What could hardly be challenged, however, was the enormous expansion in Hong Kong's textile exports to the United States, particularly when the figure of US$25 million for 1958 was replaced by the extraordinary advance in 1959 to over US$61 million. There could be little argument against the political costs of such expansion. It was sufficiently large for former Governor Sir Alexander Grantham among others to reckon in August 1959 that the Hong Kong Committee of the China Association should press the territory to open an office in New York to gain a better hearing. It was difficult, however, to fight the somewhat bizarre workings of the American government when it could announce in June 1961 that the Office of Civil and Defense Mobilization was opening an investigation

to determine whether textile and textile manufactures are being imported into the US in such quantities or under such circumstances as to threaten to impair the national security.

One-dollar blouses from Hong Kong were not normally regarded as offensive weapons in the Cold War.

The debate in 1961 was less abrasive than in the last months of the Eisenhower administration but the results were equally hard for Hong Kong to digest. In 1959 the territory had been surprised by the venom with which the US trade talks had been conducted and by 1960 Governor Black had been obliged to report to the Colonial Office that the suggested voluntary ceiling had brought forth 'violent reactions' and 'outspoken' press commentary, yet not all were prepared for the outcome. The mild and careful behaviour of George Ball as chairman of the US delegation probably helped to sugar the pill and in his role as undersecretary of state for economic affairs he displayed more sympathy towards the colony than his Republican counterpart had done in 1959. What could not be disguised, however, was the decline in support for Hong Kong's predicament among its friends in Washington. By the spring of 1961 British diplomats in the United States warned that Congress might unilaterally introduce legislation to curtail textile imports with little chance of a presidential veto saving the territory. Free trade would have to be replaced by some form of what the next generation would term 'managed trade'.

Meetings in London between the British, American, Canadian and Hong Kong governments then began. The US officials stressed that

the problem of Hong Kong exports was regarded by the United States Government as an essential preliminary to progress on a multilateral front, but they were very well aware of Hong Kong's difficulties, with a large population in a small area, and they would like to find some means of compensating her for any damage that might be done by restriction of United States imports.

This was a hopeful message but the fight had yet to move beyond initial statements of good will. In the same vein the British representatives tried to remind the meeting of the strategic and political risks involved in taking action that might undermine the territory's confidence. After repeating the familiar dangers that 'the Berlin of the East' faced, the British team emphasized that 'a conflict of policies was involved in trying to preserve the Western position in Hong Kong while attempting to take restrictive action against Hong Kong exports'.

Yet once again the United States had the stark increase in textile exports to bring into play. The jump from imports totalling $6 million in 1957 to $50 million in 1959 and $68 million in 1960 held an inescapable message. The weakness of Hong Kong's defences was further under-scored by knowledge that Japan's earlier period of self-restraint had given the territory a splendid opportunity to outsell the Japanese in the United States by 1960. While it was virtually impossible for the delegates to dissent from the Canadian view that 'we were dealing with political and social problems and not with economics alone', the eventual outcome was scarcely in doubt.

It was never possible for Hong Kong to resist instructions to 'voluntarily' reduce its textile exports. However gently the message might be put, the reality was clear. The difficulty, of course, from the Hong Kong government's point of view was to persuade its own industrialists that the game was up. Officials found this complicated by the divisions within Hong Kong's own textile organizations. The Financial Secretary, for example, was met by a boycott by the chairmen of the Hong Kong Spinners' Association, the Hong Kong Weaving Mills' Association and the Federation of Hong Kong Weavers when explaining the progress on Anglo–American talks. J.J. Cowperthwaite, the senior Hong Kong representative attached to the British negotiating team, warned that the intention of these groups was that

the cotton industry should be able to veto any proposals made by any section of industry, even if the proposals only indirectly affected cotton; and that they wanted the sole power to decide arrangements for the cotton industry even if others were indirectly affected.

He insisted that this was 'tantamount to a veto over all sections of Hong Kong industry, and Government could not possibly agree to such a proposal'.

Anger within Hong Kong stemmed both from American pressures and a concern that Britain was not prepared to stand up for the territory. This led textile groups, in the opinion of the financial secretary, to question whether Britain might not join the European Economic

Community and in doing so ditch the right of access that Hong Kong had long enjoyed to British markets through Commonwealth trade preference. Officials sensed that some in Hong Kong felt there was 'no point in acquiring United Kingdom goodwill since there could be no hope of retaining that market'. Instead of working with Britain, the growing distrust over London's intentions generated the cynical view that 'they should thus enjoy that market while they could'.

The proliferation of textile interest groups muddied the waters for the Commerce and Industry Department and showed Hong Kong's major export earning sector to be in public disarray. Governor Black, who appears to have left the greater part of the highly technical negotiations in the hands of senior officials, told the secretary of state in mid-June 1961 rather impatiently that he would welcome

in principle any internationally agreed arrangement which would remove this problem from intermittent bi-lateral dispute, provided that the basis adopted was liberal and promised to open an expanding share of the world's markets to international trade.

Black, however, had a series of reservations, including 'the danger . . . of encouraging demands for similar treatment for other commodities' that could well spell future problems for his territory.

On 21 July 1961 George Ball, as head of the US delegation to the GATT textile conference in Geneva, wrote to Cowperthwaite reminding him that the original American proposal would have restrained Hong Kong's textile exports to 'substantially below the level for the twelve months ended June 30, 1961'. He then explained to the Hong Kong official that the United States had not insisted on this in the hope that 'we could develop in discussions with you special arrangements that would meet our mutual requirements'. Ball therefore proposed that cotton textiles, other than piece goods, be restricted, 'category by category at 70 per-cent of the level of such exports during [the] calendar year 1960' and that it might yet be possible to avoid 'requesting restraint' on piece goods. In addition Ball was able to offer some hope of resolving one of Hong Kong's most serious concerns – the fear that if the territory voluntarily held back over the American market then its former share might be snapped up by its rivals. Here Ball, in a gesture that clearly indicates his considerable diplomatic skills and sympathies for Hong Kong, held out the prospect of consultations and concerted action to alleviate Hong Kong's anxieties over foreign competition. At long last the log jam had been broken. Immediate action then followed on how the details of the American package could be best secured.

Hong Kong did not repine. Governor Trench, the successor to Sir

Robert Black, made the point emphatically to visitors that 'diversification was the great cry and was proceeding', though he quietly added that 'maybe Hong Kong industrialists were worrying too much about diversification and not enough about design'. The governor was reported also to have told the American assistant secretary of labour that 'Hong Kong sought no special favours, but did ask for a fair crack of the whip from the US authorities'. Clearly textiles and the American market for them still remained a major concern of both local industry and government throughout the 1960s but the tide was gradually turning.

There were shifts in the character of manufacturing firms as more advanced technology was gradually used and electronic goods makers began to take on additional staff. Employers were often quick to spy out new opportunities; their companies remained generally small and increasingly sited in designated industrial estates rather than coping with the chaotic conditions of the past. Yet the undoubted changes of the late 1960s and 1970s deserve to be placed in perspective. The Hong Kong government's own statistics showed that even in 1979

the textiles and clothing industries are Hong Kong's largest, together employing 42 per cent of the total industrial work-force and producing some 43 per cent by value of total domestic exports.

Many workers were employed on piece work terms and naturally this encouraged a high degree of mobility within an increasingly sophisticated industry that was still the backbone of Hong Kong's economic growth. It was a large, experienced industry that could be broken down into a whole series of key units and subdivisions, varying from the production of cotton and man-made fibre yarns to weaving, knitting and finishing sectors. The Government was not boasting when it described the finishing end of the industry as capably handling

bleaching, dyeing, printing and finishing. The processes performed include yarn texturising, multi-colour roller and screen printing, transfer printing, pre-shrinking, permanent pressing and polymerising.

The industry by 1980 had come a long way from the early postwar days when wages were barely above subsistence level. Gone for good were the temporary squatter plants with workers, according to government officials in 1959, having to put in an average of 40 minutes' work to buy 20 cigarettes and 42 hours' work to earn the cash to purchase a bicycle.

Hong Kong's reaction to the Geneva Accord was one of highly qualified approval. The financial secretary listed a number of reservations that the territory held but generally it was recognized that there was no alternative to approving what was a major international agreement.

The complexities of the Accord were virtually incomprehensible to any but textile authorities, though the figures for both garments and piece goods were approximately the same as in George Ball's original proposals. What the financial press termed 'the Geneva impact' had two facets: the first, and the one that naturally received most comment, was the scaling back of textile exports to the United States but in terms of Hong Kong's growing importance in the region and beyond the fact that a colony, still officially represented by the metropolitan power and not yet a member of GATT, was being taken very seriously by larger and more influential states deserves to be noted. Hong Kong was becoming an international entity in its own right, whose interests might well conflict with those of its supposed protector in London.

The changes in Hong Kong's own attitudes to trading behaviour were also considerable. As the *Far Eastern Economic Review* noted in August 1961 when discussing the need for restraint,

those good old days of free trade are gone temporarily. The textile community has become convinced that there must be some sort of accommodation under which the textile trade between the Colony and the UK can be carried out satisfactorily.

It was increasingly recognized that the best way to cope with 'voluntary' quotas was to gradually increase the quality and therefore price of Hong Kong's textile output. This could eventually lead to increased sales once the industry realized that the vigorous price cutting of the recent past would no longer solve the territory's problems. Cut-throat competition risked leaving the industry in a worse state than one firmly based on a more regulated and higher value-added product.

Evidence that both the Hong Kong government and its manufacturers recognized that restrictions would become the norm was next seen in the extension of the Hong Kong–Lancashire pact that had first created the precedent for bilateral agreements in 1959. Certainly Lancashire felt aggrieved in much the same manner as it had towards Japanese and Indian subcontinental manufacturers, but by the early 1960s the issue was already taking on wider dimensions. There was a gradual recognition that the question of textile exports from lower-wage Asian nations was only the first part of a new wave of industrialization for which the West would have to devise a clearer strategy. As the commercial editor of the *Guardian* noted in April 1961:

The problem is seen not merely as one between Lancashire and the Commonwealth Asian countries, but between the West and the East, and as one which, though affecting cotton textiles first, will confront many more types both of consumer and of capital goods as time goes on.

The problem would indeed expand as Hong Kong and others pressed ahead with their late industrialization, though long before this dawn the reign of King Cotton had finally ended.

The issue for Hong Kong from the 1960s onwards was to calculate how best to draw on the territory's assets and devise an approximate strategy for further sustainable development. Critics certainly worried that Hong Kong was too committed to a highly limited number of industries and that both the colony's imports and exports were likewise overconcentrated on merely a handful of countries. This fear of dependency was not unfounded when approximately 60 per cent of its imports and exports rested merely on the United States, Britain, the PRC, Japan and Malaya. What some thought necessary to alter this limited picture was a greater government stress on newer industries and more attention to both financial services and tourism. Yet, as so often in Hong Kong's history, there was resistance to overcome and suspicion of formal economic councils telling industry and labour what they ought to do to achieve prosperity. Many felt that the state's role in economic development, as seen elsewhere in Asia, was not a suitable model for Hong Kong to emulate and that a better way forward might be to rely on local banks to provide the necessary financing for industrialization. This assumed, of course, that domestic bankers both had ready funds and were eager to commit themselves to the risks involved in widening the industrial patterns. The government's role could then remain that of referee, able to reject calls both for a central bank and a more planned economy.

What eventually emerged was a loose system poles away from either the rigid, state-controlled schemes of southern Asia or the directed economies of northeast Asia. Hong Kong would gradually be seen as having devised its own road to affluence – one that would prove that there was no particular advantage to be gained by slavishly linking all of Asia into one pattern of development. Hong Kong was to remain an important exception to challenge those overeager to lump Asia into a single heroic mould with shared policies and common values.

It was the small innovative firms that drove Hong Kong forward. By the late 1970s it was possible for academic texts to write approvingly of 'the quantity and quality of small factories' and to maintain that they would 'continue to occupy a very strong and significant position' in Hong Kong. In its postwar economic development as, of course, in its political life as well, Hong Kong was different. It rarely had the luxury of possessing any great number of large-size factories that might employ hundreds of workers and was therefore forced to look to what many economists in Asia have often seen as less efficient and less progressive smaller companies. The Hong Kong government's own statistics for 1971, for example, show that one-third of the territory's labour force was then working in factories employing less than 50 workers. Wages and working conditions were often lower than in the very largest firms but in terms of international comparisons with both Japan and South Korea, Hong Kong in the early 1970s had achieved higher productivity levels.

Within two decades after the Korean war boom commentators could confidently state that the colony had been transformed from 'an entrepot into an industrial city'. The same sources noted the dramatic shift in the nature of Hong Kong's economic structure, seeing 'a complete turn around of the relative importance of its re-exports and domestic exports'. This began with the restrictions imposed on Hong Kong's trade with the PRC and spurred the territory to produce manufacturing goods almost exclusively for export. No other major trading entity has been able to export such an overwhelming percentage of its products onto world markets. From 1959 to 1973 the territory averaged a growth rate for manufactured exports of nearly 12 per cent. Armed with statistics of this impressive range it was hardly surprising that Hong Kong-based economists could rejoice in comparable language to that of their contemporaries in Japan, Taiwan and South Korea. In all three societies there was much self-congratulatory talk of economic 'miracles'. In the case of Hong Kong, local economists by the end of the 1970s would explain its success through the ready availability of capital, the eagerness of the work force and 'the rare ingenuity and business flair of its average entrepreneur', able to adapt at short notice to stringent market forces.

By the late 1960s success in transforming Hong Kong was inescapable. It led to statements such as '[n]ot infrequently, economists have cited the success of Hong Kong as an example to other developing countries'. The question by then for Hong Kong was whether its visible achievements could be sustained further to ensure that the territory might shift beyond textiles to broader-based industrial growth. To many observers within Hong Kong and without the omens appeared to be favourable. Overseas economists reckoned that the territory did indeed have 'the capacity to transform' and could thereby

organize resources and apply new technology and management in the production and marketing of manufactured goods, so as to adapt to changing supply and demand conditions originating at home and abroad.

There was indeed a virtuous circle of growth whereby, as with Japan of the same era, the key factors of export growth, industrialization and capital formation all reinforced one another and in doing so enhanced the economy still further.

Hong Kong's foreign trade statistics for 1966 demonstrate the extent of the territory's transformation from an entrepôt to an export-led economy. Total exports for 1966 had reached HK$7,563 million (a figure almost double that of 1961), while imports were the highest recorded at HK$10,097 million. By 1966 domestic exports comprised three-quarters of all Hong Kong's exports; the prewar and immediate postwar patterns of trade had clearly been abandoned. The entrepôt era of re-exporting products for transshipment to other markets within Asia was over. Hong Kong's future was linked to producing its own manufactured goods for export to the United States, the Commonwealth, Europe and Asia. Clothing and textiles comprised half of Hong Kong's exports in 1966, followed by toys, artificial flowers, electrical products, footwear and metal goods. Buried within the government reports was the important item that electrical products had displayed an enormous expansion since 1959 and in 1966 comprised over 8 per cent of the territory's total of exports. Hong Kong by 1970 was no longer recognizably the same economic entity of the early postwar years. Its prosperity was no longer novel or superficial. A territory that could boast 73 banks (deploying 399 offices) was obviously being taken seriously by the region and beyond. Ambitious land reclamation schemes, still more massive government housing projects, regular increases in real wages and a belief that the territory could achieve yet more for itself and its peoples was manifestly in the air.

Economic gains, however, were not seen as likely to provoke major changes in the conduct of government. Hong Kong remained formally frozen in its Victorian mould. It would, though, be a simplification merely to note the striking continuities in gubernatorial and bureaucratic power and to neglect the quiet but substantial changes that did take place. The most important shift was surely in the range of responsibilities assumed by the government. Not surprisingly, as Hong Kong became a more affluent, industrialized entity, the demand for public services grew correspondingly with more families hoping for improved educational facilities and a wider range of welfare benefits. Yet looking to the government for practical assistance was a different matter from claiming a role in the conduct of government; Hong Kong remained very largely an administrative state run, as it had been since its birth, by its colonial bureaucracy.

In concrete, institutional terms there was indeed almost no change. There was also a degree of satisfaction widely shared by the Hong Kong government's own officials that little needed to be altered. When, for example, Sir David Trench met with US Treasury Undersecretary Joseph Barr in July 1966, the governor was reported as saying that 'the field in which Hong Kong could, he thought, really contribute in the Far East was in teaching sound methods of administration'. Such complacency would have been harder to maintain in the face of critics within the territory who complained that inadequate finance was being devoted to achieving universal primary education and in the rooting out of what the Hong Kong Civic Association in a memorandum of January 1964 to the visiting head of the far eastern department of the Colonial Office termed the 'appalling size of the narcotics problem'. Few, however, were prepared to challenge the government's view that constitutional change was out of the question. The minister of state for colonial affairs' response to Hong Kong press questions on the theme in September 1963 was:

That is an easy question to answer. You have an administration which meets the circumstances extremely well. There may be small alterations in the mechanical set-up but it will be in the best interest of the people.

The result was lack of effective debate on Hong Kong's unrepresentative political system. The *Hong Kong Standard* in its editorial for 10 January 1964 could only note that

Government is against all constitutional change because it believes not only that there is no need for change, but that change can be indefinitely avoided, that Hong Kong can remain a nineteenth-century type of Colony for ever and ever (or at least as far ahead as the Colonial Office cares to look).

Even the more sympathetic *South China Morning Post* had to acknowledge that all was not quite as Government House would have the world believe. While certainly not endorsing suggestions that the territory should move towards self-government, the paper's editor admitted that

the grumbles of discontent that are being heard today on housing, public transport, telephones and other questions should not be minimized. Complaints that the administration is in some ways sluggish and in need of tune-up are at times true and go unheeded.

The *Post* warned that

government and all those associated with it in the various councils and committees will have to demonstrate to the community at all times that they are providing an efficient and progressive administration if major changes are to be avoided.

It may be that by escaping any general censure in the provision of ever-widening public services the colonial administration had little difficulty in seeing off its potential foes. Even the Labour party's fast bowlers found it hard to argue for radical change unless there was a clarion call for reform from within Hong Kong. Parliamentary interest was generally slight. Hong Kong watchers were invariably thin on the ground and their views carefully monitored by friends of the territory in London. Such sources reported back to the Hong Kong government that the April 1963 Commons debate on the territory began with just 12 MPs present and ended with 23. In order to attempt to remedy this apathy the Hong Kong government commenced a carefully organized briefing programme for visiting MPs. Such fact-finding tours may have helped raise the territory's profile at Westminster.

What attention there was centred chiefly on the expansion of the cotton textile industry as the speed and success of the territory's industrialization inevitably damaged more established textile manufacturers in Britain, the United States and Western Europe. The British embassy's brutal description of how the American textile lobby and Washington officials saw Hong Kong in October 1965 was that 'Everybody hates Hong Kong' and that the territory was a thorough nuisance to its rivals. American officials were seen as unsympathetic and their reported attitude was to force Hong Kong to 'export something else, such as transistors, and not disrupt our textile market'. Yet, despite considerable antipathy, Hong Kong was brought into a web of bilateral and multilateral trade agreements that were intended to spread the pain of the territory's emergence as an international competitor among its rivals and enforce a degree of self-restraint on Hong Kong's own industrialists. It was never a popular process in the territory or overseas. Still, the fact that, as Governor Trench maintained in front of Secretary of State Rusk in July 1966, after one protracted period of negotiations had led to an agreement that both sides were dissatisfied with, this could only suggest how 'the recent bilateral agreement was a fair one'.

Besides the pressing need to tackle the impact of Hong Kong's rise as an exporter, there remained in the background the China conundrum. Throughout its postwar history, Hong Kong's relation with the PRC have remained at the core of the territory's external relations. It has been and will remain the critical issue for each and every administration . The territory, in Governor Trench's cautious words, 'inevitably felt under some latent pressure as a result of its geographical position' and there was 'always the possibility that trouble might develop from an incident which in itself was unimportant and he considered it his job to prevent anything like this from happening'. In a lengthy conversation with Secretary of State Dean Rusk, Trench mapped out his analysis of how Hong Kong ought to handle its vital ties to the PRC. Adopting what Trench termed a 'realistic view of the facts' he argued that Hong Kong's relations with China depended on a balance of factors. In favour of the status quo were:

(a) the economic advantage derived to China (though this was decreasing)
(b) its use as an outlet to the West
(c) the fact that it would not be easy to assimilate Hong Kong. For example, many of Hong Kong's factories were turning out products suitable only for markets which would not accept them if they were under Chinese control. Unemployment would thus result from a Chinese take-over, and it would be necessary to resettle some two million people in the same way as had been happening in the case of Shanghai.

This Trench saw as the positive side of the ledger but he could not neglect darker aspects, where

one had to recognize that the Colony did constitute a slight ideological irritant, and certain eventualities were likely to make the Chinese more disposed to try to take over:

(a) if the Government of Hong Kong did not retain strict control over what went on in the Colony;
(b) if there were considerable unrest in the Colony – though this was unlikely to occur unless there were large-scale unemployment;
(c) if there were any move toward self-government, because in such a case the Chinese could not be certain who would control the Colony.

Governor Trench, while allowing that the Chinese authorities 'had not taken opportunities which had presented themselves in the past' had still to admit to Rusk that 'the Chinese would undoubtedly intervene in the Colony if this seemed to them necessary or desirable from the political point of view'.

Shortly afterwards Trench would have to eat his words, but until 1967 it appeared that there was neither external Communist pressure nor prospect for domestic political reform. The most prominent local campaign was led by members of the Urban Council in a vain attempt to persuade the government and the Colonial Office that change was overdue. Employing fairly discreet tactics the Urban Council argued repeatedly that its role deserved to be enlarged and the franchise for electing its members ought to be urgently overhauled. Unfortunately nothing came of these recommendations, largely because successive governments were not prepared to give their blessing to the various schemes envisaged by pressure groups associated with the Urban Council. It was widely felt then and later that members of the Legislative Council were anxious not to see any encroachment on its powers.

Informal soundings by such critics with visiting ministers from London, letters to the English-language press and discussions with the Hong Kong authorities were quite insufficient to disrupt the status quo.

The attitude of the British government was more one of relief than anxiety; ministers sensed that Hong Kong was going against the decolonization grain and that the territory could be safely left alone to run its own affairs along existing lines. For colonial secretaries having to face constant political difficulties over the fate of Kenya and Cyprus it was a cause for celebration that there was at least one territory where the British garrison was not on full alert and local leaders did not take to the streets demanding immediate independence.

Parliamentary questions on the issue of political change for Hong Kong were often based on sources from within the territory and the appropriate member of the Hong Kong government usually provided the required answer for Whitehall to mould into the ministerial brief. When, for example, the Conservative government was asked in June 1957 on the possibility of extending the franchise, Governor Grantham had cabled back categorically: 'There is no apparent public demand for an extension of the Franchise and no proposals for such an extension are being considered at the moment.' Colonial Secretary Lennox-Boyd, when challenged in Westminster that Britain was maintaining a benevolent dictatorship, incorporated his governor's remarks and then added that 'if the hon. Member went to live there, even he himself would quickly absorb the prevailing atmosphere'. John Rankin, representing the working-class Govan constituency of Glasgow, for one, was not impressed and continued to prod the government, quite without success, to make Hong Kong's legislative process more representative.

At the Hong Kong end it was difficult for even the mildest of voices to win concessions from an unresponsive government. Minor changes to the Urban Council had been instituted but in a memorandum to the head of the Colonial Office's far eastern department the Hong Kong Civic Association argued in January 1964 that 'desirable modifications' were now called for to expand the number of elected members on the Urban Council and to enlarge the body's sphere of responsibilities. The chairman of the Urban Council, Brook Bernacchi, made a similar plea, noting that 'the Urban Council had no jurisdiction in the New Territories' and that elected councillors ought to hold more posts within the assembly. Mr A. de O. Sales added that 'a more frank approach to the Unofficial members' work' was required from the authorities. He feared that a 'sympathetic appreciation of the work of the Unofficial members did not seem to prevail throughout the Government' and maintained that 'the time, goodwill and experience of the Unofficials should be used to maximum advantage for the public good'. Sales, who was an appointed member, said that, while he and his colleagues 'did not advocate self-government for Hong Kong, at the same time matters should not be allowed to stand still'. But they were and Hong Kong would continue as an unreformed administrative entity for at least another decade.

At the level above the Urban Council it was the same tale of deliberate restraint on the government's part. It was invariably easier to point to Hong Kong's achievements under the existing regime and to argue stoutly that all was well. Provided the governor in Hong Kong and the cabinet in London worked in tandem there was little that pressure groups in either Britain or in the territory could accomplish, particularly as criticism was certain to be met with the accusation that apathy on the ground negated the need for change. The result was a very limited parliamentary scrutiny of events in Hong Kong. Ministers had only to handle backbench questions on the tame subjects of roof-top squatters, umbrella imports, gambling rackets and the handcuffing of prisoners. Rarely was interest much above the level of interest that led the Hong Kong government to report that 'less dog was eaten nowadays' or junior minister John Profumo's reply in March 1957 that 'modern ideas are gradually doing away with concubinage and I think that may prove the best way to deal with it'. On more central issues of government, the Legislative and Executive Councils remained unreconstructed throughout this period. Change was at best marginal with the alterations being undetectable to all not following the minutiae of government on a daily basis.

What was lacking was a debate on Hong Kong's political future that involved a wider audience than the government and those critics termed by the *South China Morning Post* in December 1958 'a small handful of political dilettantes'. Without encouragement from the authorities there was scant likelihood of the bulk of Hong Kong's population taking a firm position, though the description of the Chinese middle class in the Hong Kong of 1961 in the *Far Eastern Economic Review* as 'substantial, able, industrious and sophisticated' suggested that self-government would certainly be possible, if and when the demand was taken up. In the meantime there was silence, prompted presumably by a caution against disturbing a colonial regime that held the ring and prevented either the supporters of the PRC or KMT from running Hong Kong.

Opinion among Chinese groups on the subject of political representation varied from those few actively campaigning for a Hong Kong true to the philosophies of either the mainland or Taiwan to the silent majority who called down a plague on all government. It remains surprising, however, that there was not more pressure for change. There were demonstrations in the 1950s and 1960s on at least three occasions that ended in violence but by the standards of most British colonies during this period the events were muted and the consequences for the existing government limited. There was loss of life in both the 1966 and 1967 riots but, as Ian Scott has argued, the changes reluctantly introduced thereafter 'did nothing whatsoever to alter the existing distribution of power but rather aimed at consolidating the shaken authority of the bureaucracy and its advisory committees'. Alterations in administrative and social policies did gradually emerge later, yet the government was never in jeopardy. If the Hong Kong state could be said to lack legitimacy through the absence of organized political parties and regular elections to positions of power before 1967, the same was still clearly the case in 1977 and 1987.

The riots of 1967 were serious but not apparently sufficiently serious to lead to any immediate administrative reforms. The Hong Kong government had been embarrassed the previous year by what began as a relatively unorganized series of demonstrations over a price increase on the cross-harbour Star Ferry and then went to considerable pains to find out and analyse the possible grounds for the sporadic violence in the evenings of early April 1966. Rioting in 1966 and even more so in 1967 damaged the authority of the existing structure of government in Hong Kong, leading some authorities to describe these events as 'a watershed in Hong Kong's political history' that, in Ian Scott's view, revealed 'the weaknesses of the system and pointed to the need for change'. The Commission of Inquiry's findings on the 1966 riots disclosed to many the failings of the colonial administration. It urged the government to correct the void between itself and large portions of the Chinese population through the institution of new channels and to improve its minimalist approach to social welfare provision, yet before action could be taken the colony was faced with its greatest postwar crisis.

The more extensive 'disturbances' (a stronger term might be preferable) in 1967 were fuelled by different forces than the 1966 affair. Instead of sporadic domestic social causes, the 1967 events were the result of concerted externally-linked pressure intent on nullifying British colonial rule. Events inside Hong Kong were a reflection of the cultural revolution within China proper and the success that Chinese communists in Macao had attained by late 1966 in totally disrupting Portuguese colonial rule. Indeed, Governor Trench immediately saw the Hong Kong rioting as closely linked to the anarchy elsewhere. Trench said bluntly on 29 June 1967 that the communists' objective in Hong Kong 'is to Macau us'.

It proved to be the most violent and most destabilizing threat to government in Hong Kong in the postwar period. Yet it failed and the authorities appeared after the events of the summer and autumn of 1967 to be once more in control. Indeed, some observers went so far as to claim shortly afterwards that 'the Hong Kong government actually benefited by the disturbances. By taking a firm stand against the rioters it gained greater popularity'. William Heaton in his academic analysis on Maoist strategy and the cultural revolution in Hong Kong would later maintain that the failure of Communist sympathizers to gain mass support in Hong Kong was primarily due to the lack of 'the organizational base for action'. He could detect 'no propagandizing, uniting and consolidating before the violence was unleashed' and without stressing local issues and grievances to capture internal support it is impossible to imagine that terrorism could win over the people of Hong Kong. The stout response of the largely Chinese rank and file of the Hong Kong police force to the bomb attacks and fierce intimidation left the Maoists crushed.

Certainly, in what would later be defined as the initial phase of the campaign, there were some hopes of exploiting legitimate labour disputes but within days of the start of the demonstrations public opinion was largely on the side of the police and the government. Looting and name-calling in concert with statements from Beijing was quickly shown to be a recipe for failure and this may well have prompted the shift to more violent tactics that aimed to bring Hong Kong to a halt. Communist sympathizers in government and private companies had some success in persuading (or forcing) their colleagues to strike in June but the police handling of unionist demonstrations and the seizure of suspected Communists took the steam out of the labour campaign. The disruptions to bus services and shipping certainly inconvenienced both the public at large and the business community but neither the intended general strike nor the mass protests outside Government House and in central Hong Kong brought the colony to its knees. While some within the highest echelons of the administration failed to keep their nerve, others responded impressively and the crisis slowly petered out.

By late summer the switch to random violence was seen as a last desperate attempt to snatch victory from impending defeat. Attacks were made on prominent buildings and a death list of well known figures was released, though fortunately only one journalist and his cousin were assassinated. It was during that period that the police received very considerable public appreciation, yet casualties grew and in the highly urbanized environment of Hong Kong everyone was at risk. Fifty-one people lost their lives in these months before the campaign was called off and Maoism was widely seen to be thoroughly discredited.

There has been no end to personal inquests on the 1967 'disturbances'. Opinions have varied from government voices who argued that the steadfastness of virtually the entire community proved that all was well with Hong Kong, to critics who saw the violence as symptomatic of far deeper fissures within society. Those who pointed out that even Hong Kong's equivalent of the Red Guards were not demanding the return of the territory to the motherland and that, in all probability, Beijing did not want to be offered Hong Kong on a plate are surely correct, yet the paucity of government references to the 1967 affair suggests that the authorities wished to avoid any extensive public scrutiny. The lack of a full-dress inquiry by an independent figure was highly unusual and goes against the British colonial tradition. Neutral observers can only assume that the government, even if it did not have anything to hide, much preferred that this blot on its reputation should be passed over in near-silence. The fact that a large number of changes, albeit of less than major import in themselves, were instituted following the bombings strongly suggests that a lengthy and vigorous internal *post mortem* was conducted by the government but that for reasons of its own this debate was best kept as an internal, confidential one. It had also the advantage of avoiding official comment on the unwelcome actions of the Chinese government in the territory.

Commentators have drawn up extensive lists of reforms that are regarded as having been the products of the 1967 affair. For Ian Scott the 'aftermath of the disturbances' stretches from 1968 to 1971 and yet, as others have noted, in some important areas such as local government there was no apparent change during these years. The aftermath of the 1967 affair was to leave Hong Kong temporarily becalmed, while a rough reckoning was made of what had occurred domestically and in its relations with China. The Trench administration admittedly made some serious efforts to at least improve its lines of communication with the industrial areas and new housing estates where it sensed its support had been weak in 1967 through the novel City District Officer scheme. Yet it was felt in Whitehall that a period of near-malaise ensued in the years after the rioting; this interlude was to lead to a wish to engender new thinking under a fresh administration by 1971.

In the territory's dealings with China the resulting changes were more immediate and clear cut. The convulsions associated with the cultural revolution resulted in a near-fatal divorce between Hong Kong and southern China. Certainly the supply of food and water continued, as it had done during most of the rioting, but trade was reduced and severe restrictions applied at the border over private travel and personnel exchanges. China's internal problems of restoring order and recharging its economy after the bloodshed and dislocations left little energy for thinking about a Hong Kong that had failed to succumb to the now discredited Red Guards. Hong Kong instead would shortly turn to reviewing its own domestic achievements and starting anew.

# 4    Transformation: the MacLehose years, 1971–82

> We can now raise our sights to the achievement of reasonable conditions of life for all.
>
> (Sir Murray MacLehose, *Far Eastern Economic Review*, 8 July 1972)

> In 1980 HSBC had completed a period of extraordinary growth. Net published profits doubled between 1960 and 1967, 1967 and 1971, 1971 and 1975, 1975 and 1978, and 1978 and 1980. This indicates quite clearly an accelerating rate of growth; true net earnings were considerably higher.
>
> (Frank King, *The History of The Hongkong and Shanghai Banking Corporation*, vol. iv)

Personalities matter. In a small city-state such as Hong Kong the role of its governor is inevitably under constant scrutiny and attracts ceaseless press comment. Sir Murray MacLehose was selected from the Foreign Office to lead Hong Kong in the critical decade that saw a shift from the conventional laissez-faire approach towards economics and administration to a more interventionist era that ended with the first concerted attempt to confront the problems associated with the territory's future. MacLehose's lengthy period in office from the autumn of 1971 to the spring of 1982 was to prove a watershed in Hong Kong's postwar history. By the time he left Government House, Hong Kong was firmly established on the road to 1997.

Yet Governor MacLehose's reputation today in Hong Kong rests very largely on his domestic achievements. It is what he did to alter the seemingly set methods that determined what should or should not be attempted by the bureaucracy that has become his enduring legacy. After the somnolence of the last years of Sir David Trench's rule, it was MacLehose who attacked the complacency, corruption and callousness of an entrenched bureaucracy and its allies in the business world. There was, as editor Derek Davies pointed out in a strong piece in the *Far Eastern Economic Review* immediately after the new governor's arrival, much work to be done if past errors were to be repaired and the aspirations of a more prosperous, aspiring middle class taken with the seriousness they warranted.

The new governor soon made it clear that he was prepared to listen to voices from outside the establishment. The fact that MacLehose was the first postwar governor who had not followed the conventional Colonial Office path to the summit was an important clue as to how Westminster and Whitehall were rethinking the appropriate policies required for a changing society. While it was true that MacLehose had served in the sensitive post of political advisor to the colony, on secondment from the Foreign Office, it was assumed in the press that he had been sent to break the mould rather than reinforce the status quo. This view proved correct.

Many of the hopes of reform, however, could only be accomplished through the very bureaucratic machine that the territory's critics took such pleasure in pummelling. Derek Davies would be shown to be correct in campaigning against 'the outdated and invalid shibboleths which have so long dominated and calcified official policies', but he might have asked himself how the new broom could operate without sufficient support from within officialdom. Part perhaps of the answer to this old bureaucratic conundrum was the governor's good fortune in being able to appoint a number of his own men in key positions in the first months of the fresh administration. No doubt the promotion of such personnel assisted, but the basis for the more assertive state came from both within Government House and through suggestions from London. The agenda was long and adventurous by Hong Kong's standards. It contained both what can be seen to be corrective measures, intended to reduce corruption and crime, and more positive attempts to strengthen the avenues between the community and civil service and to improve the desperate housing situation.

Strong leadership was necessary to shape the bureaucracy to do the governor's will; so too was a steadily improving economy. MacLehose was fortunate that the 1970s proved to be an extraordinary decade for the territory. It began, as the assistant manager of the First National City Bank in the colony noted, with irrefutable evidence that 'The days of "Buy cheap in Hong Kong" are over; cheap goods are being replaced by high quality produce which will remain attractive regardless of competition'. J. Perry Wootten also argued that as the territory developed 'a solid base of intermediate industry' it would carve out for itself a regional role as Hong Kong 'not only has the necessary goods to supply these countries but, more importantly, an untapped reserve of sophisticated and experienced businessmen who have already guided the colony through 20 years of growth'. He predicted that the economic community would continue to ignore adversity and build both a stronger industrial base and develop into an energetic financial centre able to encourage the free transfer of funds. Banking profits were already sizeable and the rush to open yet more branches in the newer factory areas continued throughout the decade as savings more than matched the new prosperity. By the early 1970s government statistics could also show that the after-effects of the damaging mid-1960s on foreign investment had been reversed and vital overseas capital was being used to further expand local industry. By 1971 the territory was enjoying a boom in capital inflows, although Britain's contribution to this position was well below that of the United States and Japan; this trend would accelerate in the next generation. The banking crisis of 1965, when several smaller local banks went to the wall following a downturn in property values, the riots of 1966 and 1967, and the uncertainties of the cultural revolution in China had all been replaced in 1971 by a highly favourable investment pattern that reaffirmed the territory's attractiveness as a developing economy. High profits, low taxation and non-interference were again proving that Hong Kong's traditional policies could benefit the community.

It was Governor MacLehose's intention, however, to question whether on the basis of continuing economic growth the rewards ought not to be spread more equitably. While being careful not to damage the sources of the territory's wealth, MacLehose appreciated that substantial reforms were called for to reduce the glaring inequalities of an acquisitive but potentially unstable society. The most politically sensitive issue that the governor risked tackling was corruption. This had long been a region where only the intrepid ventured; few doubted its influence in the territory but fewer still were prepared to start any serious reckoning with the beast. The best opportunity to begin a substantial investigation into the subject of official corruption was clearly following the swearing in of a new governor. This told the entire colony that the stables were about to be cleaned out.

Governor MacLehose, it must be assumed, was well aware of the public unease within Hong Kong at the prevalence of corruption and knew equally the formidable difficulties that were involved in containing, let alone preventing, the disease. He would have been fully cognizant both of earlier legislation and the remarkably slender results that had been achieved by earlier administrations. The commissioner of police's statement during the inquiry that followed the Star Ferry riots typified the complacency that MacLehose intended to root out. The response by Commissioner Henry Heath to charges against his force in 1967 was indicative of the difficulties in store for the new administration in the 1970s. There was, admitted Heath, corruption in the police force, but . . . there is corruption in other government departments and . . . indeed in commercial life and, in fact, pretty well every walk of life here in Hong Kong . . . In terms of money the police force is probably not the worst, in spite of the fact that it is the biggest section of government.

Corruption was therefore regarded by some within the civil service as an unavoidable way of life.

The extent of the cancer in the body politic was soon exposed. The establishment of the Independent Commission Against Corruption (ICAC) in 1974 followed a whole series of initiatives whereby the police had begun the highly uncomfortable process of prosecuting their own men. It had never happened before in the history of Hong Kong; widespread campaigns against police officers known to possess incomes that were far in excess of their salaries fanned a huge public interest in the manner in which both Chinese and European police officers took bribes in order to permit triad gangs and known criminals to run their gambling joints, drug rings and brothels without official interference. It was then that the Godber case suddenly emerged to ignite public anger at the manner in which some police officers were salting away sizeable fortunes to acquire villas in Spain and to flee arrest. The Godber scandal would become the *cause célèbre* of the MacLehose era. It led to street demonstrations with the war cry of 'Fight Corruption, Catch Godber' and showed only too painfully how ingrained inside the Hong Kong police force had become the practice of requiring kickbacks.

Eventually Chief Superintendent Peter Godber was brought back to the territory, after he had escaped when about to be charged for corrupt practices, and jailed for four years. Yet it was the ability of Godber, the most senior expatriate police officer ever to be investigated for corruption, to debunk to Britain that forced Governor MacLehose to appoint a one-man commission of inquiry into both Godber's escape and the far wider question of dealing with corruption in Hong Kong. While the Blair–Kerr report tended to sit on the fence over the vital question of how any new anti-corruption agency might be organized, MacLehose took the correct decision and insisted that an independent body was required. The governor had to respond to public disquiet and needed to be seen to be in charge. The idea that the Hong Kong police could be relied upon any longer to impartially investigate instances of corruption was simply politically unacceptable by 1973. Radical change was necessary.

The ICAC was to become one of the chief legacies of the MacLehose era. With the important backing of the administration, the anti-corruption drive did make considerable inroads into the cosy world of payoffs and special deals. Its main successes over the next generation would be political and largely within the public sector. The ICAC derived its wide powers directly from the governor having, in effect, a private licence from Government House to roam at will. The arrangement was unique within the bureaucracy and was intended to demonstrate both the importance and the impartiality of the commission. Not surprisingly it claimed its first scalps from among some obvious candidates within the police force. Nothing less than the bringing to justice of the likes of Godber and his associates would satisfy a public that had in many instances been preyed upon to provide tea money out of the petty cash and knew only too well the going rate for the speedier processing of building permits and customs' clearance forms. So long as the ICAC avoided straying far from the police the new body remained in favour with the establishment, though those concerned with the investigatory powers of the commission noted that some of the methods employed were highly questionable. Godber, who had been decorated for bravery during the 1967 riots, was himself imprisoned on the evidence of two self-confessed corrupt police officers.

In October 1977 the campaign to clean up the police reached crisis-point. Many members of the force had long felt aggrieved that there was an official vendetta to get them and this led to an extraordinary challenge to the government, perhaps in part comparable to the siege of the territory a decade earlier but now, of course, with the police on the other side. Demonstrations by hundreds of off-duty policemen outside their headquarters and the roughing up of ICAC staff raised the spectre of a full-blooded police mutiny. Governor MacLehose was obliged to retreat and reluctantly ordered a partial amnesty for those suspected of corrupt practices before January 1977. This eventually led to what was seen as a dilution of the powers of the ICAC and some reduction in the instances of reporting of alleged corruption by the public. The promise of the energetic Jack Cater, who would later receive a knighthood and become the chief secretary of the territory, that the ICAC would ensure that 'the back of corruption will have been broken in two or three years' was in doubt. Corruption was certainly still alive in the years to come, though it seems reasonable to assume that the public sector is cleaner today than in the past thanks to MacLehose's ICAC. The undoubted improvement in perceptions of the bureaucracy has hinged on the public's assessment of the relative honesty of the police force. Anger at the malpractice of civil servants in the early MacLehose years has been replaced in the mid-1990s by concern that the recent standards of probity might well be unrealizable after Hong Kong's reversion. It may be worth nothing that in the infancy of the ICAC, similar instances of corruption within the

Chinese state were being described somewhat euphemistically in its official press as 'looseness in financial discipline'.

Success in the anti-corruption offensive depended on the skills of a new, all-civilian commission and the support it would receive from the public. As Jack Cater noted in his first annual report for 1974 the only means of gaining convictions was for the community to be encouraged to provide the necessary information (often anonymously) that might lead to the collection of reliable evidence admissible in court. From the start the ICAC uncovered both mundane and alarmingly systematic corruption. Cater in his report for 1975 spoke of

the titanic struggle which lies ahead. For our aim is to break the back of organized, syndicated corruption within the next year or two. 1976 and 1977 are going to be crucial and testing years for the Commission and for the Community of Hong Kong.

While petty corruption over touting at Kai Tak and the jumping of the queue for driving tests might rarely make the newspapers, it was the scale of organized police corruption that almost literally flabbergasted the ICAC officials. Cater warned that 'the sums of money taken by the syndicates were simply breath-taking, amounting to many hundreds of millions of dollars'. He explained that over half of all public complaints concerned the police and that police syndicates were so rampant that the ICAC's working assumption was that all divisions possessed such entities. Once under suspicion the syndicates redoubled their efforts to close ranks and became far harder to penetrate. The only humorous episode in this saga was the revelation that the key figure in each police syndicate, who alone possessed the fullest information on each of his colleagues and could distribute the kickbacks and bribes obtained, was known in the force as 'the caterer'.

Attempts to deal with corruption in Hong Kong's business quarters were far less successful than the indictment of police officers during the MacLehose administration, and indeed afterwards. Part of the explanation for this relative failure is probably the political influence wielded by some entrepreneurs, while it is also the case that public dissatisfaction at police syndicates and their Swiss bank accounts knows no parallel with the complex world of illegal cross-share-holdings and international property dealings. The largest scandal was perhaps the fraudulent manipulation of share prices in the Carrian affair. This tarnished Hong Kong's attempts to boost its image as a modern, open financial centre and instead confirmed the view of many inside the territory and abroad that parts of the financial community employed highly dubious get-rich-quick tactics without much overt supervision from the authorities. At the centre of the rise and fall of the Carrian empire there was nothing beyond skilful self-promotion and a booming property market that permitted the company to buy and sell at speed. The public, needless to say, purchased shares in Carrian only to discover after its collapse that it was all a house of cards. Attempts to prosecute the officers of the company were hindered by seemingly impenetrable questions of who was behind the group and who had approved the wholesale fraud; matters were further complicated by bizarre legal decisions that led to public doubts as to the competence of the Hong Kong administration. What particularly annoyed the public was the quite extraordinary costs involved in attempting to bring some of the culprits to book and the equally lengthy time it eventually took to jail a few of the ringleaders. The trial of George Tan, the chairman of Carrian Investment Limited, and his director Bentley Ho lasted literally for years and, as T.Wing Lo in his comparative analysis of corruption in Hong Kong and China has pointed out, 'broke all records regarding legal costs, length of trial and volume of materials presented' only to end when 'the principal defendants were set free because the judge made an unforgivable mistake. The public wanted justice to be done; but unfortunately, the suspect walked out of the court at the expense of the taxpayer.'

The Carrian affair dragged on throughout the 1980s but was in time superseded by fresh evidence of the persistence of corruption in the territory's financial system. Governor MacLehose's ICAC knew how to prosecute police officers but his successors have found it more difficult to contain white-collar crime. It is, of course, a pressing issue in global financial circles and one certain to reoccur in even the best regulated system, yet Hong Kong's record has been decidedly poor. For decades the stock market was seen, much like Tokyo's, as a gambling pitch where those with special information did very well, knowing that insider trading was not a criminal offence. The fact that the Hong Kong stock exchange was closed for four days following the October 1987 crash on Wall Street told the entire financial world that the territory's credibility as a fair market could be cavalierly dismissed in order to safeguard interested parties. The anger that followed led to the government belatedly taking steps to better supervise the exchange and to the prosecution of Ronald Li, the chairman of the stock exchange, for running what was held to be in effect a private club answerable to local brokers rather than an international financial centre.

It is to MacLehose's credit that anti-corruption drives were mounted from the start of this lengthy period in office. His willingness to confront obstacles head-on was also seen in his approach to the housing situation in Hong Kong. Once again earlier administrations had been well aware of what needed to be done but when faced with the government expenditure involved had hesitated to make serious inroads into the serious deprivation visible to any schoolboy or newly arrived tourist. The sprawl and squalor were obvious, but so too was the size of the problem. Immigrant families faced too many daily challenges, unless they were particularly well connected or displayed extraordinary business skills, to be able to acquire sufficient capital to purchase their own small apartment. Yet to expect the government to solve the housing situation meant a reversal of more than a century's belief in self-help and strict limitations on the powers of the state. MacLehose was not deterred and insisted on a series of housing programmes that literally changed the face of Hong Kong. Old prewar structures were largely torn down and entire new towns in what appeared to many in the territory to be remote areas quite beyond the pale began to emerge. The results can be seen both visually in the high-rise estates of today and in the political geography of the territory. As a result of the radical housing plans inaugurated in the MacLehose years there has been a huge shift in the population. In the September 1995 LegCo elections, for example, the island of Hong Kong was divided into four constituencies, Kowloon had seven and the ever-growing New Territories possessed the remaining nine. The fact that the largest single geographical constituency was New Territories East symbolizes the new demography of the territory. Whole tracts of what until the early 1970s had been farmland or coastal swamp were quickly annexed as areas for government-funded housing projects.

The complexities of purchasing sites, designing the tower blocks and providing the infrastructure might well have defeated even the most experienced town planners and engineers. It is to the credit of the authorities that a great deal was accomplished in such a short period and that the government was prepared to acknowledge even at the end of the 1970s that 'much, however, still remains to be done'. The *Hong Kong Yearbook* for 1980 suggested that

more than half-a-million households are still in urgent need of proper or improved housing. Among these are 152,500 households registered on the authority's waiting list; 57,800 households living in overcrowded or unsatisfactory conditions in old estates built more than 20 years ago; and 130,000 households living in squatter huts scattered throughout the territory.

Yet MacLehose's determination to achieve what was almost a housing revolution led to positive results. First, and most obviously, it secured stronger ties between the peoples of Hong Kong and their government through the provision of much improved, highly-subsidized housing. The city-state, using its new revenues, pushed through a huge housing drive and earned some gratitude in the process. The very visible changes also helped to show protectionist spokesmen from overseas that Hong Kong was now a more responsible, humane territory where factory workers could enjoy a far higher standard of living than only a few years before.

Closely allied to housing schemes was the construction of a new underground transportation network. Given the clogged state of traffic on the existing roads of the territory and the shortage of land, there was no choice but to dig into the granite rock of Hong Kong to design alternative means of linking the growing satellite towns to the central business and entertainment areas. The government was therefore able to report proudly that the territory

has marked its entry into the 1980s with a significant new achievement: after 10 years of investigation, design and construction, a mass transit railway (MTR) is now in operation.

With characteristic confidence officials then immediately noted

an extension of the system to the growing industrial town of Tsuen Wan in the New Territories is now underway and, when this is completed in two years' time, it is expected that passenger movement will be of the order of 1.8 million journeys daily.

The successful financing and organizing of this major engineering venture was the responsibility of the Hong Kong government; it proved to be yet another clear indication that its community role had greatly increased. Cheap, fast public transport could be shown to benefit both commuters and their companies, although continuing growth in car ownership has subsequently disappointed those who had once seen the MTR as the solution to traffic congestion. The prospect of total gridlock on the territory's roads still remains the planners' ultimate nightmare.

While the urban transformation of Hong Kong captured public attention at home and abroad, other significant reforms were also afoot. Equally as important as the housing and transport programmes for the long-term future of the territory were the educational improvements instigated during the MacLehose years. Although having little of the visual impact of the opening of a housing estate or television footage of the governor's first journey on the MTR, the almost annual announcements of the further raising of the school leaving age demonstrated the government's commitment to education. Two landmarks on this road were provision of free primary education from September 1971 and the introduction of compulsory schooling up to the age of fifteen years in September 1980. Major increases in expenditure to retrain teachers and to provide the facilities required in this huge undertaking were approved with little dissent. The expectation was that a more literate, better educated community could only be in the best interests of Hong Kong. It was noticeable, however, that this introduction of ever-wider secondary education by the government was not in the 1970s matched by any substantial increase in the number of students accepted for higher education. Undergraduate places at Hong Kong University for 1979–80 were available for no more than 4,100 students, although changes in the colony's views on tertiary education would be a feature of the following decade. Until then the structure of education, while much broadened at its base, remained decidedly elitist at the college level, with intense competition for the glittering prizes of university admission.

Linked to the education and housing programme was the issue of immigration. The government knew only too well that the waves of legal and illegal migrants in the 1970s had led to an increasing demand for public housing. The community in Hong Kong much preferred to concentrate on the resented influx of Vietnamese boat people but in truth the government's larger and more pressing concern was to control the numbers of Chinese who wished to settle in the territory. It was, of course, an old problem, yet an issue that required the closest consultation with the Chinese authorities before any successes could be claimed. Cheng Tong-yung put it succinctly in his study of the economy of the territory when he stated boldly that

people are Hong Kong's most important economic resource, and at the same time her most difficult problem. The flood of refugees entering Hong Kong before and after the [Pacific war] created the valuable pool of cheap labour without which Hong Kong's rapid economic growth would not have been possible. But a labour force, unlike other production factors, itself requires a very considerable amount of input. People must be fed, housed, transported to and from work, educated, and, perhaps most importantly, given a feeling that their lives have a meaning outside the factory walls.

It was to be the task of MacLehose's officials to begin to provide half-way decent housing for the labourers and clerks who by the 1970s had begun to expect a little more in life than merely a six-day work week and eventual bare assistance in their old age from relatives.

Yet time and again when it appeared that substantial efforts were finally bringing rewards in the housing drive, the government saw the twin devils of escalating building costs and more refugees combining to thwart their plans. Public housing programmes were a response to the trebling of Hong Kong's population between 1945 and 1951 and the further doubling that occurred between 1950 and 1970. The schemes, in effect, were an acknowledgement that the peoples of the territory had by their collective labour won the right to more adequate accommodation. It should also be stressed that the state's decision to improve living standards was intended to earn the government considerable credit within the community and dispel some of the adverse social conditions that were held to be behind the 1966 and 1967 disturbances. (The 1967 rioting, as we have seen, was very much more a response to external events than the previous year's affair but presumably any substantial governmental measure to improve housing could be said to reduce the potential recruiting ground for discontent against a colonial regime.)

Successive governments of postwar Hong Kong, however, have found it impossible to devise particularly clear and consistent policies towards immigration. The shifts have broadly reflected what were felt to be the requirements of the local economy, the hopes of family members wishing to reunite with relatives still on the northern side of the border and the need more recently strictly to curb further settlement. A territory that by the end of 1994 would have a population of slightly more than 6 million people must be reckoned to have reached a figure close to its finite limits unless still further new towns are envisaged and larger numbers of residents opt to leave permanently. The government faces obvious unpopularity from restricting the immigration of people of Cantonese extraction into the territory but has reckoned since the 1970s that this human consideration has to take second place to the interests of those already in the territory. Although some government schemes to halt illegal immigration demonstrably failed, the intention under Governor MacLehose was to send back those caught. This scrapping of the so-called 'touch base' policy, whereby those from China who crawled through the border netting and then made it across Boundary Street into Kowloon proper were safe, was necessary if the population were not to reach a figure that would endanger the stability and economic prospects of the colony. It was not, however, finalized until talks with the PRC had reached an understanding both that illegal immigrants once caught were now certain to be repatriated and that in addition a limited number of Chinese with official permits would be accepted into Hong Kong. From October 1980 it also became necessary for all residents both to possess and to carry identity cards and for employers convicted of hiring illegal workers to face substantial fines or prison sentences.

Unfortunately the government's changes to immigration policies coincided approximately with the advent of the boat people. It was, as the *Hong Kong Yearbook* reviewing 1979 stated frankly in its opening sentence, a year overshadowed by one relentless problem: the Vietnam refugees, or boat people. The influx of these refugees, together with large-scale immigration from China, raised real fears that a decade of economic and social achievement might be undermined, communal stability impaired, and plans for further progress thrown out of gear.

It was the beginning of a saga that is only now ending more than fifteen years later as the government continues to wrestle with ways of persuading the few remaining Vietnamese to return home in advance of the transfer of sovereignty.

The arrival of the boat people presented a challenge that the existing immigrant peoples of the territory preferred to duck. There was little wish in Hong Kong for its representatives to welcome or indeed do much beyond deterring future vessels from imagining that the territory was a safe haven. Yet the numbers of Vietnamese, mostly of Chinese extraction, continued to grow throughout 1979, while there was a simultaneous increase in the arrival of illegal immigrants from the north. The land and sea borders of Hong Kong were proving porous indeed, despite military reinforcements and emergency legislation that provided for stiff sentences for those responsible for organizing the shipment of illegal human cargoes into its waters. The crisis continued for months as international efforts were made to control the despatch, reception, possible resettlement and eventual repatriation of most of the tens of thousands of Vietnamese who had fled following the final reunification of their nation in 1975.

The government of Hong Kong quickly discovered, as it had in earlier times of economic friction, how few friends it possessed abroad. The entire region was intent on looking after its own best interests. Though some states made considerable efforts to assist the refugees others, such as Japan, simply ensured that their drawbridge was pulled up tight and threw money at the problem. After the Geneva conference that was urgently called by the United Nations to tackle the huge influx of boat people in southeast Asia and beyond, Governor MacLehose was able to gain some respite for his territory. He could claim that Hong Kong had treated its boat people with decency, though the camps for arriving Vietnamese not surprisingly were spartan, and he was able to make a qualified assurance that their numbers would be gradually reduced. It led him to state in October that 'if there are no further large-scale arrivals, we can hope that the problem will gradually diminish over the next year or so'. But MacLehose was careful to add that this depended on how hard Hanoi acted to prevent fresh sailings and how many Vietnamese already in Hong Kong were granted resettlement places further afield. The vast majority of the immigrants in the crowded camps that the government had hastily organized originally had high hopes of being accepted for resettlement in the United States; gradually these expectations would change as reality sank in.

By October 1979 the territory was housing over 62,000 Vietnamese. It was inevitably a confused and difficult period for Hong Kong as the community held generally that there was no space for anything like this number of new arrivals, who would be a burden on the public purse for years to come. Talk of humanitarian and international responsibilities won nothing but harsh mutterings from those already waiting for housing and fearful of challenges for new jobs. There can little doubt that had Hong Kong possessed a more democratic government with its leaders answerable in elections to the public it would have been obliged to adopt sterner measures. Only a benevolent bureaucratic city-state could or would have instituted its initial schemes. Hong Kong's lack of grass-roots' representation enabled the MacLehose administration to devise an ad hoc programme for the boat people that was light years away from public suspicions on the subject. One result of the original reception of so many boat people was that all subsequent governments of Hong Kong have had inevitably to cope with the consequences; it also remains a sticking point with Beijing since the PRC has repeatedly called for the repatriation of all remaining Vietnamese before July 1997. In this instance at least the narrow, racial concerns of China are more in line with the prejudices of Hong Kong than with undue respect for the lives of those who had survived pirates, typhoons and unscrupulous organizers to reach the territory. It is to the credit of the Hong Kong government that it has persevered in working to assist the boat people, despite being caught between domestic hostility and the views of some in the West that it has been forcibly repatriating those still living in the camps.

The numbers of Vietnamese who arrived in Hong Kong hoping to obtain either permanent residence away from the heavily guarded camps or swift resettlement in the United States nearly overwhelmed the territory. It was perhaps a perverse vote of confidence in the attractions of the colony, but the public's reaction hardly suggested that an open, tolerant community was in the process of being born. The eventual decision of the Vietnamese government in October 1991 to take back those of its citizens who were not classed as refugees by UN officials brought a collective sigh of relief. The strains on the administration, while still far from over, had at least been reduced through these negotiations and one seemingly intractable issue could be said at least to be nearer solution. The world will certainly still see television clips of Vietnamese children who have spent their entire lives in closed camps in

Hong Kong stumbling up plane gangways to fly to a country quite unknown to them but at least the territory has treated its unwelcome immigrants with some rough kindness. The government allowed capsizing Vietnamese dinghies and rotting cargo vessels to enter Hong Kong waters in the late 1970s when others were instructing their skippers to ignore all pleas for help on the open seas and then immediately deporting all those who managed to land.

Over the boat people the policies of the government were in advance of the community; in the instance of its more important dealings with China there was to be an unbridgeable gap between the aspirations of Hong Kong and what could be achieved through diplomacy. In a field where much will remain speculative for many years until the historical record is clearer, it seems reasonable to assume that the appointment of MacLehose as governor by Prime Minister Edward Heath was a conscious break with the past. The intention was surely both to revitalize the territory through political, economic and social means and to reckon with the territory's future. A trained, forceful diplomat with first-hand experience of Hong Kong was therefore the appropriate choice to shore up the colony, while starting also to consider how best to deal with the expiration in 1997 of the lease on the New Territories.

The beginnings of Sino–American rapprochement were expressed in President Nixon's surprise announcement of 15 July 1971 from San Clemente that he had 'undertaken initiatives in several areas to open the door for more normal relations between our two countries'. This in turn would lead to an improvement in Britain's ties with China. The fact that when the PRC was admitted to the United Nations in the following year its representative said that Hong Kong and Macao should be deleted from the purview of the UN's decolonization committee could also be held to have a bearing on the territory's future. The difficulty, however, with Chinese remarks that such issues 'should be settled in an appropriate way when conditions are ripe' was knowing how best to interpret them. It was possible by the early 1970s to at least argue that China was changing and that the increasing contacts might presage a more relaxed stance over Hong Kong and Macao. Yet, it could be, as the *Far Eastern Economic Review* speculated in March 1972, that 'this is nothing more than a rephrasing of what the late Foreign Minister, Chen Yi, announced in 1966: he said then that China will claim the two – "the holiday land of the imperialists" – at "the opportune moment".'

It was not only in the field of international relations that the region saw substantial change in the 1970s. The announcement in December 1978 at the 3rd plenum of the XI central committee of the CCP of a massive economic reform programme proved to have enormous consequences for Hong Kong. Deng Xiaoping, newly returned to power after being disgraced during the cultural revolution, introduced his 'four modernizations' scheme to revitalize the Chinese economy by rejecting parts of the existing state orthodoxy. Deng proposed a transitional economy where markets would become more important, decollectivization would be introduced into the countryside and institutions liberalized to create previously unheard-of growth.

In place of Maoist self-reliance, Deng ordered an open door policy that required cooperation with other nations, regardless almost of their political hue, in order to gain the finance, technology and know-how needed to create a new Chinese economy. Deng also intended to encourage also a more active foreign policy that would help build what in September 1982 he defined as 'socialism with Chinese characteristics'. External relations were now to be seen as allied to the new modernization schemes in the expectation that interested parties overseas would welcome the opportunity to trade and invest with the PRC. It was apparent from the inception of Deng's economic plans that Hong Kong could expect to be involved. Chinese government spokesmen began to make speeches that stressed the importance of the territory in the modernization drive. Although the PRC had made similar remarks in the past and its record over earlier bids to industrialize at speed had been generally undistinguished, this time the omens were better. Deng's commitment to gradually working towards a market economy and the dismantling of both the rural communes and the bureaucratic excesses of state planning remained constant. Furthermore, the establishment of a series of privileged Special Economic Zones (SEZs) on the borders of Hong Kong, Macao and Taiwan served both to reinforce the PRC's new economic ambitions and signalled to these communities that China anticipated closer political ties to flow in time from the developing economic links. Ideological opponents within the CCP might complain that the SEZs were evidence of 'spiritual pollution' but Deng held tenaciously to his belief that this late twentieth-century version of the despised nineteenth-century treaty ports system would advance China's modernization and had therefore to be carefully nurtured rather than disparaged.

Hong Kong's history since Deng's announcement in favour of a radical restructuring of China's economy, without relaxation of CCP control in the political field, has had a most significant impact on the territory's recent affairs. Sino–Hong Kong trade, tourism, and finance have boomed, while greatly expanded official and human contacts have begun to bring two different societies into at least an approximate understanding of each other's behaviour and beliefs. The territory's economic fortunes since the late 1980s have become increasingly conditional on its ties to the PRC as Hong Kong's style of capitalism and Deng's form of Chinese socialism laboured to achieve a working relationship that has since proved to be mutually beneficial.

The first significant change in Hong Kong–China affairs was the shaping of a new trade pattern. Cheng Tong-yung noted that already by 1982 the postwar one-way flow of goods from China to Hong Kong had been corrected and that 'the traditional "China Trade"' had begun to reemerge once again. Given Hong Kong's deep water port and the experience of its shippers it was hardly surprising that once Deng's economic reforms were on stream there would be dividends again for the territory. China needed Hong Kong as its window on the world, whereas Hong Kong for its part began to shut down some of its own manufacturing outlets and concentrate on providing a more sophisticated range of financial services. Both trading partners stood to gain substantially from this new arrangement. China gradually strengthened its existing banking and investment presence in the territory, while Hong Kong began to concentrate on the reexport of commodity goods, particularly to other Asian markets. The result was a seemingly unstoppable movement towards both Sino–Hong Kong attachment and regional economic integration. From the late 1970s Hong Kong has viewed its economic future as geared increasingly to the Asian–Pacific rim. It was no surprise therefore to see the territory's booksellers devoting entire sections in their shops to what would increasingly be termed the 'Pacific century'.

For Governor MacLehose there was now both the immediate prospect of warmer relations with China and the need to reckon with his territory's longer-term prospects. The records of the parliamentary subcommittee reviewing British policies toward Hong Kong during this period give at least the occasional hint as to governmental thinking. In December 1975 Minister of State for Defense William Rodgers spoke in elliptical terms of how the three parties – London, Beijing and Hong Kong itself – obviously most concerned with the possible chain of events to 1997 and beyond might envisage their futures. Rodgers referred to an 'unarticulated understanding' that suggested that all three actors recognized the 'convenience' of the status quo, but partially censored material appears to imply that this arrangement might have to be reviewed if it were to be seen as 'unreasonable' by one of the participants. The Foreign Office was already clearly thinking hard about 1997. One civil servant acknowledged that 'the year 1997 has official relevance, and one cannot just write it off. Everything would turn on the political relations between the three members of the tripartite interest'.

The picture, we must assume, was less cloudy than implied in any such gobbledegook served up to MPs and curious journalists. More considered action had to be timed to coincide whenever possible with favourable internal developments in China and the growing economic and financial interest attached within Hong Kong to the expiration of the lease on the New Territories due in 1997. Governor MacLehose would have been fully aware of the improved stability that China was experiencing with the return to power of Deng Xiaoping in 1977 after the chaos of the cultural revolution and the confusion that followed the death of Mao Zedong. The first months of 1979 were to see the initial British sally on the 1997 question.

The ploy was technical and relatively low key. The aim was to attempt to discover the thinking of Deng and his advisors on a scheme that might permit the continuation of the New Territories' lease beyond the summer of 1997, whereby British administration might be extended with China's consent. It was, as MacLehose presumably calculated, a gamble that might well fail. The risk was reckoned necessary because of growing anxieties in the territory's financial sector. How substantial, however, these fears actually were within Hong Kong remains difficult to assess.

Reviewing the complicated events that were to lead to reversion it is tempting to consider whether alternative strategies might have stood more chance of success. Some diplomats in Britain and Asia, for example, have asked whether it was essential to tackle Beijing so long before 1997 in quite so abrupt a manner, reckoning that an alternative of leaving well alone until much nearer the dreaded date might have been wiser. To such arguments the British and Hong Kong governments' response has been to maintain that it had to extract accurate information on Chinese thinking after Sino–British relations had themselves improved and, if they gained hints of a favourable reply, the lease question could then be taken further.

It appears that Governor MacLehose had been eager to gain London's approval for an overture to Beijing. The idea was to test the waters by seeing if the Chinese leadership might agree to an extension to the commercial subleases using corporations owned by the Chinese leadership and, if no objections were raised by the PRC, there was the option next to issue an eventual Order in Council extending British control. Everything, obviously, depended on how China might respond. It was MacLehose's task to find out.

Since no government in Westminster would have been prepared unilaterally to extend the lease on the New Territories there had to be official soundings. Informal discussions by senior Chinese or British businessmen were ruled out as it was deemed vital to gain first-hand information through British diplomats from the leadership in Beijing. This would, it was hoped, avoid the imprecision and confusion that could easily arise through the use of intermediaries employing casual channels.

The answer obtained by MacLehose on his official visit to Beijing was 'rebuff'. This single word by the governor to Hong Kong's Chief Secretary Jack Cater on his return to Kowloon expressed the failure to gain some assurances from Deng Xiaoping that there could still be a British administration after 1997. It was a major disappointment that would inevitably colour events in Hong Kong for the remainder of the years now to be left to British sovereignty over the territory. The hopes of some extension to the New Territories' lease appeared to have gone. China would not be tied to any British legal formula that left Hong Kong under colonial control, though Deng's remarks that investors might 'put their hearts at ease' succeeded in both boosting the local stock markets and diverting public attention from the all-important, if disguised, purpose of MacLehose's visit.

Confirmation of China's decision came in the course of subsequent ministerial exchanges in Beijing and London. It was now up to the British government to review its policies and prepare for the uncomfortable realities ahead. Action in London and Hong Kong was required to handle negotiations with China and to examine how the territory might be brought to accept its new fate. Yet before the international negotiations and the statements in Hong Kong were drafted the government of Mrs Thatcher strengthened its defences against any influx of Hong Kong Chinese into Britain. Parliamentary approval was gained to remove the right to abode in Britain of Hong Kong residents holding what became known as British Dependent Territories' citizenship. Such individuals, with the exception of a handful of favoured individuals from the civil service, were effectively barred from Britain and their future status would depend on the Chinese government. It was a deliberate device of the Thatcher government to exclude Hong Kong Chinese from imagining that they had at least a bolthole in Britain if everything else failed. The timing of the new nationality bill was rightly later seen in Hong Kong as linked to the MacLehose visit to Beijing.

This, however, was not so obvious at the time, nor were the political reforms being introduced by the MacLehose administration. The governor had instituted relatively minor changes from the start of this administration, with the objective of gradually bringing the territory out of its bureaucratic state mould into something at least more representative. The incremental reforms culminated in the elected District Boards

system that doubtless appears small beer to outsiders far from enam-
oured by the subject of local government but, as Norman Miners would
note, 'this was a very radical departure for Hong Kong, where previously
the only elections had been those for the Urban Council on a highly
restricted franchise'. In truth these elections only permitted those
gaining seats on the boards to offer advice to the government, but they
were seen as a useful means of encouraging the articulation of local
opinion. More important still was the fact that a clear precedent had
been established. It must be assumed that the staff of the New China
News Agency, in reality barely disguised officials of the PRC stationed
in the territory, conveyed in great detail the new arrangements to their
masters in Beijing. The information must have been wholly unwelcome,
since the last thing any Chinese commissar would wish to encourage in
the lengthy period before 1997 was the inception of even an iota of
democracy. A crown colony intent on reform was not likely to win any
favours with a state that had all too vivid memories of the anarchy
behind the recent cultural revolution to endorse contested elections and
uninhibited discussion. Hong Kong, despite its awareness of the reaction
from China, was moving to making appointment to at least one tier of its
government through novel means. The old ways were proving to be less
rigid than many had assumed; if the administration could alter local
government its successors could presumably consider wider changes in
due course.

Governor MacLehose was the last viceregal figure to run Hong Kong.
He knew what he wanted for the territory and he possessed both the
power and the guile to gain his objectives. He understood the need to
appear to be firmly on the side of the peoples of Hong Kong; not long
after he took office the press was noticing how he spoke in open-necked
shirt to the public of 'your government', though some officials
complained in private that it tended to be 'my government'. Senior
administrators found it hard on occasion not to draw attention to the
governor's ploy of calling meetings with carefully prepared agendas that
led inevitably to confirmation of decisions that MacLehose had already
arranged in advance. It was also the case that in some instances, such as
over the anti-corruption campaign, the governor was perhaps rather too
eager to claim all the applause when it might have been better to spread
the credit around. There was also a danger at times in precipitate
action. His moves against the police, for example, left the territory
nearly naked when the force made it clear that it would no longer
cooperate and the British government ruled out the despatch of any
additional troops to safeguard the colony. Yet, despite reservations
about the style, Governor MacLehose did largely succeed in invigor-

ating the civil service and correcting some of the faults of an administration that still possessed a very high opinion of itself. The transformation of the territory's housing stock, the serious attempts to take note of the deterioration of what was left of the natural environment, major improvements in the field of education, and the efforts to reduce corruption were rightly appreciated by the community. Confirmation of MacLehose's record can be seen through the fact that he shares with Sir Alexander Grantham the record of longest serving governor of Hong Kong: the two of them ran Hong Kong for a total of nearly twenty-two years. The remaining three successors to MacLehose were to face choppier waters and would be rewarded with shorter incumbencies and far more controversial captaincies.

Governor MacLehose's departure from Hong Kong serves as the transition point in its postwar history. The major extensions in the role of the Hong Kong government and the start of the reversion process enacted during his administration mark the end of the pristine colonial era. By 1982 the enlargement of the responsibilities of the state (and to a lesser degree in the political system itself) had combined with the overtures to China to change the territory irrevocably. The Hong Kong of cautious non-interventionism was now firmly shifting to a more open and necessarily more complex entity beginning its long journey back to China. Indeed, Hong Kong was to alter so rapidly in the next decade that for many residents of the territory the MacLehose era would shortly come to be regarded with some considerable nostalgia. The demise of all-absorbing economism and limited bureaucratic rule would be followed by wider domestic and external challenges as the 1997 deadline crept nearer.

# 5    Negotiations: Sino–British diplomacy, 1982–92

In reply to [American] questions as to how long Hong Kong would continue as a British Colony, I would say that, in my opinion, 1997 will be the fateful year, for in that year the lease of the New Territories runs out, and I could not conceive of any Chinese government of whatever complexion renewing the lease.

(Sir Alexander Grantham, *Via Ports*, Hong Kong, 1965)

You might still remember it was the signing of the Joint Declaration in 1984 that brought about the best period in Sino–British relations, during which your Queen visited China. That was an historic visit; that situation, of course, lasted until 1992 when our relationship suffered some setbacks. Of course, that happened not because of anything of China's making, but what is more important now is to look ahead.

(Ambassador Ma Yuzhen, annual dinner of the Royal Society for Asian Affairs, London, 14 March 1995)

The importance attached by successive British governments to maintaining cordial relations between Hong Kong and China cannot be overstated. Given the near impossibility of defending Hong Kong from external attack during most of its colonial history, those administering the territory invariably have wished to demonstrate the advantages that would accrue to both parties from close economic, financial and human ties. It was hardly a state secret that the British government had little in its locker to throw at the PRC if, to employ the familiar phrase, Beijing should decide to roll its tanks down Nathan Road, the main thoroughfare of Kowloon. Invasion either by military force or by encouraging mass migration into Hong Kong (comparable to the 'people's war' approach of committing vast waves of infantry into battle during the Korean war) would ensure an immediate Chinese capture of its long-lost territory.

Accepting this reality, it was general policy of all administrations in Hong Kong to work to gain and maintain the good will of the Chinese authorities. This often led Government House to grant preferential treatment to the PRC and to deny to states considered unfriendly to

China such items as landing rights or permission to open representative offices. The ability of China to delay the despatch of fresh food or water to Hong Kong left the territory ever-exposed to Chinese pressures.

Britain and China made haste slowly over resolving the 1997 question. The temptation of both Beijing and London to avoid any strenuous debate on the expiration of the lease on the New Territories was only gradually overturned. The delays were understandable, given that Britain was reluctant to undermine confidence within the colony that it had governed for more than a century and a quarter, while China appeared prepared to continue to reap the economic and financial advantages that seemingly outweighed political ideology. No Chinese government would wish to be charged by its critics with ignoring the fate of Hong Kong, given its ignominious transfer to Britain in the 1840s, but the CCP could hardly deny that its record since 1949 over the enclave had been highly pragmatic. It was its opponents within the KMT that from the late 1920s to the mid-1940s had done far more to reduce and partly end the unequal treaties associated with foreign incursions on Chinese soil; by contrast the continuation of British colonialism in Hong Kong was a reproach to the PRC's professions of nationalism.

While not the oldest colony to be maintained on the China coast (that title rested throughout these years with the less populous territory of Portuguese-held Macao) the prosperity and confidence displayed by Hong Kong was an open indictment of China. Beijing was after all in a far stronger position by the 1970s with its possession of both nuclear weapons and a permanent seat on the UN Security Council as clear evidence of its heightened status in the international system. An aspiring world power would be unlikely to wish to be seen to be overdependent forever on the conveniences provided by a minute foreign colony on its doorstep.

Once negotiations became a matter of public knowledge and commentary it is difficulty to imagine that China had any option but to insist on the reversion of all of Hong Kong. Deng Xiaoping had no wish to be branded a traitor to the cause of Chinese reunification, especially as the gaining of Hong Kong might become part of a wider process of restoring his nation to its earlier borders.

Sino–British diplomacy was to prove both lengthy and complicated. The five stages on the journey to 1997 might be said to be, first, the formulation of the Sino–British Joint Declaration in December 1984 whereby Britain agreed to renounce sovereignty over Hong Kong in 1997, second, the approval of the Basic Law for the future Special Administrative Region of Hong Kong (SAR) by the Chinese National

People's Congress in April 1990, third, the acrimonious years associated with Governor Patten from 1992 to 1995, fourth, the announcement of the first chief executive for the SAR, expected at the end of 1996 or January 1997, and finally the eventual reversion of the territory. This process is being conducted under the watchful eye of the world's media (the size and resources of Japanese newspaper bureaux in Hong Kong are a revelation to hard-pressed Western stringers), to say nothing of the daily scrutiny within Hong Kong itself from its large range of competing papers and television channels. The constant attention that the territory receives locally and overseas has ensured that each and every action by the British, Hong Kong and Chinese governments is instantly reported and analysed. Both this continuing visibility and the remarkably drawn-out nature of the transition period are rare in contemporary international relations; peaceful decolonization in the postwar period has invariably led to rapid transfer of power.

Retired British officials have suggested that the issue of reversion before the 1970s was rarely debated in depth. Sir Percy Cradock in his memoirs holds that Hong Kong's future remained 'a secondary theme' until 1979 for the Foreign Office. From London's perspective, Cradock maintains,

the New Territories lease was seen in the 1970s as an issue that would have to be faced and eventually settled amicably with Peking. But it was not yet the most urgent or the dominating issue in Sino–British relations and there was no clear view of the likely terms of any such settlement.

Whatever the territory's views on the matter, the Foreign Office felt that 'the long-term trend was probably unfavourable to Hong Kong's continued existence as a colony', though there remained the possibility that the '*status quo* might be quietly maintained, particularly if there was some bow in the direction of Chinese sovereignty'.

Hong Kong naturally enough took a very different line from those handling British relations with the PRC. The accomplishments of the territory by the late 1970s and the fact that there were less than two decades remaining before 1997 ensured that both the nervous resident and the corporate strategic planner required some concrete reassurance. The issue could no longer be ducked. What had to be attempted was clearly a sounding out of the PRC's ideas on Hong Kong. The British government's initial approach was made by Governor MacLehose in March 1979 after, as we have seen, considerable discussion on how the issue ought to be raised. The range of options was wide, varying from doing nothing to conceding sovereignty. The decision was taken to avoid enlisting an intermediary sympathetic to Beijing or to unilaterally issue leases in the New Territories that would be granted for gradually lengthier periods beyond 1997. Instead of these alternatives it was considered to be less dangerous if a tentative enquiry were made in connection with the expiry of the land leases in the New Territories. British officials have since suggested in conversation with Robert Cottrell, the author of *The End of Hong Kong*, that the objective was to see if 'a way could be found to start issuing sub-leases beyond 1997'. The ploy was to represent the question as merely a commercial question that might permit the British authorities to 'issue sub-leases which extended beyond the tenure of the head lease'. The press in Hong Kong and Britain was fed the line that the New Territories' lease would not be discussed which was perhaps technically the case, though disingenuous, given MacLehose's instructions to explore ways of looking at subleases that would run beyond June 1997.

Governor MacLehose did his best to explain Britain's wish for clarification at his meetings with Chinese officials in Beijing in the spring of 1979. Recent evidence from the Chinese side assists in confirming portions of the unofficial British record on what became the first of many Anglo–Chinese forays over the future of the territory of Hong Kong. The Governor's message that Hong Kong required a vote of confidence on the 1997 question, however, elicited little to encourage the British government. Investors in Hong Kong's stock markets enjoyed being told by MacLehose on his return that Deng Xiaoping wanted to reassure the financial community that all would be well in the future, but this public statement naturally ignored the refusal of Deng and his government to accept the British argument over land leases, with its implicit continuation of British administration beyond 1997.

According to Xu Jiatun, the former energetic head of the Hong Kong office of the New China News Agency, the Chinese Ministry of Foreign Affairs had attempted to discourage MacLehose from raising the territory's future with Deng Xiaoping during the 1979 visit. When pressed, it appears that Deng stated unequivocally that China would 'take back sovereignty over Hong Kong at the appointed time'. Clearly the British government had failed to make any impression on China's leader; the only (highly negative) consolation was that it now knew that its range of options was narrowing. Britain would have to wait for more information from Beijing but it looked increasingly as if it was fated to play the role of supplicant. It was, as Sir Percy Cradock would acknowledge later in his memoirs, 'far from satisfactory, but there the matter had to rest'. Accounts of the meeting between Deng and the British team appear to agree that the issue might have been better handled. There may well have been difficulties over the interpretation and Deng may not perhaps have been fully prepared for the discussion that ensued, yet the result presumably would not have been materially altered. Fresh soundings later were to receive the same response. The Chinese government had clearly done much of its homework and was not about to become entangled in any capitalist legalities about subleases, particularly when the entire occupation of Hong Kong, Kowloon and the New Territories had long been held by successive regimes in China to rest on unequal and, therefore, unrecognized imperialistic treaties.

Deng Xiaoping, in the words of one anonymous participant quoted by Robert Cottrell, was perhaps more in control of the discussions than others would have us believe. When tackled on the British proposal on the subleases the Chinese leader's behaviour was described as '[e]ither he was very fuzzy and he did not understand quite what was being asked of him, or he was very wily and he understood all too well'. We may never know for certain but the once the subject had been broached by the British, Deng appears to have had no great difficulty in almost instantly reaching for an approximate formula that was to endure throughout all subsequent Sino–British diplomacy. Hong Kong, it was to be repeated *ad nauseam*, should relax and take heart in the 'one country, two systems' recipe that would ensure both Chinese sovereignty and economic continuity for its soon to be liberated compatriots. For an elderly figure, Deng appears both then and later to have been remarkably able to get his way in the face of British snares. Perhaps the Chinese records have been gently touched up to convey this impression, yet it would be justice indeed if the leader who made clear his policies in March 1979, when already 74 years old, were able to visit Hong Kong in July 1997 to inspect his handiwork in person.

While Deng certainly expected Hong Kong to contribute to the success of his open door policies, he gave no indication that the economic modernization of China would be at the expense of any wavering over reclaiming Hong Kong. Sovereignty was not divisible. Once Hong Kong had rejoined the motherland, it was clearly intended that Taiwan should be enticed back under the same formula as that employed in the case of Hong Kong. The phrase that had been devised for Hong Kong in the course of the Sino–British negotiations would by 1984 be used by Deng to explain his overtures to Taipei. It is perhaps significant that when Deng met with Governor MacLehose in March 1979 he was flanked by Liao Chengzhi, the individual in charge of handling PRC policies for Taiwan as well as his advisor for Hong Kong and the often overlooked issue of Macao. Clearly the paramount leader would enjoy more success over the reversion of colonial Hong Kong than the lost province of Taiwan. Once the diplomatic deal was done with London over the future of Hong Kong, it would appear unlikely that China gave much thought to the territory's probable response to Beijing's political or military activities concerning Taiwan. Hong Kong no longer counted. After reversion it must expect to be instructed to keep quiet on the wider issues of Chinese foreign policy; defence and external affairs of the SAR would be exclusively the preserve of Beijing.

On the basis of soundings with the PRC, it was already probable that Hong Kong would cease to be a British possession after 1997, although Deng Xiaoping had given it to be understood that in some nebulous way there would still be opportunities for a returned Hong Kong to maintain its existing economic character. Capitalism would continue, apparently, but not British rule. The model for portions of the Chinese thinking on post-1997 Hong Kong was the 'one country, two systems' proposals then being prepared for Taiwan. Under this slogan it was claimed that the seat of the PRC's arch enemies could be enticed into rejoining the motherland, knowing that Taipei would be able to retain local autonomy and its economic arrangements as a special region of the PRC. It soon emerged that Taiwan was not to be so easily persuaded but what could not move the KMT redoubt was then presented by China's leaders as their blueprint for Hong Kong. The parallels in design were close and on this venture Beijing was to have far greater diplomatic success.

To be seen to have made limited headway in its very public hands across the Taiwan straits diplomacy may have spurred the Chinese leadership to ensure that the second prize in its irredentist campaign did not also elude it. After almost three years of saying very little it was suddenly apparent from 1982 that Beijing had a much clearer concept of what it intended to do with regard to Hong Kong. The message brought back by the stream of British and Hong Kong visitors to the PRC became ominously repetitive: the issues could not be left until 1997, the concerns of investors would be met, and Hong Kong, on the Taiwan model, would be converted into a special administrative region of China. The result appeared to exclude any British role beyond 1997, though Foreign Office and Hong Kong Government sources endeavoured to point out that if Beijing wished to retain the confidence of the financial and commercial sectors then it ought to permit a continuation of some form of British administration.

It was against this difficult backcloth that Mrs Thatcher visited Beijing in September 1982. It was three months since the British expeditionary force had retaken the Falkland Islands which, if popular legend is to be believed, steeled the prime minister to be sceptical of advice from among those employed to look after British national interests. Accounts by some of those present at the prime ministerial briefings tell of Mrs Thatcher's initial unwillingness to surrender British sovereignty over the whole of Hong Kong, since its possession was firmly enshrined in international law as interpreted at least by British lawyers. Her scepticism over Foreign Office advice did not extend to being able to produce a counter-strategy, however much Mrs Thatcher would have liked to have retained all of Hong Kong minus the New Territories. Unfortunately for her, the demarcation line between Kowloon and the New Territories had long since failed to signal any genuine divide. Boundary Street was now merely one more urban artery in the sprawl of tenements, offices and factories that had for decades marched north-wards from the tip of the Kowloon peninsula to encroach on what had once been the rural hinterland of Hong Kong.

Mrs Thatcher's visit was not a success. She failed to persuade the Chinese leaders that there ought to be a role for Britain in Hong Kong during the post-1997 era and was obliged to admit in her later memoirs that Deng Xiaoping had proved 'obdurate'. Mrs Thatcher's stress on the advantages of a continuation of British administration 'with the same system of law; the same political system, and the same independent currency' made no impression. Deng apparently boasted in their heated exchanges that the PLA could move into Hong Kong and reoccupy it instantly and Mrs Thatcher had, of course, to admit that there would indeed be no effective British obstacle in such an event. The prime minister's arguments on the need to retain the confidence of investors and entrepreneurs left Deng unmoved. Mrs Thatcher's comment in *The Downing Street Years* that '[i]t was becoming very clear to me that the Chinese had little understanding of the legal and political conditions for capitalism' could have been parried by their observation that the British premier had equally little understanding of the humiliations experienced by China in the nineteenth century at the hands of the great powers led by London.

Deng Xiaoping's own thoughts on the question of Hong Kong between 1982 and 1990 stress that the stain of foreign imperialism had to be totally erased (no British suggestions on shared power were countenanced in the Sino–British discussions) and that the years after 1997 would require the application of 'policies suitable to Hong Kong, under Chinese administration'. Deng then explained, in the Chinese version of his meeting with Mrs Thatcher on 24 September 1982, that while the territory's 'current political and economic systems and even most of its laws can remain in force', it would be necessary to have parts 'modified' and 'many systems currently in use that are suitable will be maintained'.

No one of Deng's generation could ignore the humiliations of Western imperialism; it followed therefore that the Chinese leader was reluctant to overstress the role of even a returned Hong Kong in China's ongoing modernization. To endorse too eagerly a capitalist enclave, albeit now as a very small part of the Chinese realm, would be to remind his audiences of China's uncomfortable past. Deng was seemingly more interested in regaining lost territory than employing Hong Kong to underwrite the expansion of the Chinese economy. He told Mrs Thatcher that 'it would be mistake to say the effect would be very great', though he could hardly suggest that 'it should have no effect whatever on China's modernization'. Yet he insisted that 'if China had decided to base the success of its modernization drive on prosperity in Hong Kong that policy decision would have been wrong'. Deng may not have personally supervised all the details of the transition of Hong Kong to Chinese rule but, if his health permitted, he had long expressed the wish to visit the new SAR to celebrate its reversion.

In the months that followed Mrs Thatcher discovered how unwilling the Chinese side were to accept her suggestion of joint discussions over Hong Kong. Twelve months after the prime minister's visit to Beijing it was apparent that rounds of desultory talks had got nowhere. Mrs Thatcher acknowledged later that the entire concept of a joint Sino–British debate on Hong Kong would collapse 'unless we conceded administration as well as sovereignty to the Chinese'. The stalling could no longer continue, particularly after the severe buffeting inflicted on the Hong Kong dollar in the late summer of 1983. The slide of the Hong Kong dollar coincided with claims in the Chinese press that the British were deliberately engineering a currency crisis to demonstrate how indispensable their administration was to Hong Kong while the British side argued that Chinese banking groups and corporations were off-loading the Hong Kong dollar for the preferred US dollar. In part, this was a speculative venture with sizeable fortunes to be made on the exchange fluctuation, but underneath the froth was a very real fear that the political divide between London and Beijing could only leave an impoverished Hong Kong sandwiched between the two parties. The sharp fall of the Hong Kong dollar was evidence of how vulnerable residents felt and their inevitable desire to switch all available spare resources into a stronger currency. Those who had lived through earlier bouts of inflation and uncertainty in China needed no persuasion to desert the Hong Kong dollar for safer havens.

By September the Hong Kong government knew it was facing a major crisis with a seemingly unstoppable run on the Hong Kong dollar. The conventional response of non-interventionism and leaving it to the exchanges to determine the fate of the local currency was quickly shown to be inadequate as the public began to stockpile emergency goods and business houses continued to shun the Hong Kong dollar. The depreciation of the currency clearly had to be halted regardless of who ultimately might be blamed for starting the mess. By 23 September it was impossible to disguise Sino–British differences in the Beijing talks. As Mrs Thatcher explained later:

Intensified Chinese propaganda and anxiety at the absence of any reassuring element in the official communique caused a massive capital flight out of the Hong Kong dollar and a sharp fall in its value on the foreign exchanges.

Observers anticipated at the very least demonstrations from residents embittered by watching the continual fall in the value of their life savings, with incalculable consequences for Britain's hold on the territory.

It was left to the economists to step in to restore the territory's perilous financial standing in the wake of the failure of the political and diplomatic imbroglio. The position was saved in two stages. The first was a tactical move that began by the Hong Kong government issuing a statement that bought time by announcing the creation of a scheme to revise the exchange rate mechanism. It was deliberately vague but deliberate enough to halt the slide in the Hong Kong dollar for the moment. It permitted the authorities to launch a hectic round of consultations involving the British government, the Bank of England and the Hong Kong government's own financial officials. On 16 October it was formally stated that the Hong Kong dollar would be pegged to the US dollar at the rate of $HK7.80 to $US1. In fact the news of some form of formal link to the US dollar had been widely anticipated and the arrangements were generally welcomed. Many families were poorer, of course, but the entire system had been saved.

The new schemes were the work of small emergency committees but behind the final details was the imprint of the Hong Kong-based economist John Greenwood. He had to a large extent anticipated the difficulties that the Hong Kong government found itself in during the September crisis and his proposed solution gave at least a fig leaf of credence to those who preached their dislike of an interventionist government. The new peg could be interpreted as avoiding the necessity of a central bank for Hong Kong, though in reality the government's commitment to fix the rate for the territory's currency and to purchase the Hong Kong dollar at the appropriate rate surely conformed to what would be expected of any such institution.

The British government managed to hold the line on the Hong Kong dollar; it had next to determine what steps to take to reengage the Chinese government in the tense standoff over the future of Hong Kong. Unpleasant decisions were called for that would gain few immediate supporters in the territory. The most unwelcome comment came from Sir Percy Cradock, who warned members of ExCo that London had no option but to yield with as much finesse as it could achieve in the face of Chinese power. Cradock stated bluntly that Deng intended to retake Hong Kong and that he would not be hindered by concerns for the territory's economic health. It was necessary, in Cradock's view, 'to look into the pit' and reckon with China. Not everyone appreciated this bluntness.

Since Beijing was not prepared to alter its determination to regain full sovereignty in 1997, Mrs Thatcher and her advisors were required to draw up a new approach that might yet save something from the reversion process. Cradock took the line that his colleagues 'were negotiating for the best we could get', although others held out for conditions. The new aim, in Cradock's later words, was dependent 'on what we could inject into the final document in the way of binding and detailed legal obligations defining the structure and way of life of Hong Kong after the hand-over'. The devil, as was constantly noted, would be in the detail.

Yet the switch had been made; the Chinese government now needed to be persuaded to cooperate in the wake of the British concessions. It was up to the PRC to reckon with the grudging but nonetheless real changes of mid-November when London expressly hoped 'to explore the Chinese proposals' for the territory, while emphasizing that it would hold 'no links of authority' after 1997. Such clarity after the confusions and contradictions of both sides in the previous weeks was highly reassuring and marked the end to what the British side had scathingly termed 'megaphone diplomacy'. From now on Beijing would have the whip hand.

In charge of Hong Kong negotiations in the Foreign Office from January 1984 was Sir Percy Cradock, the recently retired ambassador to Beijing, who had been asked by Mrs Thatcher to serve as Britain's leader in what would become a highly controversial and lengthy series of talks and eventual agreements. The appointment of Cradock clearly left many within Hong Kong's political and business circles disappointed. His insistence that defying the Chinese would only compound Hong Kong's difficulties was not what Hong Kong wished to hear. The territory preferred to believe that Hong Kong's economic and financial strengths were such that it could effectively defy Beijing, if the Chinese leaders insisted on unsatisfactory terms over reversion. Cradock would have none of this. He wrote later that some individuals in Hong Kong, including both members of ExCo and the government, were deluding themselves and that they had no means

of retrieving the situation and getting back into talks if, as was all too likely, their theory proved wrong and we found ourselves facing a breakdown and unilateral Chinese decrees on Hong Kong.

Cradock saw the Unofficial members of ExCo as particularly ready to take a leap into the unknown and felt it his responsibility to counsel prudence. Unfortunately, in the opinion of the Foreign Office at least, the prime minister was attracted to what Cradock terms 'their extreme ideas' and Mrs Thatcher's sympathies for Hong Kong had also to be tempered. It can hardly have been an easy task and clearly there were moments when Cradock was outmanoeuvred by the combined forces of Hong Kong's financial and bureaucratic leadership, particularly when allies were found within Whitehall and Westminster.

The first challenge for the British negotiators to confront was the changed tactics of their Chinese counterparts. It was increasingly clear that the PRC was shifting its ground to introduce more detail on how it wished to see Hong Kong evolve prior to 1997. In February 1984 the Chinese side at the protracted Sino–British talks produced documents that spoke of a joint commission to monitor developments in the territory in the immediate period prior to reversion. Nothing could have been less welcome to the British and Hong Kong governments; nothing could better illustrate the nakedness of the British position when Deng Xiaoping had already spoken unilaterally of a September deadline for completing discussions with London.

Knowledge of the Chinese moves acted to undermine remaining hopes of a united front that might keep Britain and Hong Kong fighting on the same side. The risk was now of fragmentation and public name-calling that would only further strengthen Beijing's offensive. Demor-alization could lead to rout. Hong Kong's ExCo, though kept informed of Sino–British talks through Governor Youde, felt largely excluded from the negotiations and Hong Kong's financial world was equally dispirited, particularly when Jardine Matheson announced on 28 March that it was moving its headquarters to Bermuda. Since Jardines' name had been largely synonymous with Hong Kong in the public's mind for more than a hundred years, the decamping was regarded by Beijing as a government-concocted act of treachery.

In an attempt to restore a degree of confidence in the territory, Foreign Secretary Howe visited China in mid-April. He hoped to demonstrate to Hong Kong that Britain could still protect its territory even after the difficult sessions with Deng, but the initial signs were hardly reassuring. The foreign secretary's subsequent press conference on 20 April marks the moment when the British government openly acknowledged that there would not be any British role after 1997 in the running of Hong Kong. Howe could no longer paper over the twin truths that the British were leaving and there had yet to be any concrete agreement with the PRC over ensuring the future social and economic well-being of the territory. Certainly Howe could refer to the fact that both Britain and China hoped 'to see the continuation of Hong Kong as a society which enjoys its own economic and social systems and distinct way of life', but actually gaining an internationally binding agreement acceptable both to London and Beijing was far from probable. The omens after months of inconclusive Sino–British negotiations were hardly favourable.

The situation was muddied further by strong interventions from within Hong Kong that cautioned its present and future masters against ganging up to manufacture arrangements that excluded adequate consideration of the territory's own opinions on reversion. Hong Kong had suddenly found its own voice and began an extensive campaign warning of the pitfalls ahead for the negotiators and demanding that the public be entitled to determine the acceptability of any future agreement.

The question of where and how the Chinese-proposed Joint Liaison Group would operate became the next major issue to confront the British government. Once again, as Mrs Thatcher would later confess in *The Downing Street Years*, 'we were dealing with an intransigent and overwhelmingly superior power' and, the prime minister might have added, the pattern of British negotiations was becoming an all too familiar succession of retreats. Even Sir Percy Cradock's later remark that the idea '[c]oolly considered . . . was not an unpractical suggestion' begins to look less convincing when the head of the British team was obliged to note how 'bitterly' Hong Kong resented the Chinese intention to have the Joint Liaison Group operate from within the territory prior to 1997.

To work round the roadblock presented both by the Chinese insistence on stationing the Sino–British monitoring commission in Hong Kong and the delays on final agreement on how the returned territory would be run, the foreign secretary was again sent to Beijing. It was during the July 1984 round of talks that the breakthrough in negotiations was finally achieved. The Chinese side did, it is true, make concessions but the alacrity with which they were promptly grabbed by the British officials strongly suggests that yet again the bargaining had been between two very unequal partners. Cradock's account of events sees Wu Xueqian's agreement to delay the involvement of the Joint Liaison Group in Hong Kong's business until 1998 and to extend its powers to the year 2000 as particularly important, but this is doubtful since the Foreign Office was under no illusion as to Beijing's ability to intervene if and when it wished in the territory's affairs. There were also to be alterations to the small print in what would eventually be termed the Basic Law and it was agreed that the both sides would ensure that any future deal would be enforceable under international law. But few of these changes could be easily seen as dramatic. Certainly Howe, by all published accounts from the British side of the table, worked efficiently to claim and digest morsels that Beijing had jealously retained in the past but the unevenness of the process is unescapable. Mrs Thatcher would later refuse to put a gloss on events: she admitted that '[i]t was no triumph.'

The negotiations at last began to gain a head of speed. The frustrations of the previous two years were seemingly now behind both parties. There was to be a Joint Declaration binding on both sides with a later Basic Law to clarify the administration of post-reversion Hong Kong as agreed to in the Howe talks and blessed by Deng himself, who added the unexpected bonus of then inviting the Queen to China. The terms were announced by Secretary Howe in Hong Kong to widespread approval. His claim that 'Hong Kong's economic and social systems, its distinctive way of life and its position as a financial, trading and industrial centre will be secured' was applauded, though his next remark that 'there is still a lot of work to be done' was more prophetic than some listeners may have initially realized.

The explanation given to Hong Kong by Howe inevitably accentuated the positive. It offered hope to the community that there could be a reasonable prospect of continuity in legal, economic, financial and social affairs. It was not, of course, a final statement on what the territory could expect after 1997, since a number of issues clearly had yet to be decided upon by the two parties, but it was probable that the emerging Joint Declaration would serve as the sheet anchor to ensure that Hong Kong would be recognizably the same place before and after 1997.

Negotiations continued apace to this goal. The Sino–British working groups had the unenviable task of pressing ahead along the lines agreed at the Beijing meeting to produce both a main text and what eventually became three lengthy annexes (see appendix 4). It was an exhausting round-the-clock process for the British side, since it would first negotiate with its Chinese counterparts before reporting back to Cradock in London and to officials in Hong Kong, but there was also considerable pressure on the Chinese to complete what must have appeared to be an interminable process. The detail of some of the questions proved complicated in the extreme and in a number of instances, as in the sensitive area of nationality, it was only solved through an 'exchange of memoranda' device that was deliberately excluded from the binding Joint Declaration.

The end result left over 40 per cent of the population of the territory possessing documents as British Dependent Territories' citizens in Hong Kong that might be recognized by the PRC for travel purposes abroad after 1997 but did not, in the eyes of the Chinese authorities, influence the fact that all Hong Kong Chinese 'compatriots, whether they are holders of the "British Dependent Territories citizens' Passport" or not, are Chinese nationals'. Such individuals would not have the right of permanent residence in Britain after 1997, nor would those unfortunate individuals, often from the Indian subcontinent, with neither a Chinese nor an alternative passport.

Yet the initial assessments of the Sino–British Joint Declaration suggested that Mrs Thatcher and her negotiators had won something of a victory for themselves and Hong Kong. One anonymous Foreign Office source even went so far as to claim that 'what we have done is strike a deal that virtually gives Hong Kong independence'. It did indeed appear that the prime minister had at least stood up for the peoples of the territory and in preparing Hong Kong for its now inevitable future under the PRC serious efforts were to be made to construct a more democratic government prior to 1997. It should be noted that the absence of elected members to LegCo and ExCo during the lengthy and intricate Sino–British negotiations in 1983–4 assisted the British government and permitted it to claim that criticisms from within the two bodies by its unofficial members could be disregarded. Foreign Secretary Howe repeatedly stressed that it would be the members of the House of Commons rather than possibly unrepresentative opinion within Hong Kong that would be the final arbitrators of any Sino–British accord. This was hardly a fine illustration of Hong Kong's claims to the enjoyment of virtual self-government; nor was the subsequent pace of political reform much of an advertisement for democracy. The announcement in July 1984 of planned indirect elections, proposed almost certainly with barely the minimum of advance notice to the Chinese authorities, served both to antagonize Beijing and divide the local community between those in the business world who feared the wrath of China and the more liberal elements in Hong Kong who complained that measures were unacceptably timid.

The Joint Declaration has been subject to a great number of conflicting interpretations. The text consists of eight paragraphs and is remarkable for its brevity in describing what will ensue for Hong Kong after its reversion to the PRC. While it is true that in annex I to the Joint Declaration the Chinese government 'elaborates the basic policies' established in paragraph 3 of the main text, there has remained considerable imprecision surrounding portions of the document. Commentators in the territory were quick to note, for example, that Hong Kong in its post-1997 form as a SAR was to enjoy 'a high degree of autonomy, except for foreign and defence affairs which are the responsibility of the Central People's government'. Yet this promise to run its own affairs, under what in annex I was described as its 'capitalist system and lifestyle' for the next fifty years, did not derive from the concept of divided sovereignty. The Hong Kong SAR was still to remain the vassal of the PRC since, as annex I insisted, the authority of Beijing was not to be questioned.

There was a vagueness too in regard to paragraph 4 where both parties spoke of leaving the UK government with responsibility for running Hong Kong until June 1997, yet in the following paragraph agreed to a Sino–British Liaison Group in order to ensure 'the effective implementation of this Joint Declaration'. Equally imponderable was the elliptical statement in the Chinese elaboration of its policies for the SAR contained within annex I of the Joint Declaration. This said that the future 'chief executive of the Hong Kong Special Adminstrative Region shall be selected by election or through consultations held locally and be appointed by the Central People's Government'. It went on to note in perhaps the most controversial sentence of the entire document that the 'legislature of the Hong Kong Special Administrative Region shall be constituted by elections'. This statement was intended, of course, to please each and every Chinese, British and Hong Kong interest, since the method of elections was deliberately not specified and could satisfy both those who imagined it implied a Westminster-style process and advocates of a single-party one-candidate Chinese communist arrangement.

Any prospect of a Sino–British era of good feelings continuing after the ratification of the Joint Declaration in May 1985 was short-lived. Disagreements between Britain and China over political change for the territory were to remain the greatest impediment to effective cooperation over the next decade. It was, in essence, a long battle over whether the British government and its Hong Kong administrators should determine the course of events until 1997 or, as China insisted, the only way forward was to align London with the Chinese version of how ambiguous agreements ought to be interpreted. Once the initial euphoria within the territory began to dissolve, Hong Kong discovered that its increasingly disparate voices would not determine the outcome.

Britain, at times in a decidedly cautious manner during the late 1980s when it supinely followed the Chinese warnings over electoral change, and China, insisting as always that any British alteration must conform to its sense of both the Joint Declaration and the eventual Basic Law, settled down to an exhausting war of attrition. Even when the two sides were obliged to negotiate, the evidence was unavoidable that London and Beijing were both united at least in being prepared to settle their differences in private without open consultation with the peoples of Hong Kong. Rival officials might claim to articulate the interests of the entire community but both Britain and China preferred that their supporters stayed on the sidelines until mobilized in the often heated debates over Hong Kong's future.

In this contest the Chinese government had the advantage of being better able to speak with one voice and to orchestrate public displays of unity. It was, of course, vital to Beijing's goals that this be so and that as many as possible of the peoples of Hong Kong should be satisfied with the PRC's interpretation of the Sino–British agreements. It was to ensure that there was to be only a minimum of constitutional reform that the 'convergence' concept was introduced, in the expectation that any piecemeal British reforms would meet the criteria established by the Basic Law. Until the Tiananmen Square massacre it was the Chinese government that had been generally gaining its way over constitutional developments in Hong Kong, assisted by the differences within ExCo over how to respond to Chinese insistence that all important reforms be stalled until 1990 when the draft Basic Law was to be published. Beijing, on the advice of its officials in the Xinhua News Agency under Xu Jiatun, also had the sense to coopt at least a number of nominally independent residents from within Hong Kong to its carefully guided Basic Law Consultative Committee.

The Basic Law of the Hong Kong Special Administrative Region of the People's Republic of China was considerably longer than the Joint Declaration. When published in a PRC booklet by its semi-official Hong Kong research outlet it comprised 160 articles, three annexes, a coloured illustration of the regional flag of the SAR and twenty pages of supplementary text elaborating on how the National People's Congress had drafted the Basic Law (see appendix 5). The result was clear. Hong Kong now knew for certain that its chief executive would be selected by the Chinese authorities and that the new legislature would have only a minority of its members subject to direct elections. It looked very much to be the construction of Chinese cadres in love with the Hong Kong of the early postwar colonial era. It did little to reassure those more democratic elements in contemporary Hong Kong who hoped that the

SAR might incorporate features from the recent political reform period. Martin Lee pithily defined the Basic Law as the reverse of 'Hong Kong people ruling Hong Kong' under their own steam with the intrusion of 'Hong Kong puppets ruling Hong Kong with a high degree of control'.

Those who pleaded for near-autonomy for the SAR would remain disappointed. The political arrangements for the enclave's management make it certain that if the PRC were challenged in the period after 1997 it would much prefer Hong Kong to be Red and dead than liberal and alive. The only possible consolation that can be tentatively offered over the territory's prospects is that precise policies hinge on fluctuating membership of the PRC's politburo and its key working groups for Hong Kong. Textual analysis of the Basic Law tells us only the outlines of the story. Despite its length and seeming precision much will depend on the victors in the succession struggles following the death of Deng. His imprint on Hong Kong, however, has been so substantial that neither President Jiang Zemin nor Premier Li Peng will wish to be seen to be dismantling his architecture. While both individuals appear presently to be hardliners, they have also to take note of the more moderate views of Foreign Minister Qian Qichen.

The initiative rested with China. For all the British government's talk of introducing a more representative system, little was being accomplished. Governor Wilson's discussions with the PRC leadership had yielded only a few crumbs for pro-democracy groups in the colony, since the Hong Kong authorities had agreed with Beijing that elections be delayed until 1991 and all sides knew that the changes proposed would not seriously impair the government's built-in majorities in LegCo and ExCo. The manner in which the Hong Kong government chose both to draft and interpret public opinion surveys on the political future of the territory in 1987 was further evidence of British hesitancy. The White Paper of February 1988 was only able to refer to a 'prudent and gradual' democratic evolution and Secretary Howe went out of his way in the Commons to stress the overriding necessity of cooperation with China.

While the territory was discovering what its post-1997 future was likely to be, the Hong Kong government had begun to institute far-reaching domestic changes. The precedent of open elections was indeed followed up and three years after MacLehose had left Hong Kong the expansion of LegCo was underway. Again, the changes may appear almost trivial to some readers but the number of elected members to LegCo was considerably increased, though the elections were indirect through so-called functional constituencies and electoral colleges. LegCo by the autumn of 1985 was a different institution from any of its predecessors. While far from fully democratic in a city-state where the legislature had never been the fount of power, the 24 members who had gained their seats through elections were an important indication of changed thinking in Whitehall and Government House. This represented a major break with the purely appointed system of the previous hundred years. It again must be assumed that these developments were calculated to bolster the territory as it began increasingly to calculate its positions over reversion.

It is true that these reforms to LegCo were made before the PRC's publication of its Basic Law but doubtless the Hong Kong administration of Sir Edward Youde had hoped from their inception that this would not unduly impair what had been created in the interim. Yet it did and the territory has continued to remain divided in its last years between those who prefer to press ahead and those who fear the wrath of Beijing. Governor Youde, who had succeeded MacLehose in the spring of 1982, was now caught between the British and Hong Kong governments' wish to increase democratization at the local and central levels and the concerns of Beijing that all political change must conform to its as yet unpublished Basic Law. It was an uncomfortable period but it does strongly suggest that the origins of change within the territory's political structure predate both the Tiananmen Square massacre – others prefer to term it merely an 'incident' or 'event' – and the more dramatic shifts of the Patten era.

The 1980s saw the gradual emergence of political groups that were established to take sides within Hong Kong, following publication of the Sino–British Joint Declaration in 1984. The territory's first elected members to LegCo have been defined by Jane C. Y. Lee of the Hong Kong Policy Research Institute as 'conservative-cum-moderate in their political outlook, with no clearly identifiable political affiliation at all', yet what might be called an opposition party to the business establishment did evolve. Barrister Martin Lee, for example, gained a seat in LegCo in 1985 and shortly afterwards began campaigning against the Chinese government's view that Britain was guilty of 'deviating' from the Joint Declaration. His stance was opposed by both the conservative groups and the moderates who feared that it would be against Hong Kong's best interests to openly demonstrate in favour of greater democracy before 1997 in order to safeguard the post-reversion position of the SAR. Most businessmen and professional groups felt that there was little to be gained and a great deal to be lost from making public any concerns they might feel over the SAR. China, they reasoned, would certainly not be deterred by a few marches through the streets of Hong Kong or by mere petitions advocating the direct election of LegCo. A formidable streak of pragmatism was also at work: those wishing to develop close personal connections to Beijing in order to smooth their business operations would much prefer to keep on the good side of China. There was too a common view, shared generally by expatriates, that the entire subject of reform was arcane and remote from the apathetic horizons of the peoples of Hong Kong. This condescending stance was destroyed for good in June 1989 when the slaughter in Tiananmen Square told the world only too clearly that Chinese state power would brook no challenges to its iron rule. It was as Chris Patten would later note 'understandably cathartic' for the peoples of Hong Kong and its legacy continues to plague the community. Hong Kong's current history may be dated from this event.

Demonstrations in Beijing in May and June 1989 that were crushed by the Chinese authorities drastically altered Hong Kong's perceptions of China and changed the entire nature of the territory's politics. The sight of PLA tanks and troops purportedly at work to restore order in the face of counter-revolutionary activity led to a huge outpouring of anger and demands that the British and Hong Kong governments rethink their entire dealings with China. Even conservative business groupings that had long resisted a more democratic system felt obliged to propose schemes that had at the very least a stronger directly elected element than any pre-1997 bicameral legislature.

While pro-democracy associations gained fresh support inside Hong Kong, the Tiananmen Square massacre galvanized the British government into taking a far stronger line with China and led to the reconsideration of some of its previously controversial measures. Comment in Hong Kong was, of course, highly critical of the Chinese state but London was chastised too for only making slight changes in its existing stringent restrictions on the entry of Hong Kong Chinese into Britain. While it was necessary for the West to reckon with what Winston Lord, the former US Ambassador to China, described as 'the big chill' in Sino–American ties, something of the same dimensions threatened to engulf Hong Kong and its sovereign power. The peoples of the territory now pressed the British cabinet and parliament to appreciate the depth of anxiety throughout the territory over its future under socialism. The guarded changes, however, that the Thatcher government announced later in 1989 satisfied only the fortunate beneficiaries (a small number of largely senior officials and key businessmen) and left the bulk of the community to fend for itself. Editorials and speeches that spoke of Britain's moral responsibility were largely unheeded, even on behalf of those with close links to the Crown. It was readily apparent that large-scale Asian immigration into Britain was not the kind of platform that very many MPs would risk endorsing, whatever the evidence on television screens of Chinese inhumanity.

The concern of the communities of Hong Kong that the Beijing government might ignore any constitutional provisions that conflicted with the priorities of the state and communist party were seen at their starkest in June 1989. Nothing in the years since has removed the stains surrounding the Beijing massacres; it is improbable that the very deep reservations held within the territory during the weeks and months after Tiananmen Square have dissolved. The fact that the staff of Xinhua and pro-Chinese newspapers in the colony joined in the huge demonstrations is indicative of how widespread was the shock. As the commentator and former official John Walden wrote shortly after the crisis:

what happened on the night of 3 June and the morning of 4 June 1989 is that all Hong Kong saw on television, heard on radio and read about in newspapers, horrifying events in Beijing that they feared might well be repeated in Hong Kong, any time after 30 June 1997. The bloody crimes against humanity taking place before their very eyes were being carried out on the orders of the regime into whose hands British officials were working so hard to deliver them.

He reminded readers of *The Other Hong Kong Report*, an annual publication intended to provide a critical analysis of local events, that

much of what they saw being done by soldiers and security police was in direct violation of the Chinese constitution. If that paper guarantee of civil and human rights could so easily be torn up by China's leaders before 1997, so could the Sino–British Joint Declaration after 1997.

The Foreign Office in Whitehall would dispute this view, but it has remained the conventional wisdom in Hong Kong since 1989 and deserves at the very least to be recalled when analysing the legal and political background to reversion. Governments, industrialists and trades unionists elsewhere may afterwards have adopted a much less critical stance on Chinese human rights violations in order to secure economic ties to the expanding China market but many in Hong Kong are still sceptical. Chinese Premier Li Peng has had to steel himself for occasional protests when visiting Europe or north America but his officials are fully aware that the hope of lucrative business opportunities has largely replaced the earlier reservations of Western governments. The argument, employed by Canada's prime minister in October 1995, was that 'the best way to improve the situation there is by not letting a country like China become too isolated'. Jean Chretien argued that 'if they were to be completely isolated, there would probably be more problems in that country'. Similar remarks have been frequently used by the British, American and Japanese governments in their haste to finalize trade contracts with the Chinese authorities.

In response to muted opposition from human rights groups in the West, the Chinese government invariably adopts a set piece to match the equally predictable remarks of its foreign hosts. Li Peng, for example, would later assure his audience in Montreal, for example, that 'although Canada and China differ in their respective social systems, historical backgrounds, cultural traditions and values, this has not and will not hinder fruitful cooperation between the two countries'. This constant reminder by China that it had its own governmental system that was not to be tampered with by outsiders, if they expected a share of the spoils in Beijing's modernization drive, leaves Hong Kong facing difficulties. It is feared by many residents that Western public opinion is likely to be muted in the event of a crisis in the future SAR. There appear to be strict limits on any possible overseas criticism of the PRC. Much will depend on the overall state of Sino–American relations and whether a future US administration would be prepared to continue linking China's most-favoured-nation (MFN) status over trade to Beijing's human rights record. Difficulties in Washington's ties to the PRC, particularly with regard to Taiwan's status and the strengthening of Chinese military forces, may leave the United States less willing to take up other more tangential issues involving the SAR.

The British government, however, was obliged to take note of the changing political realities within Hong Kong following its anger at the Chinese government's butchery in Beijing. The cabinet recognized, as junior minister Alastair Goodlad would later write in June 1994, that

political life in Hong Kong could not be the same again. A new maturity, a new political awareness had been born. Pressure for democratic change was expressed in, for example, successive motions passed by the Legislative Council. The British and Hong Kong governments had a clear responsibility to respond to that pressure.

While such realities could be easily recognized, it was far harder to devise new arrangements that, in Goodlad's words, responded 'to the palpable desire in the Territory for greater democracy; while ensuring that the changes were compatible with what had been agreed with China thus maximising the chances of the "through train" remaining on the rails'.

The eventual reforms proposed by Governor Patten attempted to square this circle. Clearly the British authorities after Tiananmen altered their entire approach to dealing with the PRC. In the period before the student protests in Beijing Sino–British affairs had been relatively smooth as the Joint Liaison Group functioned adequately and Britain slowly introduced a modicum of democracy to Hong Kong. Afterwards there was always going to be controversy, unless the way forward was to bow to China and adopt the approach that Chris Patten derided of believing that 'the only way you can stand up for something is to lie down'. The contrast between Governor Wilson and Governor Patten was more one of changed circumstances than different professional backgrounds and personalities. Whoever was governor had no choice but to respond to the new realities within Hong Kong. Wilson was held to have reacted with less than total aplomb but he had the unenviable task of attempting to reassure a divided community after the Beijing massacres. It would have taken an extraordinarily gifted individual to simultaneously hold the territory together while urging London to shift policy and still maintain channels of communication with the PRC. There clearly was no easy means of accelerating political reform within the territory in conjunction with China. Its government's anger at Hong Kong's defiant response to events in Beijing in the early summer of 1989 obviously could not be reconciled with the voices of those inside Hong Kong who called for the abrogation of the Joint Declaration. Alastair Goodlad's thesis that weary negotiations with China demonstrated the improbability of any Sino–British accord after Tiananmen is convincing. Goodlad noted that

experience of the 17 rounds of talks with China, and of earlier exchanges on constitutional development in Hong Kong suggest that whatever our approach, the Chinese position was one of great suspicion and inflexibility. Their concept of what criteria those wishing to ride the 'through train' needed to satisfy was fundamentally different from ours.

He doubted if the peoples of Hong Kong would have been prepared to accept any such one-sided deal and under the radically changed post-1989 circumstances Goodlad saw that disagreement with China was the price to be paid for accelerating constitutional change within the territory. Yet again, however, it appeared that Hong Kong's future would rest with those monitoring events beyond its borders.

It is this sense of possible neglect by the international community that has spurred groups in Hong Kong to strengthen their position in the last months before July 1997. Only if clearly defined and firmly established constitutional and legal processes are in place will the territory have the necessary self-assurance to maintain its promised autonomy. Fears of Chinese intimidation, greater corruption, a creeping self-censorship and harsher economic circumstances could gradually undermine the hopes of the pro-democracy parties. It would be foolhardy to deny the challenges that Hong Kong faces in the years ahead; the great experiment of one country, two systems is an unknown vessel. The territory in the last fifteen years has had to move at speed to prepare itself as best it can for a future that most of its residents are approaching with concern. Few in Hong Kong, aside from those most committed to the communist cause and some businessmen who are incorrigible pragmatists, welcome what may be in store for them. The need shortly to operate an untried political system with relatively inexperienced leaders and a civil service that is still wrestling with a series of rapid promotions and dislocations would be a difficult battle in itself, but to do so when uncertain of the personalities and policies of the sovereign power only compounds the test.

# 6 Confrontation: the Patten years, 1992–5

> My goal is simply this – to safeguard Hong Kong's way of life.
>
> (Governor Chris Patten, address to LegCo, 7 October 1992)

> Today's Chinese Government is not the Qing Dynasty Government and today's Chinese people are no longer the 'sick man of East Asia'. Whoever has a wrong concept of time, and of whom they are dealing with, and tries to force history backward, will surely have lifted a rock only to drop it on his own foot.
>
> (*People's Daily*, 20 November 1992)

Chris Patten became the twenty-eighth governor of Hong Kong in July 1992. There can be little doubt that the five years of Governor Patten's stewardship from 1992 to 1997 will prove to have been the most controversial in Hong Kong's postwar history. He is the one individual associated with the territory who has won widespread international attention for Hong Kong. The very date '1997' is now known across the globe. From the summer of 1992 Chris Patten made it apparent that he saw it as his responsibility to make a stand for Hong Kong; he wished therefore to enact legislation that might ensure that the territory was better equipped for its post-reversion future. In one of the most publicized speeches ever given by a governor of Hong Kong, Patten on 7 October 1992 outlined his policy programme to LegCo. If accounts by others are to be believed, there appears to have been a deliberate bid to exclude the Chinese government from all but the most perfunctory advance briefing of what the British cabinet now expected its new appointee to carry out. The former senior member of first LegCo, and until 1988 ExCo, Sir Sze-yuen Chung, has stated that China's request for delay and full discussion over the portions of Patten's intended speech was the beginning of the protracted confrontational period that would endure for the next three acrimonious years. Since the Hong Kong government was only prepared to debate the proposed constitutional changes at the heart of Patten's programme after they had been first announced to LegCo this was taken as virtually a declaration of open warfare.

Chris Patten's appointment was the first time in the postwar period that a non-bureaucrat had become the governor of Hong Kong. Having helped secure John Major's success in the British general election but failing to retain his own parliamentary seat in the process, Patten's move to Hong Kong appeared to be both a reward for his campaign direction and a signal to Beijing that change was afoot. Patten arrived in the territory determined to represent Hong Kong more vigorously as he and the community debated the Joint Declaration in detail. The governor later explained to an audience at the University of Hong Kong in 1994 that 'it is because we believe Hong Kong's interests to be worth standing up for that we do sometimes have to differ over how best to interpret and implement the commitments made in the Joint Declaration'. The British government, in other words, would no longer wish to downplay the interests of the peoples of Hong Kong when negotiating with the Chinese authorities over Hong Kong's future. A senior British politician was felt to be better equipped than his immediate predecessors to represent Hong Kong during these transition years. The emergence of a more open political system in Hong Kong combined with unprecedented demonstrations at the behaviour of the Chinese government over the Tiananmen Square massacre in 1989 had irreparably altered the familiar administrative system. It was to be Chris Patten's difficult task to operate within the context of worsening Sino–British relations and increasing domestic pressures for substantial constitutional reform. It was always likely to be a turbulent period.

Governor Chris Patten inherited a situation where his freedom to manoeuvre was highly constrained. He was boxed in from the start both by past Sino–British agreements and knowledge that there was only a short period remaining before he would hand over his territory to jubilant Chinese dignitaries. Clearly Patten intended to make the most of what chances there might be, but it has to be said that his ambitions and the opportunities available appeared at times to be mismatched. He had been appointed by his close friend John Major with the task of better uniting the peoples of Hong Kong and better representing their interests in the continuing debate with China over preparing the territory for its post-1997 era. It was surely a near-impossible task to attempt to promote cordial relations with Beijing and simultaneously press for political changes in Hong Kong that were certain to produce fierce attacks from China.

All postwar governors have regarded their annual addresses to LegCo as a well publicized opportunity to present policy programmes to the community. Chris Patten was no exception. He spoke forcefully in October 1992 knowing that media attention would be intense and as a politician throughout his entire working life he needed no reminder of the advantages that accrue to pithy speeches. Governor Patten's replies to questions from LegCo members on the day after making his policy statement indicated that he had already fully digested the initial press response. Yet to be doubly certain that his message would dominate the airwaves he pointed out that he had already the same morning taken part in a phone-in and was claiming that his proposals for constitutional reform had received public support. Since there was certain to be a contest with Beijing over the Patten proposals, the governor was determined to ensure that his case was not lost by default.

Patten stated without a moment's hesitation that he had got it 'just about right' in 'trying to find a point of balance in the community'. He felt that the aspirations of the peoples of Hong Kong were clear in that 'they do want more democracy' and as the new governor of the territory he saw it as his responsibility to work towards that goal. He told Emily Lau, when answering the first question on his speech, that he intended to 'broaden democracy' through a 'coherent package' that he was prepared vigorously 'to defend and argue for in Peking'. From the first days of his administration, the message to the hesitant within Hong Kong and the critics in China could hardly be in doubt: Hong Kong should be encouraged to press ahead with political change though this would also be 'entirely consistent with the Basic Law'. Governor Patten went out of his way to inform the territory of his personal beliefs and how he intended to guide Hong Kong within that philosophical framework. There was, Patten insisted, no excuse for standing still, since the Joint Declaration refers to the holding of elections and the Basic Law identifies the increasing proportion of the legislature that will be directly so elected. While not wishing to see the peoples of Hong Kong succumb to being used as 'heroic pawns' of outsiders' 'doubtless well-meaning preconceptions', Patten intended to provide 'a greater measure of democracy'.

His proposals for vastly enlarging the franchise for LegCo, the demotion of ExCo to a relatively minor constitutional role, and the lowering of the voting age to eighteen represented a dramatic change in the government of Hong Kong. It is not surprising that the Chinese government was swift to protest and has repeatedly vowed to undo the arrangements in 1997. Governor Patten and his advisors were obliged to employ highly technical devices to prepare reforms that could at least be said to conform superficially to past agreements reached with Beijing. It was, however, a questionable procedure to claim that the reform package bore much resemblance to earlier Sino–British understandings. The cooperation of the late 1980s no longer existed.

Competing international law specialists will offer rival interpretations on whether Governor Patten was in the right or wrong. In the event, Chinese and British officials held seventeen inconclusive rounds of talks in 1993 before LegCo made up its own mind by approving the governor's reforms. The change from largely limited and indirect elections (only eighteen of the sixty seats in LegCo up to 1995, it may be recalled, were directly elected, despite public pressure for reform) to twenty popularly-elected geographical constituencies, thirty huge industry-wide functional seats and leaving the remaining ten members to be drawn from members of the District Boards could be guaranteed to anger China. It was certain to lead to stronger political parties and confirm the death knell of conservative-run informal government. Beijing's response was to dismiss the entire exercise as a violation of Sino–British dealings. China was no longer interested in the earlier 'through train' analogy. Reversion would now require new Chinese-only institutions staffed by compatriots loyal to the party.

Patten's announcement in October 1992 that he intended to propose changes to LegCo led to charges from Beijing that the British had reneged on their agreements to honour the Basic Law and were set on instituting democracy by stealth. For outsiders the entire debate may appear petty, since the changes were far from earth-shattering in the first place and few would immediately imagine that the move warranted the Chinese description of 'extremely irresponsible and reckless'. Yet the proposals were to lead to an unprecedented period of Sino–British acrimony and must as a result be analysed at some length. Chris Patten arrived in Hong Kong making it clear that while 'good co-operation with China is my sincere aim and my profound wish', there was to be no return to the humiliations of the recent past that had culminated in John Major reluctantly having to fly to Beijing in the aftermath of the Tiananmen Square massacre to sign the agreement over the new airport. Patten wished to be seen to be as mounting a more vigorous defence of Hong Kong's own interests.

The new governor was quickly embroiled in controversy. His plan was to make up for lost time and to press ahead to ensure that at least a partial form of representative government might yet be installed in Hong Kong prior to 1997. Patten's aims immediately collided with the opposition of an outraged China. The scene was set for trial by newspaper headlines and what was frequently termed 'megaphone diplomacy' as both sides fought to prove their points on how Hong Kong should be treated. The views of the British government were spelled out publicly in the correspondence columns of *The Times* through Minister of State Alastair Goodlad in replying to criticisms from Lord Shawcross that the Patten proposals contravened the Joint Declaration and the Basic Law. Goodlad, who had had first-hand experience of working in the territory, insisted in December 1992 that Governor Patten's proposals 'fit squarely' into the Joint Declaration's agreement that LegCo be elected by 1997 and that his design conformed to what was stated in the Basic Law; he further underlined the point that Patten's ideas could be discussed with the Chinese government through 'calm and constructive dialogue'. This did not happen. Beijing continued to complain that the rules had been broken. It was a package that no Chinese officials could possibly accept, since it was contrary to their understanding of Sino–British convergence for LegCo, as seemingly listed in the Basic Law and agreed to by both London and Beijing in 1990, prior to the public unveiling of the details of the Basic Law.

China's wrath and Governor Patten's equally caustic rebuttals plagued the territory from November 1992 until after the eventual LegCo elections of September 1995. Neither side would stop measuring out the vitriol in the three years that were to follow. It was certainly at times far more than merely a case of Hong Kong being subject to 'divergent tensions'. Patten spoke repeatedly of his intention to leave in 1997 as the last governor having guided his territory 'honourably and honestly', but while the rhetoric was loud, the realities of his predicament could only serve to deflate some of these boasts. Patten clearly did wish to be seen to be the loyal defender of Hong Kong and his visits overseas gave the territory an international exposure that it has rarely, if ever, experienced on such a sustained basis in its history. But China has an equally strong vested interest in reminding the governor and the world that its wishes could not be ignored and that it would be final arbitrator of events both prior to and after 1997. The attempts to exclude Beijing in the autumn of 1992 from consultation over reforms to LegCo, for example, only served to increase existing suspicions that the British had plotted to maintain a lever over Hong Kong into the next century. Equally, the financing of the new airport at Chek Lap Kok was viewed by China as an extravagance that deliberately ran down the territory's sizeable reserves in order to benefit Western enterprises. Capitalism, it was alleged, was devious to the end.

Indicative of the disputes between Britain and China had been the long-running controversy over proposals to fund and construct the airport development scheme. There had long been proposals for a new airport in Hong Kong. Possible sites and planning outlines were in existence from the early post-reoccupation period. Kai Tak had obvious difficulties in its location and operation; traffic on the perimeter had to be stopped, for example, in the 1950s when planes were about to land and the limitations on the extension of its only runway encouraged officials to commission consultants to report on possible alternatives.

Nothing, however, came of these schemes until the days following the Tiananmen Square massacre. Then, in a very determined exercise to boost public morale, the governor of Hong Kong announced in October 1989 that a mammoth new airport construction project was to be instituted in order to solve the inadequacies clear to all passengers who used Kai Tak. The evidence that Hong Kong needed a new airport was not in doubt, but the timing and scale of what would be defined shortly afterwards as 'one of the largest infrastructure programmes in progress anywhere in the world' had immediate repercussions on Sino–British relations. As journalist Kevin Murphy would write later, it 'appeared extravagant, politically charged and arrogantly announced'.

While the British government saw the proposed new airport at Chek Lap Kok island off the northern coast of Lantau as part of what Sir Percy Cradock termed 'efforts on our side to restore confidence in Hong Kong', the reaction of the Chinese government was very different. Beijing took umbrage at not being fully consulted over what may have been genuine fears that the territory's exchequer would be depleted by a project that involved a new airport, six transportation links, two land reclamation schemes and the start of a new town adjacent to Chek Lap Kok. China's anger grew as its government consolidated its position in the months after the Tiananmen massacre.

What followed from the autumn of 1989 to the autumn of 1994 can best be described as a very slow, bitter process of protracted airport diplomacy. Only in November 1994 was it possible for the two sides to agree on arrangements that appeared to signal the ending of the dispute, though even then there remained financial hurdles to overcome. The broad 'preliminary' agreement over how to pay for the US$20 billion airport was greeted with considerable scepticism, since pledges to cooperate in the past had led only to disappointment.

From 1989 commentators were quick to note how the airport project was seen by the Chinese side as a valuable weapon with which to belabour Mrs Thatcher and the Hong Kong government. Of course, the huge financial implications of the schemes and the very tight construction deadlines announced in the original statements made Chek Lap Kok almost certain to arouse controversy, yet even the most battle-hardened of British officials might have doubted that the bilateral negotiations would generate such venom during the succeeding five years. The airport core programme, defined by its media relations division as 'Hong Kong's gateway to the future', centred on replacing

Kai Tak with a new airport able to handle 35 million passengers and 1.5 million tonnes of cargo a year.

The ambitions of the Hong Kong government and the professional skills of a large number of international consortia in preparing and then starting to build both the airport itself and the associated projects were soon eclipsed by China's criticism of the entire development. If the British authorities had imagined that the new airport would restore confidence in Hong Kong they were soon to learn the error of their ways. The frustrations felt by the PRC in turn would hurt both the territory and Sino–British relations; it is also probable that the ensuing airport imbroglio contributed to John Major's decision not to reappoint Governor Wilson when his term of office ended. Certainly public debate over the delays at one stage left journalists in Hong Kong predicting that the entire Chek Lap Kok project would have to be cancelled as the demands for concessions by China appeared to undermine the remaining credibility of the government. It was Hong Kong that ended up demoralized, not the PRC. Beijing's successes in reminding all and sundry that it had ultimate control was a lesson that Britain and its representatives in Hong Kong were reluctant to accept. The airport negotiations had become by 1994 a metaphor for the inability of the Hong Kong and British governments to combat the burgeoning influence of China in the political and financial affairs of the territory.

The Hong Kong government might have saved itself from some of the ensuing rancour by taking the PRC into its confidence earlier in the day. This is easy to suggest with the advantage of hindsight but the sheer initial size of the new airport project was bound to put Beijing on guard. This was made doubly certain by the Hong Kong government's financial proposals. It was, as Cradock explains in his memoirs, 'a big project, worth over £8 billion and extending well beyond 1997'; but his assumption that 'the Hong Kong budget could readily carry its share, and 40 percent of the money would come from the private sector' was to prove cavalier. No Chinese government could be expected to wave through such an expensive project, which it had only recently seen, without subjecting it to minute scrutiny and most certainly not so soon after what it regarded as subversive elements had been demonstrating in Hong Kong against their future masters. The PRC was also very aware that private financiers would only lend sums on such a scale with cast-iron guarantees from Beijing.

The Hong Kong authorities blundered. The ensuing delays inevitably increased the costing, seriously damaged Sino–British relations and at the moment of greatest animosity in the summer of 1991 led the British government to inform the PRC that the entire airport programme would be cancelled unless cooperation could be quickly promised. Yet to proclaim that enough was enough and to achieve together a compromise of sorts, the Chinese government exacted its pound of flesh from London. John Major was made to travel to Beijing to sign an airport memorandum of understanding in September 1991 that many observers outside the Foreign Office have termed humiliating. It was in the event not the end of play that Hong Kong had hoped for. Disagreement persisted. The prime minister's visit did indeed look very much like 'a tribute-bearing occasion' and the Chinese leaders no doubt relished the sight of the British discomfort and were not about to relax their grip on the future of the airport thereafter. The details were made the source of limitless frustrations to Hong Kong. Lengthy meetings ensued where each side took it in turn to state its official position, without much hope of breaking the logjam of issues that continued to pile up.

The result was a series of missed deadlines for the construction schedules on what were termed the airport core projects. As the *Financial Times* noted in May 1993 the airport plans and the proposal to enlarge the booming container terminals were 'obvious targets' for the Chinese authorities; together they represented an attempt to go for 'Hong Kong's jugular'. The Hong Kong government saw the funding of these mixed (public and private) projects in a very different light from the PRC. The Chinese side was eager to limit the borrowing requirements and to avoid what it reckoned might be overexpensive facilities. The Joint Liaison Group's airport committee for long remained the battleground for disputes on the funding of a remarkable series of engineering feats. Certainly Hong Kong needs a new airport – it could have been built sooner if earlier governments had been braver – to maintain its competitiveness as an international centre, but what its officials failed to fully appreciate was the fury of Beijing at the manner in which the plans were presented and the costs calculated.

Differences over Chek Lap Kok were paralleled by a series of problems over port facilities. The issues were again ones of finance and the involvement of the PRC in what it claimed to be a matter where its approval was necessary, since the new port extensions would have an important bearing on Hong Kong's post-1997 future. Although the financial costs have never approached those of the new airport core programme, the disagreements over who should build the projected container terminals have a familiar ring to them. The Chinese side took particular objection to the inclusion in container contracts of Jardines, arguing that the company was receiving preferential treatment from the Hong Kong government and did not deserve to participate. What was less difficult to dispute, as with Chek Lap Kok over air transport, was the clear need for additional harbour facilities. The entire axis of Hong Kong's port was shifting westwards by the 1980s as the territory concentrated on the development of new container systems that contributed mightily to the enormous expansion in tonnage handled by the port. Only container terminals will be able to provide the cheap and efficient services needed for Hong Kong's intended strengthening of its ties to southern China. The traditional focus on ships moored between Hong Kong and Kowloon and in outer channels is becoming far less important as fewer vessels use buoys and lighters in the more profitable container era.

It was this insistence on safer, faster, handling of cargoes through containerization that led the government, in conjunction with private companies, to press ahead with its port reforms. The port development strategy drew on all available data on cargo and shipping movements to forecast impressive growth rates in port traffic. Estimates suggest that by 2006 there might be 33,000 vessels annually arriving in Hong Kong, in comparison with 20,363 in 1990. To cater for this rapid increase the government pressed ahead with container terminals 8 and 9 and proposed that new terminals might next be built at Lantau and anchorage for river traffic sought at Tuen Mun. The planners developed their schemes to match the new airport infrastructure; indeed the Lantau port cannot function until the Lantau fixed crossing suspension bridge is in place (scheduled to be in 1997). In the meantime enormous construction work is underway at Stonecutters Island (terminal 8) and Tsing Yi (the controversial terminal 9).

Both the Hong Kong and Chinese governments were quick to cry foul over their opponent's interpretations of what was or what was not permissible under the terms of the 1984 Joint Declaration. The charges made by the British were that China had deliberately employed delaying tactics over considering the airport project, while the Chinese side insisted that the British handling of the requirement to consult on issues that had consequences beyond 1997 was perfunctory and therefore humiliating. The PRC case against the Hong Kong government is stronger than the British press has long maintained. The subsequent foot-dragging by Chinese officials is almost certainly intended as a riposte to British unwillingness to take the PRC into its confidence in the initial, formative period. William Overholt has suggested that the 'Hong Kong government informed Beijing about the airport decisions through a letter written in English that was sent to Beijing only two days before the Hong Kong governor, David Wilson, publicly announced the decision'. Following this, apparently, the Hong Kong government procrastinated for three months and finally 'sent a huge technical report in English'.

Everything that seemingly could go wrong, did so. After more complaints from Beijing, a consultative group from the PRC was timed to land in Hong Kong at the moment when the rearranged financial details were to be announced. Governor Wilson next stated emphatically that his administration was under no mandate to consult with the PRC and the *Far Eastern Economic Review* weighed in with the comment that if Beijing were to get its way this 'would mean surrendering the territory's autonomy on financial and economic affairs, areas which were guaranteed under the 1984 Sino–British Joint Declaration on the future of Hong Kong'. Yet the British government was already weakening its stance. On 20 September 1990, Lord Caithness, the newly appointed minister responsible for Hong Kong, stated on his first visit to the territory that the PRC would be given full information, since 'they are going to take on a liability through the project, a project that continues into the next century'. The united front between London and Hong Kong was in jeopardy with colonial bureaucrats and lawyers tending to claim that Hong Kong's future autonomy left it with responsibility for its financial liabilities post-1997, whereas international bankers were vitally interested in gaining Beijing's approval before agreeing to funding.

The Foreign Office appears to have generally sided with those who wanted to bring Beijing into the game, provided terms could be agreed. Sir Percy Cradock, when reviewing the chapter in his autobiography that is rather ambitiously titled 'The Airport Agreement', noted how talks in 1990 and 1991 failed. The Chinese, he claims,

used the talks for propaganda purposes and advanced a series of extravagant demands as preconditions for their agreement. These demands were for considerable sums to be set aside from the Hong Kong fiscal reserves and for veto powers, not only on the airport authority, but also widely in the financial sphere.

Final agreements over the new airport were eventually realized in the autumn of 1995. By then the accords excited little of the earlier passion, both because the negotiating parties had tempered their previous positions and because of the introduction of newer issues into Sino–British negotiations in the interim. Fresh disagreements elsewhere left the press with choicer stories than the final financial details over Chek Lap Kok.

The result was an almost daily round of harsh words and a general reluctance to cooperate. Obviously the interests of Hong Kong were in jeopardy while the two powers fought their battles out in public. The process was precisely the opposite of how earlier governors and Chinese officials from Guangzhou and Beijing had gone about their business.

Instead of carefully prepared British overtures convened as far as possible away from press scrutiny, the territory now stood divided over how to respond to the gladiatorial contests supposedly staged on its behalf. Business groups were appalled by the new governor's confrontational approach. One toy manufacturer when asked by *Asiaweek* in December 1994 to assess Patten's plan replied simply: 'it stinks.' Others might take a more considered opinion but, as pro-Beijing property magnate Vincent Lo asserted in the same article, conservative industrialists and financiers were agreed that 'the community is calling for more cooperation'. If so, it did not get it. Throughout the first three years of the Patten administration the business lobby made appeals for conciliation, yet it began to discover that its firmly held assumption that because Hong Kong was its creation the government of the day would automatically respond to its petitioning was no longer the case. Vincent Lo, a member of the China's preliminary Working Committee for the SAR and initially thought by some as likely to be the first chief executive in 1997, objected both to Governor Patten's dealing with China and his attempts to improve the social infrastructure of the territory. No longer, however, was the business of Hong Kong merely business; the community was now seen to have important interests that might even take precedence over trade. For Hong Kong in the last decade of the twentieth century this was mildly daring stuff. Patten, for example, in his October 1995 speech at the opening of the LegCo session, stressed that 'improved social services are one of the rewards for our economic success'; earlier governors might have preferred to wax lyrical on the slim nature of budgets.

Complaints arose from other quarters, too. Former Foreign Office figures made it clear in print and through private interview that Governor Patten's handling of China was to be faulted on the grounds of breaking agreements solemnly entered into with Beijing and through the likelihood that by antagonizing its future rulers the main sufferer from the exercise would be Hong Kong itself. (The fact that British trade also faced constraints in the important China market was another factor in the equation.) Ex-diplomats generally felt that attempts to pressurize the PRC would leave Hong Kong more vulnerable to a possible reduction in the freedoms and opportunities originally promised under the Sino–British agreements. There would, of course, be little that any outside power could do in that eventuality, though some optimists hold that perhaps the United States might see itself prepared to take up the SAR's cause. Congressional attention to the fate of Hong Kong as expressed in the US Hong Kong Policy Act of 1992 has encouraged some in the territory; others sense that possible sanctions by the United

States in the case of human rights violations in the SAR would depend very largely on the overall state of future Sino–American relations.

The immense difficulties of interpreting the 1984 Joint Declaration must make any foreign government hesitate before deciding to criticize China. One instance of the legal minefield that would have to be crossed before action might be mounted was seen in the Senate hearings of the Clinton administration's nominee as ambassador to Beijing. Former Senator Jim Sasser's remarks, later reversed, that the 'Chinese have indicated that they are not going to abide' by the LegCo elections of September 1995 and that 'clearly by the covenant of 1984 they are not required to' further weakened the case of those hoping for strong American support. It should also be noted that Chris Patten had long attempted to discourage any coupling of criticisms of Beijing's human rights record with the withdrawal of its MFN status on trade. Patten had argued in front of the Washington press corps during his visit to the United States in May 1993 that trade ought not to be treated as a weapon against China. Clearly thinking of the consequences that US sanctions would have on his territory, the governor maintained that if trade were restricted on China 'you reduce your communication and your ability to influence'. He pleaded with congressional opponents of China to think again, stating that those who 'would like to help Hong Kong to protect our modest aspirations by linking MFN renewal to the political developments of Hong Kong' should desist. Employing the style that had already become familiar to listeners in the territory he said bluntly: 'I hope that anybody who thinks that would actually be helpful will take it from the governor of Hong Kong that it certainly wouldn't.'

Patten's own confidence in his approach to political reform also won him fewer friends among liberals than he had probably anticipated. Loose political groupings associated with the likes of Martin Lee had frequently expressed disappointment at the gradualism behind Patten's changes. Whereas businessmen tended to agree with the headline comment of *Asiaweek* in December 1994 that 'for many corporate chiefs, 1997 cannot come soon enough', those who looked to Patten for defences against China also accused him of backsliding. Lee's criticism of Patten's constitutional proposals was that 'we believe they do not go nearly far enough'. Responsibility for this situation was, as Lee explained in a lengthy article in the *Far Eastern Economic Review* of 26 November 1992, partly the fault of earlier timidity by Britain and partly the nature of the governor's own modest democratic reforms.

The September 1995 LegCo elections were the most democratic in Hong Kong's history and the successes of Lee's own Democratic Party suggested that many in the territory shared the party's stance. The results indicated that the pro-China parties had underestimated Lee's popularity and demonstrated that even if the earlier talk of a 'through train' were to be derailed by Beijing large portions of the electorate were still prepared to support the Democrats. Lee was quoted in the *South China Morning Post* on the eve of the poll as stating that he shared no responsibility for the collapse of a dialogue with China. While his opponents made great play of the fact that Lee was *persona non grata* with Beijing, Lee enjoyed turning his back on the PRC by pointing out that 'dialogue with China is not a bad thing, but it is not an end in itself'. Lee insisted it was 'a means to an end: safeguarding Hong Kong's way of life'. Lee could be scathing in his attacks on the more cautious groups hoping to remain conciliatory with Beijing. He argued robustly: 'Our opponents say: "Don't confront China." We say: "If you cannot defend Hong Kong, why be in politics at all?" We believe we owe it to Hong Kong to speak up, to say what we may not always feel free to say, but wish someone would say for them [*sic*].'

The results from Hong Kong's first ever directly-elected LegCo revealed a community uncertain of how to handle relations with its future Chinese overlords. The extent to which pro-democracy candidates were able to defeat politicians standing for close cooperative ties with the PRC suggested that the final days of British rule could be uncomfortable. Within hours of the start of balloting the New China News Agency had issued a fierce denunciation of the parliamentary elections masterminded by Governor Patten. The blunt message was that once British sovereignty over Hong Kong was terminated in the summer of 1997 all Patten-inspired attempts at democratic government would stop functioning.

The leader of the pro-democracy movement and Hong Kong's first ever media politician remains Martin Lee. His long record of outspoken statements in the years since the Tiananmen Square massacre has enraged the authorities in Beijing. Yet his coalition's triumph in the LegCo elections by winning twenty-five of the sixty seats left the PRC in a quandary. Those preferring to put their trust in China did less well than their organizers initially expected. The defeat of the Democratic Alliance for the Betterment of Hong Kong's leader Tsung Yok-shing was a resounding rebuff for the pro-Chinese forces and observers feared that it could seriously undermine hopes for a smooth transition to Chinese rule. It may also lead to Beijing introducing new electoral schemes after 1997 that effectively prevent any possible repetition of the humiliation experienced by pro-China figures in September 1995.

Once the results have been digested it appears possible that both the groups linked to Martin Lee and the DAB may begin to modify their respective views. Beijing will not wish to publicly retract its words forbidding the newly-elected LegCo to survive after July 1997, but it is possible that at least some legislators may yet be reappointed to whatever new body is instituted to help run Hong Kong as an SAR in greater China. Likewise some in the pro-democracy camps may feel that their constituents will recognize that there are limits to standing up to China. A degree of pragmatism from both sides should not be ruled out in the final months to the handover of sovereignty.

The results suggested that the pro-China DAB, and the Hong Kong Progressive Alliance failed through being seen as too eager to intimidate the territory's voters. The electorate, particularly in the more representative geographical constituencies, was not prepared to do the bidding of Beijing. For Martin Lee the September 1995 LegCo elections were his finest hour. The New China News Agency's statement made on the morning of polling day that China would disband the assembly about to be elected once it assumed power in 1997 was widely felt to have been counter-productive. In the winter of 1996 it remains unclear, however, if Martin Lee's Democratic party will be able to utilize its strengths against opponents in LegCo and the administration of Chris Patten. The challenges by Lee to the executive suggest that all political parties in LegCo and the government will be subject to considerable strains. Loose coalitions on specific issues may gradually evolve; Government House will have to take sides to maintain its authority.

Lee's doubts over the Patten administration are legion. He has spoken out frequently about the need to strengthen not only the electoral process but also the human rights structure and the arrangements for the Court of Final Appeal (as a practising barrister this might have been expected). In neither case can it be said that he has fully gained his goals, since the Hong Kong government has been reluctant to press for reforms that would greatly antagonize Beijing. While, for example, a Bill of Rights was enacted in June 1991 in order to damp down fears of how a future regime might operate after 1997, the recommendation of the House of Commons Foreign Affairs Select Committee to establish a human rights commission for Hong Kong was shelved. The idea that as a substitute there might be public education in the territory to promote awareness of human rights and a section under the local ombudsman to monitor possible governmental deficiencies in this field was almost derisory; such action is unlikely to be regarded with anything but extreme displeasure by China after reversion.

A number of changes to common law in Hong Kong followed the introduction of the Bill of Rights but perhaps more serious than this has been the Chinese government's ruling in October 1995 that it would scrap sections of the Bill itself. Beijing clearly dislikes any weakening of the territory's emergency powers over security and broadcasting regulations and has announced that recent changes, made to conform to the Bill of Rights, would be invalid after 1997. It has also said that it will not file human rights reports to the United Nations Human Rights Commission (UNHRC), since China is not itself a party to the international rights covenants. The view of the Chinese government's Hong Kong and Macao affairs office is that the future SAR has 'resolved' the issue through the Joint Declaration and the Basic Law. What should not be overlooked, however, is that until recently the postwar statutory powers of the colonial police to prevent subversion and maintain immigration controls were indeed extremely wide.

It is the unwillingness of Chinese officials to think too sympathetically of how the peoples of Hong Kong might react to their future sovereign power that has left not only Martin Lee's Democratic Party but some conservative politicians as well fearful of the proper continuation of the rule of law after 1997. The anxieties of many in the community that the colonial system, for all its faults, might be replaced by arbitrary state power have not been adequately addressed by Beijing or its local cadres. Business groups doubt whether the settling of commercial disputes will be necessarily possible in the SAR courts and are therefore taking great pains to ensure that all parties to commercial contracts accept that English law be the medium for any possible recourse to arbitration and mediation.

Local human rights organizations have even more cause for alarm than the financial interests of property magnates and fund managers, since concern for their clients could indeed bring arrest and imprisonment if the authorities after June 1997 so determine. To imagine that the protection accorded to civil liberties in China proper will be much assistance to those wishing to take to the streets of Hong Kong to demonstrate against officialdom in the near future is chimerical. Martin Lee and Emily Lau know this perfectly well; it must be assumed that restrictions and interference in the traditional manner in which individual citizens in Hong Kong have exercised Western concepts of freedom will grow once the SAR is established.

Certainly there have been faults with the legal system in Hong Kong, an arrangement that appears remote both culturally and linguistically from the lives of many in the territory, but China's promises that 'laws currently in force in Hong Kong will remain basically unchanged' after reversion is little comfort. Equally, the Sino–British agreement to limit the role of overseas judges with common law backgrounds in the court of final appeal in the SAR has angered liberals. The concern that civil rights and an independent judiciary may both be impaired by external pressure exists widely in the community. To expect vigilance from the people of the SAR under possibly intimidating circumstances, as suggested by some authors, is again somewhat unrealistic. It is more probable that silence will be the conventional response to any erosion of a judicial system alien to the thinking of the sovereign power.

Martin Lee has long maintained that 'just as free markets and free trade are the lifeblood of Hong Kong's economic success, so a free market of ideas and free competition in the political sphere are the keys to successful government'. His calls for 'democratic and accountable government' to be combined with continuation of the rule of law ensured that he would win few friends among the business community, the Hong Kong government or the Chinese authorities. He further damaged his standing with the conservatives by repeatedly calling for far greater liberalization of the restraints on entry to Britain for residents of Hong Kong. Unlike most corporate directors safely in possession of second passport Lee has made it clear that he intends to stay on in the territory after 1997 and few doubt that he means what he says. This gives him a strong moral and political platform from which to urge London to permit the entry of more Hong Kong citizens. On this issue Lee is in general agreement with Chris Patten, as both have endeavoured to press for the right of far greater numbers of Hong Kong peoples to visit and reside in Britain. There is little evidence, however, that the present Conservative Party government will accept the arguments that over 3 million residents in the territory be granted British passports other than for use as temporary travel documents. It is also highly improbable that any change in political fortunes following a general election would lead to greater sympathy from an incoming Labour cabinet.

Public opinion surveys conducted within Hong Kong in October 1995 suggest that the bulk of the peoples of the territory is resigned to being refused the right of abode in Britain. While Governor Patten made highly publicized remarks urging London to think again in the autumn of 1995, the clear response from the home secretary that the issue remained closed and was not subject to review can have surprised no one. No British political party is likely to consider even marginal changes to the present highly restrictive regulations with an election in the offing. Survey findings within Hong Kong strongly suggest that the public reluctantly accepts this position and has little interest in pursuing the matter when the British political climate is so opposed to giving residency rights to an estimated 3.3 million holders of British Dependent Territories citizens' passports.

While the tripartite debate over access will doubtless continue and there is at least the possibility of minor shifts over Asian ethnic minorities who risk becoming stateless after 1997, most Sino–British issues were in the process of being resolved by the winter of 1995. The outcome was often a disappointment to the government of Chris Patten but it was hardly to be expected that Beijing would wish to be seen to be actively cooperating with the colonialists so soon before the handover of power. The installation in Tiananmen Square of a clock registering the days before reversion and the opening of talks on the actual ceremony for the transfer of sovereignty were reminders to all that Hong Kong was entering the last phase of its European rule. The local media also reported a large number of symbolic changes, from the issuing of bank notes within the territory by the Bank of China to the scrapping of the royal prefix from the title of the Jockey Club. Indeed, as if to underline this process of change, statistical information from the Bank of China group was released in November 1995 that indicated that it controlled a quarter of all deposits and dollar loans within Hong Kong. Its reported assets of HK$700 billion (US$90 billion) will undoubtedly grow once the territory reverts to the PRC. In 1996 the Bank of China assumed the chairmanship of the Hong Kong Association of Banks which necessarily requires close cooperation with the Hong Kong Monetary Authority. It is these financial and economic ties that are felt to be the best informal guarantees for the SAR's future. Capital inflows from China have been extremely important in maintaining a reasonable degree of confidence within Hong Kong's business community, which suggests the prospects for the post-1997 era ought not to be seriously impaired, despite the obvious political uncertainties. The high stake of mainland financial concerns in Hong Kong's property, trade and stock exchange dealings has indeed acted to the advantage of the commercial establishment. Relatives of senior Chinese cadres are known to have considerable personal involvement in this process.

Integration, of course, between Hong Kong and the southern China region has a lengthy history. From the territory's early days, as we have seen, the attractions of Hong Kong were widely appreciated to the north. The postwar economic linkage was clearly a vital factor that constrained Beijing from all but occasional action against the colony. The experiences of the Korean war may have played an important part in underlining the value of Hong Kong to a China supposedly under siege from the United States and its European allies. The contraband trade helped provide the PRC with materiel to withstand the might of American arms. Hong Kong also quickly proved its worth in more legitimate transactions as China began to reconstruct its economy. From the export of primary products (including the pumping of large volumes of water as the territory's own reservoirs were unable to provide a constant supply in the summer months) to the shipment more recently of low-cost manufactured goods from the Pearl River Delta the economic relationship has undoubtedly strengthened. This has lead some commentators to ask whether the border has not already lost most of its importance for the two economies. The concept of a 'greater China' appears to have taken root in the fertile financial and commercial soil of interdependence. The Hong Kong dollar now circulates freely in southern China.

Yet Chris Patten has had other goals besides maintaining economic growth and political reform. Like most recent administrators, he wished to identify areas within Hong Kong that appeared to be in particular need of improvement. For Governor MacLehose it had been 'two million houses', for Governor Patten it was improvements in social welfare. In his initial speech to LegCo outlining his agenda for the next five years, Patten stated that his second objective, following on from continuing 'to generate the economic success that has made Hong Kong one of the wonders of the world', was to ensure 'proper priority to the protection of the disadvantaged'. He therefore proposed an extraordinarily large, though affordable, increase in funding 'to meet the community's needs in rehabilitation, social welfare and social security'. Patten, clearly using language that reflected his own social conscience, saw that Hong Kong, for all the regular trumpeting of its growth statistics, 'is not without its darker side'. While rightly dismissing the extreme critics who would identify the territory only with the 'crassly materialistic', Governor Patten noted that 'much remains to be done to honour our obligations to the deprived and the disabled'. In the years since 1992 the Hong Kong government has made social welfare reform a priority issue; it is an area where the benefits are likely to outlive much of the sound and fury over constitutional change. Patten's legislation over communal welfare responsibilities may yet prove to be his main legacy to Hong Kong.

Yet the peoples of Hong Kong will judge their governor by more wider and more individualistic measures than desirable social policies. Patten as an experienced politician needs no instruction on how best to satisfy the aspirations of his territory. He will not be surprised to learn from his advisors that his popularity depends more on economic results than political reforms to LegCo. The public, like the public in Britain or Germany, thinks first and foremost of its own economic condition when voicing an opinion on its government. The advent of more sophisticated and regular opinion polling has enabled researcher Robert Chung to track the relatively shallow knowledge of many citizens on Sino–British negotiations and the public's rating of the governor. By the end of 1994 Patten's score was approximately where it was when he was designated governor. His popularity had first surged following his policy statement to LegCo in October 1992, only to slump after the failure of subsequent Sino–British talks. While the distrust of China has remained high, the widening involvement in local politics by many in the territory has generally reduced the standing of the government. Perhaps this is a healthy sign of greater maturity but it is not a fact of much comfort to Chris Patten. For the remainder of his period in office he is obliged to work for economic improvement (in 1995 unemployment was the key issue in the territory, much as in the previous year it had been property prices) and strive to ensure a stable transfer of power.

Governor Patten takes pleasure in speaking up for Hong Kong and attempting, in effect, to correct the world's opinions of what even for Britain remains a place largely of peripheral interest. While careful not to present the territory as a model for faltering European states, he could hardly be faulted for gently suggesting that the newly industrialized Asian economies might have at least some lessons for Britain. Hong Kong, as he explained in the correspondence columns of the *Spectator* in January 1996,

is not a value-free zone. It is a thriving community with values and freedoms which it cherishes and which underpin its economic success. Hong Kong people believe in working hard, in saving, in education.

He went on to claim that neither these attributes nor those of representative government should be seen as the exclusive preserve of any one part of the globe. During Chris Patten's last months in office, it may be that this role as diplomat and spokesman for Hong Kong will be his final contribution to the community. The adversarial and leadership years are now seemingly behind him. Events after 1997 will soon tell us if he has been successful in preparing the territory for its uncertain transition.

# 7    Future: to 1997 and beyond

> In its short but dazzling history, Hong Kong has demonstrated what hardworking men and women can achieve. The People of Hong Kong are walking tall and looking forward to the 50 years beyond 1997, which will no doubt be even more successful than the prior 50 years.
>
> (David H.T. Lan, principal representative of the Hong Kong Economic and Trade Office, Tokyo, 24 January 1995)

> To say that one country, two systems can work has always required an article of faith.
>
> (Henry Kissinger, *Far Eastern Economic Review*, 16 November 1995)

Hong Kong is glamour and misery. It has always been a place of such stark contrasts but in the last generation the space between the extremes of mega-wealth and destitution has been filled increasingly by a better educated, more confident middle class. The city-state's present position in the international order owes a great deal to the energy of the sons and daughters of those who escaped from China after the war. The recent prosperity of the territory has enabled hundreds of thousands to join, however perilously, the ranks of the more fortunate in a manner that was almost inconceivable only thirty years ago. By a host of standards, material, technological and cultural, the lives of many, perhaps the majority, of the residents in Hong Kong have shifted from gaining the basic necessities of existence to joining the growing ranks of the bourgeoisie.

In the process the role of the Europeans has been marginalized in Hong Kong. Their status has been undermined as the British domination of the political, administrative, economic and social life of the territory has drained away. The realities of this decline were very evident by the mid-1990s. Plans were then afoot to ensure that all senior posts in the Hong Kong government would shortly be held by non-Europeans, with the exception of the governorship itself and a small circle of advisors and seconded expatriate staff from Whitehall. The reins of power in Hong Kong's bureaucracy, traditionally seen as the heart of the territory's governmental and political system, were at last in non-

European keeping. The chief secretary was both Chinese and female, a combination that even a short decade ago would have been hard to imagine. The running of Hong Kong for the first and last time in its colonial history was very largely the business of those drawn from its overwhelmingly Chinese communities, with one solidarity post being held by a representative from the Indian subcontinent for good measure. The fact that some of those remaining Europeans in the civil service wished to take legal action against the government on the ground of discrimination was ironic indeed; after a century and a half of entrenched British power the boot was on the other foot.

The extent of Britain's nakedness in maintaining sovereignty could hardly be in doubt. By 1995, there was no British regiment in the territory to undertake garrison duties, the Royal Navy was reduced to a handful of patrol boats and the RAF had only a few Wessex helicopters. Security was the responsibility of the Hong Kong police, who could count in emergencies only on the remaining gurkha units, whose fate was itself unclear in the light of the forthcoming reversion of the territory and successive defence reviews by London. The public in Hong Kong knew full well that not only were the British forces leaving as fast as their stores could be sold off and their properties auctioned away to enhance the government's budget surplus but that their place would be taken soon by large numbers of Chinese troops. Efforts by the British government to discourage a sizeable, armed PLA presence after 1997 had already failed.

The symbolic undermining of British military prestige in Hong Kong was the decision by Chris Patten shortly after he arrived in the territory to remove the general officer commanding the garrison from his *ex officio* membership of ExCo. This action told the entire colony that the military had no more than a token role in the remaining years of British rule. It was the Royal Hong Kong Police that provided the guard of honour for Governor Patten when he arrived in 1992 to take up his post and it is to the police that the public instinctively look for internal security and protection. The force is virtually on its own in the unenviable position of attempting to reassure the residents of the territory over crime and immigration at a time of very real unease about personal safety and the sanctity of property in the less safe atmosphere of the mid-1990s. Increases in robbery with violence and the influx into the territory of additional triad gangs from south China left the police, now under a Hong Kong-Chinese Commissioner, in some difficulties.

If the British role in defence and law enforcement was clearly being eroded, the same trend was apparent on the economic and financial fronts. The era of Foreign Office attention to the interests of the major

British merchant houses and banks was now well and truly over. The idea that there might be preferential treatment for long-established European hongs that in some cases could trace their roots back to the early years of the colony was merely a distant memory by the 1990s. The fond image of power in Hong Kong being shared by expatriate stewards of the Jockey Club and select members of the Hong Kong Club was another fiction as the deadline for the handover of sovereignty fast approached.

But perhaps the best example of the now constrained position of British traders in Hong Kong was the highly publicized and much criticized decision of Jardine Matheson to move its domicile to Bermuda and then later to delist its shares from the Hong Kong exchange. The announcement that it would switch its registered office in 1984 came at a time of uncertainty during the Sino–British negotiations and was widely seen as a sign of funk within the territory and without. The timing was remarkably inept and the decidedly mixed fortunes of the conglomerate in the last decade has given great comfort to Jardines' adversaries. Supposedly purely commercial decisions by the virtual founders of Hong Kong have been shown to have major political repercussions.

Others have adopted the reverse strategy and reckoned that the best way to avoid anything comparable to the expropriation of Western assets that followed the Communist victories in the Chinese civil war is to work with the PRC. Instead of fearing Chinese interference after 1997 and possible takeover bids from Hong Kong's increasingly confident Chinese multi-millionaires, two British groups demonstrated some of their predecessors' flair and resilience. In terms of financial clout the Hongkong and Shanghai Bank has continued to maintain a prominent stance in the territory, while using its wealth to expand far beyond its east Asian base. The bank, like Jardines, has had its share of misfortune but the strength of its involvement in an increasingly prosperous Hong Kong has provided it with a launching pad for expansion in north America and more recently to acquire control of the Midland Bank to raise its profile on the high streets of Britain. Yet this wider international presence should not be seen as the beginning of the Hongkong and Shanghai Bank's abandonment of the territory, since the group retains a formidable hold on local developments. Certainly its management is under no illusion that it faces increasing competition from rival banks and the fact that in May 1994 the Bank of China became the third bank in the territory to issue locally denominated currency is very much a sign of the times. It must be assumed, however, that the substantial linkage between Hong Kong and the southern China region will provide fresh opportunities for the Hongkong and Shanghai Bank to strengthen its ties with its neighbours, though the particular skills required to work throughout the region must necessarily alter. Attention to personal contacts and connections will be essential in the future if the fierce race to provide capital for a rapidly developing China is to succeed.

The other British group to have the financial and entrepreneurial abilities to stay and fight is Swires. Although far smaller than either Jardines or the Hongkong and Shanghai Bank, it had the sense both to use its assets carefully and to ensure that it would not be easily subject to the surprise stock market raids that weakened others. It has displayed the Yorkshire grit of its founder in cautiously husbanding resources, while diversifying out of shipping into civil aviation (Cathay Pacific was to become the flag carrier for the territory) and joint ventures within China proper. The group's extensive dealings within the region were rightly interpreted as a determination to prosper in its own backyard. All this is on the credit side of the ledger; it remains to be seen how prepared it is to encourage a more cosmopolitan management intake and structure.

It would be absurd to suggest that Hong Kong is about to disappear overnight. It may still prosper but the going is likely to get tougher as it attempts to adapt to substantial changes in the way it will be governed. Hong Kong's ability to influence events has always been circumscribed and yet it has flourished in the face of challenges that would have felled many a less determined city-state. Unfortunately, its freedom to manoeuvre and adapt at speed to external rebuffs will be greatly curbed after 1997. No one who saw the curt, negative reply by China's foreign minister Qian Qichen when on a visit to London in October 1995 to a question on whether the democratic institutions of the Patten era could survive the transition to PRC rule is likely to feel optimistic about Hong Kong. The Chinese government's determination to ignore the territory's electoral changes of the early and mid-1990s bodes ill for its future.

Hong Kong's prospects are far from encouraging if responses by senior members of the Chinese government exhibit comparable insensitivity in the years ahead. Of course, an historical case can be made in defence of the PRC's uncompromising attitude but to imagine that this can possibly assist in gaining the active cooperation of peoples who are wary of their new leaders displays evidence of a disturbing mind-set. Unless the attitudes of the Chinese politburo and its party cadres undergo an unexpected sea change, it will be decidedly harder for Hong Kong to maintain either the governmental or economic policies of the past two generations.

It is illusory to hold out much hope for the preservation of financial and economic freedoms if there is an imposed, regulatory political framework devised by Beijing to force its diktat on Hong Kong. The idea, shared in public at least by a considerable number of the territory's business leaders, that it will be possible to divide issues into the two relatively simple and separate categories of politics and economics is highly improbable. An urban, mobile and educated population is most unlikely to take kindly to being told how it must behave in one area, while feeling unfettered to go about its business in the marketplace. The implausibility of each and every Beijing-appointed bureaucrat being prepared to submit to a form of self-control over boundaries to his or her job is an illustration of what is in store for Hong Kong. The temptation to use official postings for personal political and financial gain may also be hard to resist.

Historians of international relations must expect the worst; their training inevitably leads them to an ingrained scepticism over human motives and finely-worded agreements, particularly when the cultural gulf between those who will assume ultimate power in the territory after the summer of 1997 and the experiences of their wards is certain to be hard to bridge. Even if one were to assume an improbable amount of mutual good will, the difficulties would still remain substantial and the occasions for misunderstanding frequent. Evidence from mainland Chinese sources on their government's thinking is available in sufficient quantities for outsiders to suggest how uncertain Hong Kong's prospects are likely to be. Semi-official material from Beijing is on sale in the territory to provide at least clues on post-1997 developments.

Deng Xiaoping was clearly proud of his role in negotiating the return of Hong Kong. His pleasure in seeing the 'one country, two systems' formula enacted in the Basic Law was immense. He pointed out to members of the drafting committee on the Basic Law in April 1987 that their work was 'something new, without precedent in world history', since it would not only pave the way for the reintegration of Hong Kong within the PRC but also 'serve as a model for Macao and Taiwan'. The underlying nationalism that has long motivated Deng's actions over Hong Kong has important ramifications for its future. Deng in June 1988 reminded his audience that above all else it was stability that must be maintained 'when the people of Hong Kong were administering the region after China resumes its exercise of sovereignty'. It was 'crucial' that there be both 'stable economic development' and 'a stable political system'. The great patriarch stressed 'the close relation between the prosperity and stability of Hong Kong and the strategy for the development of China', which is not perhaps the common view in Hong Kong in 1996 where attention inevitably remains narrowly focused on the territory itself. Deng sees Hong Kong as merely a part of China's

need 'to open wider to the outside world'; this must not be at the
expense of permitting the 'arbitrary copying of Western systems'. For
Deng the dangers of Hong Kong shifting from a colonial form of
government to a more democratic one before 1997 have long been
apparent. He made it clear in 1988 once again that the returned territory
'will not copy any Western system in the future either. This is a most
practical and serious problem.'

The evidence inside Hong Kong conflicts overwhelmingly with such
Chinese governmental thinking. There is no easy manner in which the
increasingly democratic nature of government in the territory can be
squared with the statements from Beijing on its plans. Vows to abolish
the three-tier system of political reform and to insist that only 'patriots',
defined in the past as 'people who love the motherland and Hong
Kong', participate in the post-1997 political process are not reassuring
to a community that is doubtful of Beijing's handling of the territory.
The apparent determination of China to control the key appointments
within the SAR's government and to abolish legislative assemblies that
predate 1997 is a poor omen. How future elections will be conducted
and the character and composition of the next administration of Hong
Kong is not yet known, but the denunciation of Governor Patten's
handiwork has been total.

The Basic Law was intended to assure Hong Kong residents that their
fears of future difficulties when part of greater China were groundless.
The evidence suggests that it has failed to do. Short of a last-minute
change of heart by the Beijing leadership, it is likely that the broad
appointive powers of the PRC granted by the Basic Law will conflict
with the opinions of many of those individuals and their political parties
elected to LegCo in the autumn of 1995. Any Chinese volte-face would
involve a most considerable loss of prestige and given the strident
remarks of some Hong Kong leaders, notably Martin Lee and his
colleagues in the Democratic Party, this is unlikely to occur. Indeed, the
influence of Lee and his supporters is almost certain to polarize politics
after 1997 and his party's behaviour in the last months of British rule
could provide exactly the confrontational display that Beijing says it
wishes to avoid.

Deng Xiaoping has frequently expressed fears of disturbances in the
transition period and after. In October 1984 he spoke menacingly of
'potentially disruptive forces' in front of visitors from Hong Kong
touring Beijing and he stated categorically that Chinese troops will
garrison Hong Kong to prevent disturbances. Definitions of such
instability, of course, will be determined by the PRC government; Deng
did not mince his words, however, in pointing out that

knowing that there were Chinese troops present, people who intended to incite disturbances would have to think twice about it. And even if there were disturbances, they could be quelled immediately.

Such thinking hardly suggests any particularly sympathetic appreciation of Hong Kong's right to local autonomy and leaves one wondering how broad will be the leeway for effective exercise of the promised freedoms of speech and assembly. It recalls the restrictive colony of the 1950s with its emergency police powers and frequent resort to deportation orders rather than the Hong Kong of the mid-1990s where demonstrations are the norm. Those who have watched the rush-hour traffic of central Hong Kong brought to a standstill by pig farmers protesting against government legislation or interviewed Christine Loh as she canvassed in Wanchai on the eve of the last LegCo elections may be sceptical of promises that it will be plain sailing for the territory under China's benign rule.

Even those more favourably disposed towards Beijing may occasionally admit that a great deal of well intentioned action by the new SAR authorities could be misunderstood. Unless there is a most unlikely change in the attitudes of the residents of Hong Kong after July 1997, it is probable that the existing cleavages within the territory's political spectrum will persist. The September 1995 LegCo returns presage precisely the divided views that will be hard to contain should the new chief executive of the SAR and the equally untested provisional legislature react with what others may interpret as impatience at excessive direction on the community. The possibility of restricting rights promised under the Basic Law and limitations on democratic freedoms now accepted as commonplace in Hong Kong would almost certainly lead to the outcome foreseen by Deng Xiaoping in repeated comments over the last decade and more. Confrontation can hardly be wished away; those most likely to suffer will be the individuals who have voiced the loudest support for what may yet turn out to be the forbidden fruit of representative government. The pessimists' case gained further weight by other developments in the autumn of 1995 besides the LegCo elections. Announcements by the British government on the composition of the final court of appeal that will replace the Privy Council following Hong Kong's reversion to Chinese sovereignty were greeted with anger by pro-democracy groups.

China's hopes of administering Hong Kong effectively after reversion hinge on the active cooperation of its residents. While sizeable numbers of businessmen and financiers are prepared to state publicly that in their field at least Chinese policies will not change, it is equally clear that their need to repeatedly reassure the peoples of Hong Kong and mount publicity campaigns abroad is indicative of how real the doubts of others have become. The purchase of newspaper space and television footage is hardly the way forward; only more concrete attempts by the Chinese authorities will begin to alter public perceptions of the post-1997 future. For Hong Kong executives to imagine that well funded advertising projects can lessen the unease increasingly felt among the community is a sign of the remoteness of the commercial elite from those less fortunate than themselves. Many without the means to leave the territory in an emergency through the holding of second passports see only too clearly how Hong Kong's wealthiest have for years been cultivating the PRC leadership by word and deed to ensure that their own privileges are maintained after 1997. Such cooperative behaviour worked well in the colonial era and may succeed in the future, though any mass desertion of the territory by Chinese businessmen after 1997 would ensure the collapse of PRC plans for the SAR to serve as a dynamo for the wider Chinese economy.

Second only to the vital need to anchor Hong Kong's entrepreneurs in place is the importance of securing the loyalties and talents of the existing bureaucracy. The Basic Law notwithstanding, it is hard to imagine that cadres newly arrived from Beijing could run the SAR with the skills and style that the peoples of Hong Kong have long been familiar with. The composition of the bureaucracy will make or break the SAR. Yet the difficulties of retaining key personnel and ensuring that professional standards are maintained has already become a major concern for the Patten administration. The need to persuade senior Hong Kong officials to stay on is pressing. The PRC has made known its views on the suitability of certain figures and it is widely believed that substantial files have already been built up on the backgrounds of many presently serving the Hong Kong government. Some of those who have recently resigned from the bureaucracy were felt to be trying to calculate where their best prospects might lie and therefore have distanced themselves from the British in order to gain employment when the SAR comes looking for its first chief executive. Senior government official John Chan, for example, felt it expedient to resign in 1993 because his close ties to Governor Patten were seen as an impediment to his career prospects after 1997 and because his presence was felt to be damaging to hopes of improving Sino–British relations. Others have moved laterally from highly visible posts to ones where there might be hopes of maintaining a lower profile; the secretary of the civil service was transferred in September 1995 to the less taxing job of director of the Trade Development Council, while the former secretary of education took over gentler responsibilities as the first-ever local commissioner of the Independent Commission Against Corruption.

These rapid transfers within and without the civil service can hardly be said to strengthen the British commitment to ensuring stability in the territory prior to 1997. Any hopes that Government House might have initially possessed in persuading Beijing to accept a high degree of continuity in the upper echelons of the civil service had dissolved by 1996. Hong Kong Chinese bureaucrats were voting with their feet; the repeated promise by Communist spokesmen that officials wishing to remain in post after 1997 would not have to answer for their behaviour in the British portion of their careers appeared to convince few of its intended hearers. For the deputy director of Xinhua merely to announce after a recent shuffle of senior posts within the Hong Kong civil service that 'after the 1997 handover, the appointment, dismissal and retention of Government officials will be handled according to the Basic Law' was not perhaps quite the way to win friends and influence public opinion.

Some lowering of morale within the territory's bureaucracy was probably inevitable as officials and their families calculated their futures in the late 1980s and early 1990s, yet the enforced changes by 1996 were too large and too frequent for Hong Kong's own good. The switches left commentators openly discussing the probable decline in efficiency as posts were filled only briefly before the Patten administration was obliged to shuffle appointments yet again. The career changes of the new senior officials reached its most extreme in the case of Lam Woon-Kwong. He had been moved from deputy secretary of the civil service to deputy secretary of education and manpower to director of education before being catapulted to civil service secretary all within in the space of less than five years; not even Japanese cabinet ministers expect such a revolving door approach to government. The fact that Mr Lam was only 44 years of age suggests how desperate the government has become in its need to fill its most senior and sensitive posts with relatively inexperienced figures. Not surprisingly Hong Kong's trade unions felt disgruntled at the inability of some of their supervisors to master their briefs before being rapidly transferred.

Under the Hong Kong system of government it remains the case that it is the governor, his advisors and the bureaucracy that have the greatest responsibility within a highly centralized administration. The very considerable changes of recent years to ExCo and LegCo can hardly be said to have dislodged the importance of the bureaucracy in the running of the territory. Its functions are so extensive and its size so large that with a total staff of 180,000 in the summer of 1994 it is both a huge employer and an important influence on the entire community. Aside from a very few exceptions, its most senior administrators are now all Hong Kong Chinese. The effects of localization in the past two decades has ensured that there is now almost total domination of the highest posts by 'local officers'. In the winter of 1995 only one departmental headship was held by an expatriate and even this exception to the comprehensive policy of localization came in for criticism from those who saw this as a slight to the goal of Hong Kong being ruled by Hong Kong people after 1997. Governor Patten, while defending the selection of a European for the post of director of civil aviation, stressed how rapid had been the process of localization and its advantage to 'the future chief executive of the SAR to have a good choice of local officials for the principal official posts here in Hong Kong'.

By January 1996 the territory, however, was still waiting to learn who might be selected for the critical role of running post-1997 Hong Kong. The speculation was unlikely to be halted before the last months of 1996, when it is assumed that the Preparatory Committee for Hong Kong and its Selection Committee will have forwarded a short list of candidates to Beijing for final approval. Beijing will then probably make certain that its chosen son (or daughter) is the person selected by the committee. The possibility that an experienced Hong Kong civil servant may be selected as the first chief executive of the SAR has been periodically raised in the territory as the Basic Law envisages a quasi-parliamentary system of government at best. It follows, in the opinion of constitutional experts, that a governing structure which appoints rather than broadly elects its members will rely heavily on bureaucrats. The names of Hong Kong's present chief secretary Anson Chan, the former bureaucrat John Chan, and ExCo member C.H. Tung have been widely canvassed for the post but the opinions of local residents will not have the final say in 1997, any more than they had in Governor Patten's selection in 1992. It is likely that loyalty to Beijing will be the deciding factor in this highly sensitive selection process. Press speculation within Hong Kong has also noted that there may be differences within the Chinese government between those felt to be supporting the candidacy of C.H. Tung and others who may prefer a chief executive with fewer business connections with the territory.

It is premature at this stage to make more than intelligent guesses on how the SAR may function. Only with the selection of its first chief executive will the PRC's own thinking be clearer as the long years of criticizing the colonialists from the sidelines end. Published material to date by Chinese leaders and their officials attempts to minimize either changes of personnel and policy within its government or development inside Hong Kong itself. The well documented and repeated assurances that the SAR should possess a high degree of autonomy have been stated too often to be easily overturned and are reflected in Deng Xiaoping's insistence that the residents of Hong Kong in dispensing with British rule will then demonstrate to the world that they do indeed possess the full capacity to run their own affairs. The Chinese people, Deng maintains, stood up in the creation of the PRC on 1 October 1949; the Hong Kong Chinese will do likewise on 1 July 1997. Deng's determination to 'have faith in the Chinese of Hong Kong' is apparent. He said in 1984 that the prejudice that

Chinese can not manage Hong Kong affairs satisfactorily is a left-over from the old colonial mentality. For more than a century after the Opium War, the Chinese people were looked down upon and humiliated by foreigners.

Deng's belief that the Chinese of Hong Kong share the common culture and pride of the wider Chinese communities in the region has enabled him apparently to place his public trust in their abilities. He argued that the

prosperity of Hong Kong has been achieved mainly by Hong Kong residents, most of whom are Chinese. Chinese are no less intelligent than foreigners and are by no means less talented. It is not true that only foreigners can be good administrators. We Chinese are just as capable.

While this general vote of confidence does indeed provide encouragement that the SAR will not be entirely dominated by Beijing, it could not begin to solve the important details of how power within the SAR would be constituted. Central to the PRC's misgivings over permitting a democratic legislature after 1997 has been the rapid pace of political change in Hong Kong since the Joint Declaration was signed by Britain and China. The vehement criticism levelled at Chris Patten is based on the dangers of what his open encouragement of political reform might presage for the SAR and perhaps by extension within southern China and beyond.

Vocal critics of Governor Patten, such as Sir Percy Cradock, maintain that the ironic result of insisting on political change that was certain to anger the PRC has been to bequeath to Hong Kong a less representative system of government in 1997 and thereafter than if the original, limited reforms had remained unaltered. Beijing's deep suspicion of many Hong Kong politicians is hardly a new story but the international publicity attendant on the likes of Martin Lee in recent years is bound to complicate China's handling of the SAR. Lee and other highly vocal advocates of a democratic Hong Kong can no longer simply be branded as counter-revolutionaries and dealt with in the time-honoured manner, as any such treatment would damage Beijing's relations with the West both politically and in the international trading arena. The influence of the overseas media in scrutinizing future events in the SAR may well prove to be an inhibiting factor of considerable weight. Yet to minimize the role of what the PRC regards as disruptive busybodies, the Basic Law left unclear the vital details on how elections should be conducted following reversion. (It is generally held that the British negotiators had attempted but failed to press the PRC to be more specific in this area during the often tedious rounds of Sino–British talks.) It was disturbing for the increasingly politicized residents of the territory to read that the Basic Law stated merely that the 'Legislative Council of the Hong Kong Special Administrative Region shall be constituted by election' and that 'in accordance with the principal of gradual and orderly progress' at some remote date in the twenty-first century there might perhaps be an assembly where all members shall be selected by 'universal suffrage'. The time scale and the complexities involved in attempting to gain this objective have not yet received the attention they deserve in European and North American circles.

Many in Hong Kong sense that the Chinese authorities, while more than willing to encourage the economic advance of the territory, will ensure that political arrangements are made that severely limit even a gradual process towards a more democratic form of government in the SAR. The difficulties of finding an area of common ground between the Hong Kong-based political parties that have campaigned against the PRC and the leadership of the CCP are going to be formidable. Yet unless some efforts are made to achieve a reconciliation the SAR's prospects look decidedly uneasy. Commentators have been quick to suggest that the issue should not be exaggerated and may be rather simply solved by the purely cosmetic touch of dissolving the territory's LegCo on 1 July 1997 and then reconvening what can be technically seen as a new body on the following morning. This would enable the PRC to display its full authority in the SAR and demonstrate that its powers have been complied with in front of its new citizens, but the forcible removal of even a handful of legislators could sow the seeds of lengthy confrontation. Any banning of democratically elected figures will inevitably spur their supporters to protest, though the SAR authorities may calculate that this would pose only a temporary problem. Its cadres will doubtless point to the steady decline in the number of Hong Kong residents prepared to join demonstrations on the anniversary of the Tiananmen Square massacre during the 1990s to illustrate the supposedly underlying political apathy of the territory. Yet the new chief executive of the SAR might well find him or herself in an immediate dilemma, caught between wishing to comply with instructions from Beijing but sensing widespread resistance through accurate first-hand knowledge of the sentiments of Hong Kong. It would hardly be an auspicious start to the long anticipated reunion of patriots to the motherland.

At the heart of the problem for the PRC was the unwelcome truth that Hong Kong by the mid-1990s had changed. Its political culture was certainly not revolutionized in the last years of British rule but it was sufficiently altered to make most of the textbooks of even the previous decade ready only for pulping. If this reality was hard enough for some within Hong Kong itself to accept, it can be readily imagined how unpalatable this message must appear to CCP officials, whose education and indoctrination took place in a very different world. Cultural commonalities do little to bridge this divide and may indeed leave the Beijing authorities only disappointed when their appeals to nationalism are left unheeded. The evidence, admittedly fragmentary, hardly suggests that the PRC wishes to recognize this fundamental shift or has detailed proposals for fleshing out how the one country, two systems rhetoric will cope with a newly politicized society. Even when Deng Xiaoping spoke in 1984 to visitors from Hong Kong, it was obvious to his listeners that the assurances that the territory's 'current social and economic systems will remain unchanged, its legal system will remain basically unchanged, its way of life and its status as a free port and an international trade and financial centre will remain unchanged' deliberately omitted reference to its political arrangements. Only briefly would Deng add that provided the future administrators of Hong Kong were patriots and thereby possessed 'a desire not to impair Hong Kong's prosperity and stability' then they were qualified to govern the SAR.

Less exalted figures have made the same point more recently. The official position of the Chinese government remains as stated by its ambassador to London Ma Yuzhen in March 1995 to the Royal Society for Asian Affairs that Beijing 'more than anybody else needs Hong Kong as a bridge, as a link to do business with the rest of the world'. He was not prepared, however, to comment other than with disfavour on events since Chris Patten took up his post. Ma Yuzhen expressed the view of his government that after 1992 'our relationship suffered some setbacks'. Following this understatement, he returned to the familiar stance that these occurrences were 'not because of anything of China's making' and that 'what is more important now is to look ahead'. Unfortunately Ma Yuzhen could reveal little on how Beijing will cope with its responsibilities for Hong Kong, beyond repeating the familiar litany that the territory 'will be prosperous, will be stable, and we will have a smooth transition in 1997'. All three claims are questionable.

The economic prospects for the SAR are no more than mildly encouraging. It could be foolhardy of the PRC to imagine that Hong

Kong is an overbrimming honeypot that can be used effortlessly for the greater good of the Chinese nation. It would be another in a possible host of ironies if the reversion of Hong Kong coincided with a faltering southern Chinese economy and the ex-colony had to go cap-in-hand to its new compatriots for assistance. Such a measure is certainly unlikely but the difficulties that Hong Kong might face are linked to its increasingly close ties to China; problems for one are guaranteed to impact on the other. Interdependence risks turning into overdependence. The Hong Kong economy, however considerable its growth rates, is slowing down, while unemployment has increased and inflation remains disturbingly high. The potential problems for Hong Kong centre on how the city-state will be able to replace its less productive jobs with a sufficient number of service-oriented and high-tech posts. It must also tackle the increasing expense of doing business in the territory as it faces competition both from other centres in Asia and from China proper. The *Far Eastern Economic Review* suggested in July 1995 that 'Hong Kong's most pressing problem isn't politics but costs. And these costs are starting to bite'. The paper warned that the extraordinary prices still being asked for rented property and the rapid inflation across the border has led to huge increases in labour costs in Guangdong that may eventually result in further migration northwards of the industrial plants and products that the territory relies on for the exports from the PRC. As always the prophets are divided on the extent of possible damage this may cause to the SAR, but overinvolvement in a faltering China and a lackadaisical approach to improving domestic productivity in the all-important service sector may yet cause serious dislocations for the economy.

It would be doubly difficult if any substantial downturn coincided with political tensions within post-1997 Hong Kong. The old rule of thumb that substantial economic growth, currently in excess of 5 per cent per annum, conveniently acts to curtail any widespread public interest in the political field no longer applies. Recent reputable studies have shown that the community has reached the stage of at least monitoring events done in its name by its leaders, if not yet being overprepared to actively participate in the political arena itself. This change in public perception (and expectation) has been reached at the very moment when such future political activity is now in serious doubt. The combination of a more aware community supporting its elected representatives and a suspicious and possibly illiberal outside sovereign power might become unpleasant, since Hong Kong's fresh democratic roots can be said by 1996 to have become indigenous. While it took a considerable period for the same type of imposed Western political system to be assimilated within postwar Japanese society, it appears that the transplantation has been more rapid for Hong Kong. The uncomfortable truth remains, however, that only when this new plant it tested will we know the real loyalties of the SAR.

The temptation to backslide should not be discounted. Hong Kong's new persona is undoubtedly a very recent phenomenon and there are many sceptics who continue to insist that the pursuit of economic growth is still the defining element in the Hong Kong soul. It is, of course, precisely what the PRC leadership appears to believe and undoubtedly would wish to see encouraged in the new SAR, as it is within the rest of the subcontinent. Yet even those who applaud the spirit of capitalism in Hong Kong might concede that the scale of public protest against the butchers of Tiananmen square and the careful monitoring of the unhappy experiences of residents subject to inhumane sentences inside the PRC's desolate labour camps is indicative of a positive shift in attitude.

The character of Hong Kong society in the last years of British rule has altered through the injection of controversy over its future. This new politicization has reversed some of the past behaviour of what the British academic Hugh Baker in 1983 defined as 'Hong Kong Man'. Then this 'unique social animal' appeared to be interested above all else in the short-term economic gain characteristic of migrant societies. Today 'Hong Kong Man' can be seen as an increasingly political animal prepared to stand up and make his (or her) opinions known. Of course this remains a stereotype but the need to redraw its largely acquisitive traits strongly suggests how the Hong Kong public has reacted to its difficult predicament. It is at least possible that in his future evolution 'Hong Kong Man' might, if sorely tested, now be prepared to resist.

The half-century between the first slight calls for constitutional reform and the eventual LegCo elections of 1995 indicate how much ground had to be covered before the peoples of Hong Kong could all participate in an improved political system. The *South China Morning Post* of September 1946 poured scorn on the very idea of limited reform by arguing that 'Hong Kong cannot have self-government, because it has no self'. In September 1995 the same paper thought now that democracy had triumphed and that if China wished to see Hong Kong 'contented and stable, not defiant and angry, it should listen to the very clear voice of its people'. Hong Kong Man undoubtedly changed some of his characteristics after the late 1980s. The emergence of political parties, the mass demonstrations against Beijing in 1989 and greater willingness to participate in a series of local and territory-wide elections are powerful evidence of this shift in public opinion. It was Chris

Patten's encouragement of Hong Kong's new interests in politics that has both angered China and left Hong Kong Man in a dilemma. He is now required to choose from among a number of unpalatable options. He can emigrate, and thereby lose his sense of attachment to the place where he was born, educated and works, support the future communist regime, as most major Hong Kong Chinese corporations have actively done, campaign for more democracy or lastly remain neutral and disregard rival appeals to his patriotism, his pocket and his political conscience.

The Chinese authorities will doubtless continue to regard the Patten reforms as a colonialist Trojan horse designed to preserve British influence in the years after 1997, but it is impossible to see how the democratic process can now be reversed. Beijing will insist that the imperialists and their supporters broke the rules of the Basic Law, yet short of physical assaults on those it dislikes, the genie cannot be put back into the bottle. Some Hong Kong residents, it might be wiser for the PRC to recognize, are not about to go quietly in the night. Several prominent political figures, including Martin Lee and Emily Lau, are prepared to organize and campaign for what they hold to be essential to the well-being of Hong Kong. The successes of the democratic groups in the September 1995 LegCo elections may be partly reversible but they can hardly be wiped away. To refer to Martin Lee as a counter-revolutionary is no longer part of the language that many in Hong Kong can take seriously; anyone willing to risk wrecking his lucrative career and health for political ideals is seen to be a figure of respect. Hong Kong has dozens of millionaires; in the last decade it has begun to acquire politicians who have also gained regional reputations.

The change in Hong Kong's political consciousness since the early 1980s leaves the Chinese government in obvious difficulties. It wishes to ensure a smooth transition and a prosperous SAR, yet events within Hong Kong in the Patten era have clearly alarmed Beijing. It is indeed possible that Chinese policy for the post-reversion period has still to be finalized and may well be subject to change as the succession to Deng Xiaoping is resolved. What can perhaps be assumed with some confidence is that in any stark choice between permitting Hong Kong to remain relatively autonomous and safeguarding the greater interests of the Chinese state, the party authorities would sacrifice Hong Kong's growth to preserve their control. No one hopes that events will take this course, but any challenge within the future SAR, however peaceful and cautious it might appear to outsiders, that questioned the hegemony of the Chinese system would be seen as subversive and therefore unacceptable. Opposition within the SAR would, of course, then be quickly assessed for its political implications throughout China and across the Taiwan straits.

Political uncertainties may in turn have important economic and financial consequences for Hong Kong. The Chinese authorities have already announced that after reversion the Hong Kong dollar will remain tied to the American dollar. It is unclear, however, whether this arrangement, first introduced during the monetary crisis of October 1983, can last for long. One school of thought among economists and brokers holds that the link may be broken within two years and that thereafter a new arrangement with the Chinese yuan might replace the US dollar once the yuan becomes fully convertible. The possibility of a future depreciation of the Hong Kong dollar was already being recognized in the autumn of 1995 by the British government. A parliamentary bill was expected in the next session that would specify London's responsibilities in order to minimize hardship for Hong Kong government pensioners in the likelihood of the post-1997 dollar weakening. This could occur through concerted international currency speculation, which in turn might be fuelled by the rapid movement of assets out of the SAR by Chinese enterprises to safer havens and by any parallel collapse of property prices. Obviously any major change in the exchange rate would affect Hong Kong's export-oriented economy and, to a degree, the entire Chinese economic system.

Ambiguity is the cobbler's last of diplomacy. The result, unfortunately for Hong Kong, is that it is obliged to live between two different interpretations of parts of the Joint Declaration. Officials will suggest that there was no other way forward but to be told this is hardly much of a consolation to the peoples of Hong Kong. Sino–British negotiations produced at times a remarkably ill-fitting shoe. The 1984 Joint Declaration – Beijing preferred not to be seen to be signing a treaty through the document remains internationally binding on both partners – was intended to reassure Hong Kong that its way of life would not be in jeopardy after 30 June 1997. Yet to achieve any such vote of confidence was never going to be straightforward and, as Michael Davis has argued, successful implementation 'raises profound and difficult constitutional questions' arising 'from the convergence of several constitutional traditions and political value systems'. The perhaps unavoidable imprecision of the Joint Declaration has in turn left 'considerable creative room for the Basic Law drafters'. In part the British common law jurisdiction and the state-determined Chinese legal tradition have had somehow to be merged, but the Joint Declaration is a considerable, if incomplete, victory for the status quo in Hong Kong. Annex I of the Joint Declaration states that after the establishment of the Hong Kong Special Administrative Region the socialist system and socialist policies shall not be practised in the Hong Kong Special Administrative Region and that Hong Kong's previous capitalist system and lifestyle shall remain unchanged for 50 years.

The second paragraph of the same annex both elaborates on the post-1997 legal system and to a degree restricts some of the practices of the previous era. Concern over the composition of the final court of appeal illustrates the fears of the territory that interference from the central government could yet override the frequent promises of a high degree of autonomy. Whether the courts will prove vigilant enough in the active protection of the rights and freedoms expressly confirmed in the Joint Declaration and Basic Law will soon be evident.

Hong Kong will have to draw on all its available talents to disprove its detractors. Obviously it can hardly be certain of the outcome when many of the factors in the equation are still unknown. In the process it is perhaps unwise for even its closest friends to take refuge in the comforting official rhetoric that somehow it will be all right on the night. The Hong Kong government and its business leaders are doing the territory a disservice in trumpeting the future successes of the SAR in almost messianic terms. While there may indeed be enticing economic and financial prospects for some sections of the community, it should not be forgotten that the domestic and national political foundations for the SAR are as yet uncertain. Economies – even liberal ones of Hong Kong's rare calibre – cannot function in a vacuum. Only when Hong Kong begins to grapple with running its own government and dealing with its new overlords will a clearer picture emerge. Until that day Hong Kong needs to adopt a more modest style of presentation, while drawing what confidence it can from the achievements of the past half century. Ultimately it will stand or fall on the skills and strengths of its peoples, since it has precious few alternative resources or reliable friends overseas. As always it must react with alacrity to economic opportunities, but this in itself will no longer suffice. As the last British administrators prepare to leave and the Chinese government prepares for its great day, Hong Kong has to find the self-confidence and unity to go it alone. Survival this time could be even more daunting than in the postwar decades.

# 8    Conclusions: endgame

Only the French and the Chinese keep through twists of fortune a firm confidence in their own future.

(Douglas Hurd, *An End to Promises*)

It is ironic that Hong Kong, under British rule, has always given Beijing the best of all possible worlds: vast economic gain, political neutrality and no responsibility. But once Hong Kong is Beijing's responsibility, China will find itself with the worst of all worlds: an economic burden, a political thorn, a cultural contaminant and a threat to the very unity of China.

(George Hicks, *International Herald Tribune*, February 23 1994)

Hong Kong's postwar history is without parallel in Asia. It has been a strange tale of confronting successive domestic and international crises, intermixed with lengthy periods of stability resulting in considerable affluence. No one surveying the dilapidated territory of August 1945 could have dared imagine the prosperity and sense of identity that Hong Kong would exhibit half a century later. Few even would have risked betting on Britain retaining sovereign power for so long, particularly against the tidal wave of global decolonization and Europe's own inward-looking quest for federalism.

Hong Kong has survived for fifty years since 1945 as an off-shore speck on the South China coast under British administration. This has been the first and most important foundation for a range of unexpected achievements. Hong Kong, until the summer of 1997, remains a British colony. Although diplomats and lawyers prefer to describe the political arrangements under which it has been governed in more neutral terms, it serves no historical purpose to disguise this reality. Decisions since 1945 and, of course, in the hundred years between occupation and its capture by Japan, were taken by the metropolitan power purportedly on behalf of the inhabitants of Hong Kong. Recent attempts to downplay the source of ultimate authority have reached surprising proportions. Official correspondence is still embossed with the letters OHMS and postage stamps display the sovereign's head, but the official *Hong Kong*

*Yearbook* for 1995 prefers to refer to 'the three-tier systems of representative government' and takes pain to emphasize the indirect, relaxed nature of overseas rule. Political correctness has much to answer for in suggesting that Hong Kong long ago virtually declared independence from Britain and that the 'territory largely controls its own affairs and determines its own policies'. The reality is otherwise. Hong Kong does indeed conduct very much more than merely routine domestic and trade business by itself, but over most of the critical issues since 1945 the roles of Whitehall and Westminster have proved decisive. When, for example, a Chinese official branded Governor Patten a 'big dictator' in November 1995 for expanding social security benefits it was the British government who summoned the Chinese charge d'affaires in London to the Foreign Office to receive an official protest. The Chinese side made a similar point over sovereignty by maintaining that Patten 'was sent to Hong Kong by the British Queen' and was therefore, in the eyes of Beijing, 'not eligible to comment on the budget because he does not represent the people'.

The colony is undoubtedly encouraged to believe that it is 'governed by consent and through consultation with the community', yet this impression can be misleading. It remains a very recent and still incomplete phenomenon. The role of the British government is certainly far more circumscribed that any rehearsing of its formal absolutist powers might suggest, but the overwhelming importance of the transfer of sovereignty in the last two decades has been a constant (and at times unpleasant) reminder to the peoples of Hong Kong of ultimate authority. Sino–British negotiations determined the future fate of Hong Kong. Equally, since the territory has never been represented directly in the House of Commons and there are only a handful of life peers who have been appointed to the Lords because of their links to Hong Kong, the argument that Westminster provides an adequate forum for full and open discussion of its affairs is tenuous in the extreme. It is rather the British cabinet, in consultation with the Foreign Office, that both selects Hong Kong's governor and issues instructions on what London wishes to see broadly accomplished. There were, as we have seen, periods after 1945 when some governors were given considerable opportunities to run the colony without excessive supervision, but those days are long over.

The oft-cited decision to describe Hong Kong as a territory rather than a colonial possession of Britain hides as much as it reveals. The change was largely cosmetic, though it gave rise to the frequently recalled incident when one senior civil servant spluttered with rage that, if he had now to term Hong Kong a territory, he was fully entitled to 'terrorize' its recalcitrant local Chinese banks. It certainly conveys the impression that Hong Kong is governed, administered and run politically and economically from within but the fact that no governor has ever been appointed with a mandate from any of the electors of Hong Kong is a very considerable drawback to the local autonomy school. Hong Kong can point rightly to its own status as a separate member of WTO and APEC, yet it is the British government, after consultations with Hong Kong, that signs international conventions on its behalf.

Certainly there have been instances of governors being able to persuade London to alter important prescribed policies. Governor Grantham's stonewalling over the intended introduction of a measure of representative government surely remains the classic example, but in more recent decades the Nelson approach has rarely been accepted without demur in Whitehall. Governor MacLehose brought with him a detailed agenda when he was sworn in that must already have been discussed in London and Governor Patten's reform package announced in 1992 is widely felt to have been crafted in London and Hong Kong by differing bureaucrats and politicians prior to the governor's personal stamp being applied to the programme. Continual consultation between Hong Kong and London makes it impossible for the outsider to identify particular policy inputs with any confidence, but the consequence in recent decades has been a great deal of largely hidden direction from overseas. Instant communications and frequent scheduled flights between Heathrow and Kai Tak have reduced the ability of recent governors to resist and delay. The era when Sir Alexander Grantham could rest reasonably secure until challenged by his masters in the Colonial Office during an occasional visit to London when on home leave predates the careers of today's most senior civil servants. John Major and Chris Patten share a very different working relationship from the semi-isolationism that persisted in Government House in the 1950s and 1960s. Policy for contemporary Hong Kong has become too important a business to be left to the governor, even a governor with the reputation of the present title holder.

The suggestion that Hong Kong has become almost a 'non-colony' left to cultivate its own garden received its greatest rebuff during the Sino–British negotiations on the territory's future. Beijing, to the obvious discomfort of the British diplomats, made great political capital out of emphasizing that Hong Kong was indeed still a colony and that therefore its senior officials could not be recognized as other than members of the British negotiating team. Such reminders of imperial responsibility led the Chinese side to emphasize that Hong Kong would be passing in 1997 from one particular overlord to another. It was also an argument that the Chinese government were intent on deploying to marginalize any role for Governor Patten in the ceremonies planned to mark the end of British rule.

Reversion to China has been understood by the Chinese government to mean that, in the words of the preamble to the Basic Law of the Hong Kong Special Administrative Region of the People's Republic of China adopted by the VII National People's Congress on 4 April 1990, the PRC

will resume the exercise of sovereignty over Hong Kong with effect from 1 July 1997, thus fulfilling the long-cherished common aspiration of the Chinese people for the recovery of Hong Kong.

It then graciously repeated that since Beijing 'has decided . . . upon . . . resumption of the exercise of sovereignty over Hong Kong, a Hong Kong Special Administrative region will be established'. The views of the peoples of the future SAR were studiously avoided throughout the preamble and in the following eleven general principles. China made it clear in the subsequent chapter on the relationship between the central authorities and the SAR that Hong Kong's status 'shall be a local administrative region'. It would enjoy 'a high degree of autonomy', but article 12 stressed also that the SAR will 'come directly under the Central People's Government'.

Hong Kong's self-confidence and pride in its postwar accomplishments may have prompted an exaggerated opinion of its own role and risks ignoring external factors that have contributed to the fate of the territory. Clearly, it was British arms and voices that rather fortuitously won the day in 1945. The reoccupation and reconstruction programmes rested on service personnel and young, relatively inexperienced administrators. Equally, it was small amounts of British governmental assistance, as well as important local financing, that got the colony back on its feet. Hong Kong's restoration by 1949 with its promise of political stability and an equitable system of justice were major factors next in persuading Shanghainese magnates to decamp from the mainland. In many cases these textile bosses made careful advance planning before deciding to relocate to the territory and both the administrative structure and the deliberately loose hand of the state in economic matters were evidently appreciated in the course of these preliminary reconnoiterings. Obviously, however, the outcome of the prolonged civil war in China was the first determinant in this diaspora. Defeat for the KMT on the mainland would soon turn into economic victory for Hong Kong. Yet the reaction of the United States to what was then regarded as this 'loss' of China initially weakened Hong Kong both by the imposition of draconian trade embargoes and equally seriously for the inhabitants of the territory by suggesting that the fate of Hong Kong could easily be determined by great power manoeuvering in the region. The US Seventh Fleet could be seen both to offer protection from Beijing and act as provocation to the PRC in the uncomfortable years between 1949 and 1962. The fact that Mao Zedong would later be rightly viewed as a 'continentalist', then lacking in naval power for almost anything larger than motorized junks and thereby incapable of liberating Taiwan, was cold comfort in the 1950s. Hong Kong felt highly vulnerable during the tense decade of the Korean war and the periodic off-shore shelling that prompted international crises over the Taiwan straits.

The remark of Secretary Bevin to Dean Acheson that Britain stood ready in the autumn of 1949 to 'defend Hong Kong from external attack, economic boycott or internal trouble' was fortunately never put fully to the test in these years; whether concerted efforts in league with the Pentagon might have acted to deter any PLA massing near the border is conjectural. The role of the British garrison remained one of assisting the police as a ready reserve against internal subversion. The available British records remain largely silent on the nature and extent of official and unofficial dealings with the PRC during the post-1949 period. It is not yet possible to trace adequately the soundings that may have been undertaken from the early 1950s to attempt to reassure the authorities in both Beijing and Guangdong that Britain had limited aims for Hong Kong. The frequently stated suggestion that the British government explained through its Chinese contacts that it intended that Hong Kong should remain an unreconstructed colony for the foreseeable future with, at best, a quasi-democratic facade has yet to be fully documented. Equally unclear, too, is the thinking of the Chinese government, though the advantages of strengthening its economic and financial ties to Hong Kong could hardly have gone unnoticed in its central committee. If both legitimate and contraband Hong Kong trade with China can only be described as modest in the 1950s, thanks to the substantial adverse effect of American-led controls on Western dealings with the PRC, the fact that some at least continued at the height of the Cold War did eventually permit subsequent improvements.

By the 1960s the value to China of its increasing economic links to Hong Kong were hard to overlook, though the very obvious political embarrassment could only be partly reduced by removing the colony from all maps of the region and by stating that while Hong Kong was temporarily under unrecognized British occupation it still remained subject to Chinese sovereignty. It would appear that the PRC, like the Nationalist government in earlier days, was content to enjoy the economic gains that were accruing substantially through expanded trade in the 1960s and, of course, afterwards, while seemingly biding its time over committing itself to any final decision on the future of Hong Kong. Events appear to have followed generally in line with the statements attributed to Mao Zedong in 1957 that 'Sino–British relations should be kept running like a narrow winter stream, cold at the official level and uninterrupted in people to people contact'. The patience and pragmatism of the PRC's leadership over the reversion issue is noteworthy, given that it is known that several senior British figures had raised the question of the New Territories' lease by the early 1970s. While the KMT in office after the Pacific war had necessarily to attempt to solve China's huge problems stemming both from the Japanese occupation and the continuing civil war the PRC, once it had survived the Korean fighting and transformed the Chinese political economy, had no such excuses for inaction. Aside from a single, confused border incursion at the height of the 1967 crisis Beijing, however, elected not to employ direct military force to retake its lost enclave.

Writing after the anxious months in 1967 when Hong Kong was subject to mass violence, Edward Rice, the American consul-general in the territory described the territory bluntly as 'an anachronism'. It existed, said Rice,

as a colony, in an era of decolonization, on the doorstep of the world's most vocally anti-imperialist power. In an age of high taxes and deficit spending, it had low tax rates and had been producing, in most years, a budget surplus. Almost entirely lacking in natural resources, it had a thriving economy, based on industry and trade, which was growing at a rate of roughly 15 percent per year. Originally created for the benefit of the mother country and British subjects, it turned over no revenues to the treasury in London, although it did help to cover the cost of maintaining British troops stationed in the colony. Instead, the substantial sums left over, after covering operating costs, were largely plowed back into public works, such as the low-cost housing projects in which over a quarter of the colony's population had been resettled. The colony, in short, was being governed for the benefit of its inhabitants, and it was governed well.

Comments by third party nationals a generation later would probably convey much of the same type of information and perhaps approval. Admittedly the days of double-digit growth are gone for good but the continuities in the manner in which the territory is administered are striking. Rice's view, contained in his lengthy work *Mao's Way* that 'Hong Kong's normal atmosphere is one of amicable bustle, and it is a place where one ordinarily can walk the streets in perfect safety, day or night' remains also largely the case in 1996.

What is more difficult to explain, however, is why postwar Britain retained Hong Kong for over half a century. For London to hold onto its colony has taken political guile, administrative skill and good fortune, yet that said we are still little nearer discovering why the endeavour was attempted. What was there to gain from going against the decolonization grain? Why did the British stay on? It is not as if Hong Kong served any particular strategic purpose for Britain after the ending of the Korean war, though it could still pay dividends to the present by providing intelligence-gathering facilities and safe anchorage for visiting US carriers and nuclear-powered submarines. Nor can British merchant and financial houses be seen to have done particularly well out of the territory. Some institutions, of course, prospered but the British share of Hong Kong's imports is relatively small and its slice of the major construction contracts is far from outstanding. The richest individuals in Hong Kong for the past century have been Chinese and no British government has seen fit to attempt to direct the territory's economy into channels beneficial to its own exporters or investors.

One explanation that can satisfactorily address the question of the British retention of Hong Kong is in terms of history and sentiment. Having held the colony for a century, the British government in 1945 was eager to remove the humiliating scar of Japanese occupation from its record by regaining the territory. Once this had been accomplished and Hong Kong, to the surprise of many observers, demonstrated its remarkable economic prowess the incentive was to ignore events in the wider Afro–Asian third world. Provided the Chinese authorities could appreciate the advantages of Hong Kong to its exchequer and later modernization schemes, no cabinet in London appears to have considered doing much to alter the colony's status, given that no internal demand for independence arose. There never was a British masterplan; events were usually in the saddle.

Yet, as has been suggested earlier, the date 1997 was for some at least an unstated but fixed impediment, whose importance inevitably grew as the remaining time shrank. Although Mrs Thatcher challenged her advisors on the question of retaining Hong Kong (much as she did on a host of other issues), it proved impossible in the end for her to withstand the insistence of Deng Xiaoping that the British must fold their tents. The prime minister's supporters, however, could argue that at the very least she had demonstrated to the peoples of Hong Kong that their rulers had made a concerted effort to persuade Beijing of the special character of the territory and its entitlement to local autonomy. Perhaps all along there was an unarticulated opinion within successive Hong Kong administrations that British rule was inevitably going to be finite.

This led paradoxically to a determination to stay because few doubted that they would have to leave in 1997.

If the probability of a Sino–British negotiated settlement and a non-violent handover of sovereignty was high even from the earliest postwar years, then it followed that the interval might be employed to run the territory efficiently and painlessly. The arrangement has worked because it satisfied in the main all three interested parties: the British government could point to its administrative successes, the Chinese had the satisfaction of knowing that over half its trade passed through Hong Kong by the early 1990s and the residents of the territory could expect to be left alone to get on with their own affairs. Hong Kong's postwar accomplishments have been the consequence of these three forces of domestic stability, external non-interference and economic dynamism.

Yet, as events in the final years before the handover have made clear, the conventional triangular set of arrangements no longer operates as smoothly as in the past. Changes within the political culture of Hong Kong through the decline in apathy and the growth of political movements holding various opinions on the wisdom and terms of the Sino–British Joint Declaration and the Basic Law have forced the British government to alter its stance towards Beijing. Governor Patten stated frankly within months of arriving in Hong Kong that, while he would like to be seen in 1997 to have served his term 'honourably and honestly', he recognized that it was impossible to imagine 'everybody cheering in the grandstands'. After receiving strong criticism from Chinese spokesman at the time of the September 1995 LegCo elections Patten was characteristically quick to respond in kind. It may be, however, that in the aftermath of these elections a more gentle tone is gradually reemerging in the diplomacy required to ensure even an approximate solution to the issues surrounding a highly complicated reversion process. The final months of British rule could yet revert to what Sir Alexander Grantham had predicted over three decades ago would be the Chinese government's reward for its self-centred patience – the return of Hong Kong in its 'complete and intact' state.

The ability of the government of Hong Kong and its coopted business and professional elites to maintain social cohesion for the last half-century also requires some explanation. The continuing economic advancement of the territory with discreet steering from officialdom and the improvement in the range of public services provided by the Hong Kong authorities (the government remains the largest landlord and employer) are two factors behind the remarkable stability since 1967. The past, however, is not necessarily a reliable guide to whether the existing social order can or should be prolonged. The warnings by

Leung Chun-ying, an advisor who has served both the Hong Kong and Chinese governments, that Hong Kong must itself adapt to a range of changes is timely. The onus on the PRC to tread carefully and respect the way of life of its new ward after July 1997 risks neglecting the changes required also of the citizens of the SAR. Their knowledge of China may be less accurate and more prejudiced than some imagine and Hong Kong's bureaucracy will have to make its share of adjustments. There will certainly be economic challenges too that are less discussed than perhaps they should be. Leung cautions over taking for granted that the large income differentials between the SAR and other parts of China will necessarily persist. Competition from within China may reduce the Hong Kong edge and only if the territory is 'quick off the mark, identifying and filling new niches in China's economic development' will the SAR succeed. There is, in other words, little to be gained by complacency. Hong Kong's present domination of the Pearl River delta and its hinterland should continue but such extensive integration is also contingent on an open international trading system and subject to changes in Chinese national policies. The Greater China concept does not necessarily provide all the answers for Hong Kong in the future; other parts of the region must be expected to develop with active encouragement from the Chinese state and the emergence of what might be termed 'mini-Hong Kongs' early in the next century should not be ruled out.

It was the convenience of Hong Kong to China that won the territory its lengthy reprieve. Hong Kong's combination of postwar economic advance and political backwardness acted to underwrite its existence for two generations. Both the authorities in China and Hong Kong saw mutual advantage in developing economic and financial connections that drew the two very different entities into what could become an increasingly close relationship. To take but one trivial example, Mao Zedong's wife Jiang Qing used the territory as a source of both medicines and pornographic films then unobtainable inside China proper. By the late 1960s the territory was proving its worth to China by not only importing huge quantities of food and water daily but also by demonstrating its skills as an expanding financial centre. Mainland companies and banks prospered from the profits of their Hong Kong offices and branches. Once Deng's modernization programme was in operation the Hong Kong–China linkage became irrevocable. Statistical proof of this was seen through the PRC's vital role as an exporter to Hong Kong. In the 1980s China was comfortably the largest source of the territory's imports and in turn it provided the largest market for Hong Kong's re-exports.

Unfortunately for many in the territory this explosion in Sino–Hong Kong trade did not continue in a political vacuum. The era when Hong Kong could decently ignore both the 1997 question and leave its domestic administration in safe, expatriate hands was already in doubt by the late 1970s. Once the British government in London began to glance nervously at the calendar on the wall and simultaneously consider introducing a more representative political system for its colony the familiar game was up. New soundings and ground rules in turn prompted Beijing to reconsider its strategy.

While some discussion of the expiration of the lease on the New Territories had taken place before the Second World War in Whitehall, it was only after 1945 that the subject gradually worked its way up the official agenda and eventually required cabinet consideration. Once the initial soundings with the PRC leadership had been taken by Governor MacLehose, however, it was apparent that the trial balloon of recognizing Chinese sovereignty but having Britain continue to administer Hong Kong was doomed. Mrs Thatcher had pressed this now familiar suggestion on Beijing without success during her visit in 1982, arguing in vain that there were nothing but advantages to both Hong Kong and China in retaining the territory's affluence through a continuation of British rule. The remark to the press by China's prime minister Zhao Ziyang during Thatcher's September 1982 talks with the PRC leadership that 'of course China must retain sovereignty' indicated conclusively what would follow. Zhao's promise that following reversion his government 'will certainly take a series of measures to guarantee Hong Kong's prosperity and stability' was hardly the reassurance that either Mrs Thatcher or the peoples of the territory were hoping for but it was almost certainly the best that might be forthcoming from China.

Dissatisfaction with London also involved other issues. The colony's efforts to persuade China to alter important sections of the Basic Law were hampered by Britain's awareness that any change was very largely dependent on Beijing's good will. Given the PRC's vehement criticisms of Hong Kong's highly public support for the student movement during and after Tiananmen, the British negotiators were dubious from the outset that this was likely to be obtainable. Proposals, for example, from a more strident OMELCO (Office of the (non-governmental) members of the Executive and Legislative Councils) on a sizeable change in the democratically elected membership of LegCo were rejected. The British government preferred instead to endorse the Basic Law's scheme of February 1990 that permitted only eighteen directly elected seats (out of sixty) to LegCo in 1991, twenty in 1995, and thirty by 2003. In the opinion of the Foreign Office this was the best deal that could be wrung from a Chinese state deeply worried about even the introduction of modest amounts of democracy in what would soon be an addition to its own territory.

The adoption of the Basic Law by the VII National People's Congress on 4 April 1990, however, failed to produce the Sino–British rapprochement that British officials were hoping for. New issues simply replaced older ones as the long-standing acrimony continued, while at the same time the differences between what were now recognizable political parties inside Hong Kong with highly diverse objectives made the British commitment to the maintenance of social order a much more challenging task than in former decades. Governor Trench's proud boast of an earlier era on the competence of British administration in the territory was now at last to be put fully to the test.

The first half of the 1990s were to be the years of greatest British controversy with China and a period of unprecedented political change within Hong Kong itself. Yet for all the initiatives shortly to be associated with a more openly antagonistic British cabinet and its new governor, the unpalatable truth remained that, as the Chinese People's Institute of Foreign Affairs bluntly stated in 1994, the 'days for British rule in Hong Kong are numbered, and there is no force in the world that can turn this round'.

While it remains premature for any but tentative hypotheses, it may be that the period from Chris Patten's appointment in July 1992 until December 1995 has a recognizable unity. It could be that the remarks by Lu Ping, the PRC's most senior official in the territory, made on New Year's Day 1996, that a 'new dawn' in cooperation with Britain was in the offing will prove accurate as marking the end to recent turmoil. Any such reality would suit the Chinese government, of course, since its successes of the recent past could then be consolidated without overmuch concern for further protest from London. Objections certainly will continue from voices inside Hong Kong but these will doubtless be disregarded, as in the past. The announcement of China's nomination of the grouping responsible for the selection of the first chief executive of the SAR in December 1995 has already underlined Beijing's near-total disdain for its vocal opponents in the territory, since no members associated with Martin Lee's party have been included.

The years from Governor Patten's first policy statement in October 1992 to the winter of 1995 are likely to prove to have been the era of maximum tension in Hong Kong's postwar story. It was a relatively short but tumultuous period when Britain and China clashed repeatedly over what each party saw to be its opportunity to mould minds and construct institutions that would endure long beyond 1997. Chris

Patten rarely disguised the fact that his overriding intent during these years was to equip the territory for the post-reversion decades when Hong Kong would have to soldier on alone. (Sir Percy Cradock also made the same claims for his own position, arguing that 'the long-term welfare of Hong Kong must be the sole criterion' for making British policy over the territory.) Although Patten spoke proudly to LegCo in October 1995 of the convening of 'an historic Council, the first fully-elected legislature in Hong Kong's history', it remains the case that the decades of dilatoriness exhibited by cabinets and civil servants in both London and the territory itself have resulted in an extraordinarily slow advance to this objective. For most of the postwar period and all of Hong Kong's first century under British control, debate over the prospects for local self-government had been deliberately discouraged. It is surely reasonable to suggest that a stronger, more confident territory with greater political acumen might have been in place at least a generation ago, if the Young Plan had been adopted and had further political developments then followed in its wake. In the context of the Chinese civil war and the first years of reconstruction following Mao's victory in 1949, it is hard to imagine that either the KMT or the PRC leadership would have had the time or energy to mount an effective campaign of destabilization within Hong Kong. Much of what Sir Robert Kotewall suggested in terms of political reform in 1945 was barely in place when Patten saluted his new LegCo in 1995. There would indeed have been risks in any such venture and speculation of this nature must remain unsatisfactory, yet senior officials within Hong Kong and their business supporters were surely guilty of excessive timidity. It was certainly safer, in the medium term at least, to damp down what was hardly more than an occasional plea for greater autonomy, but the consequences for post-1997 Hong Kong appear profoundly disturbing.

   With the historian's great luxury of hindsight, it may be suggested that if the territory by the late 1970s had been moving towards self-government it might have exhibited sufficient self-confidence to make the Chinese state wary of dismantling what might then have been a well established system two decades later. Of course, this was not the way Hong Kong evolved and, as we have seen, the advice from Government House was to avoid any such tendencies, partly out of concern for Beijing's reaction but also, and perhaps equally importantly, out of a wish to appease the territory's business and financial elites in order to ensure that their investments were not transferred elsewhere in the region. It made little difference in the long run as most of these gentlemen were among the first to desert the ship when Governor Patten proposed his constitutional changes and had little interest in encouraging political initiatives that might cause economic disruption. The owners of a sizeable percentage of companies listed on the Hong Kong stock exchange moved quickly to reach out to Beijing, and to form the heart of a somewhat improbable capitalist–socialist alliance likely to determine the bulk of the SAR's forthcoming policies. This strange marriage is clearly made out of mutual necessity; it remains the most satisfactory way for Beijing to ensure the future prosperity of the territory for the benefit of the Chinese state as a whole, while reassuring local magnates that the SAR will avoid excessive intervention in the affairs of private sectors. The arrangement bears all the hallmarks of conventional government–business thinking in the Hong Kong of the 1950s and 1960s. Whether there will be an actual regression through any reduction in the role of the local state after 1997 is still uncertain, though changes in the level of new housing starts and welfare spending from the reforms of the Patten years would provide one important indication of where officials of the SAR and local business supporters stand.

Recognition by the British government that the first three years of the Patten administration are likely to have achieved only limited success was seen in January 1996. Foreign Secretary Malcolm Rifkind stated unequivocally in the territory before visiting Beijing that the British government could not 'suddenly produce some formula which will deal with the determined Chinese desire to dismantle institutions'. Rifkind in October had lamely called for Beijing to have a 'proper respect' for Hong Kong's way of life after reversion but the general fear that the PRC will act as it has frequently promised and unceremoniously end the painfully constructed LegCo edifice of 1995 appears to be well grounded. Equally convincing is press speculation that London is, in effect, preparing to throw in the towel and accept that further contests with China are now a thing of the past. There is simply insufficient time or desire to refight what must inevitably be unequal contests over human rights and issues of nationality: there had been too many humiliating defeats in 1995 over the territory's future judiciary and civil liberties for the British government to consider fresh troubles. What the Hong Kong civil service is now describing as 'the outstanding issues' are subjects where China can be expected to make up its mind by itself. The game is almost up and all sides now recognize this reality.

Throughout these nearly two decades of often difficult discussions with China over the future of Hong Kong it should not be overlooked that the territory's economy continued to grow. Despite the controversies and setbacks, the Hong Kong government could invariably point to this reality as an effective means of demonstrating the successes of what

Governor Patten called 'a highly-rated economy' that 'has flourished mightily'. The statistics that he listed confirmed many of his administration's claims. It would be churlish to deny Hong Kong its position as perhaps the least restricted economy in the world with *per capita* GDP at US$23,800 or to challenge the territory's switch to a modern service-based economy increasingly reliant on its status as the fourth largest international financial centre for its prosperity in the future. With larger foreign reserves and higher annual growth rates (averaging 6 per cent over the last decade) than Britain, France and Italy, the economic story remains impressive. The critics who stand ready to gloat at Hong Kong's impeding doom have yet to be heard from in this field, though warning signs may be appearing over the rise in unemployment levels and the stubbornly high rates of inflation.

The idea of many in the West that Hong Kong, in the opinion of the authors of the 1993 edition of the *Dictionary of Cultural Literacy*, is still only 'home to many international corporate offices and a world-famous tailoring industry' ignores a great deal, particularly the declining importance of the manufacturing sector and the territory's increasingly close links to the Chinese economy. It is Hong Kong's strengthening ties to the China market that continue to lure overseas companies to the colony, more than offsetting in the process those who have shifted their regional headquarters to Singapore or Bangkok. The business community, as we have seen, has been among the most vocal of groups within Hong Kong in supporting the reversion of the territory to China. The pessimism of many local political organizations is downplayed by both domestic and overseas enterprises, who calculated nearly two decades ago in some instances that the 'open door' policies associated with Deng Xiaoping's modernization of China could provide vast advantages for their Hong Kong-based companies. The continuing growth of the territory's economy since the 1970s is certainly in good measure attributable to the China factor. The lure of this huge, developing economy has brought sizeable benefits to Hong Kong and the management of corporations that have expanded in the real estate, banking, retailing and shipping industries have no wish to endanger this prosperity. The impressive geometric Bank of China structure designed by I.M. Pei is a confident symbol of China's increasing financial power over Hong Kong.

By 1995 there was a general sentiment in most business circles that the reversion to China would prove to be less of a destabilizing issue than earlier prophets had predicted. While public statements by businessmen could indeed be concocted to ingratiate themselves with Beijing, much as their fathers and grandfathers had done when dealing with local bureaucrats in the days of British control, the prospect of Chinese sovereignty aroused few open fears. The close investment and trade relationships between Hong Kong and China would only be damaged to the detriment of both partners if the Chinese-appointed chief executive of the SAR and his staff were to intervene excessively in the affairs of the economy. The statement, drawn from Chinese sources, in December 1995 by Paul Cheng, a senior figure through his roles in LegCo and the British traders Inchcape, that Beijing was determined to avoid the over-involvement seen in its dealings with Macao typified the current atmosphere. Cheng would claim that such remarks indicate 'that China intends to give Hong Kong the autonomy it needs to be successful'. Most executives assume that the new post-1997 administration will keep any temptation to meddle within manageable limits.

Sceptics, however, will weigh the evidence carefully after reversion before endorsing what others may be more willing at present to take on trust. While local businesses are hoping for preferential treatment from the SAR, some executives at least wish to go a step further and attempt to convince the Chinese central government that Hong Kong's importance to the economic health of the entire nation could be put at risk by state policies that looked to the promotion of alternative SEZs and financial centres. This suggests long-term anxieties over which it is far from clear that Hong Kong's private sector will have any major influence. The post-reversion economic and financial future for Hong Kong proposed by professor Leonard K. Cheng of Hong Kong University of Science and Technology offers a healthy correction to both the school that imagines that the SAR is certain to develop further regardless of PRC rulings and the pessimists who are already referring to Hong Kong as 'a second-class Shanghai'. Cheng's picture of Hong Kong's future conditional 'on what it has to offer China and to the world as well as how well it exploits opportunities as they emerge' follows almost to the letter the musing of David MacDougall at the start of the reconstruction period in 1945. Hong Kong, in other words, might be advised to put its trust in its domestic talents and energies without imagining that either its future sovereign or the rest of the global economy will display any particular magnanimity towards this new upstart. The next decades rest on the territory continuing to demonstrate that it can still determine its own road to economic salvation.

Political change and economic development in postwar Hong Kong have necessarily had a profound impact on how the peoples of Hong Kong see themselves and how the community has adjusted to uncertainty. The tendency to simply assume, however, that society will behave generally as directed by whoever its administrators and managers happen to be at any given moment has been implicit in much of Hong Kong's entire history. The impression that Hong Kong presents of frequently accepting the decision of those in authority and preferring to avoid confrontation with such superior powers is inescapable. The brief period recently when the public has had at least the opportunity to be consulted on major issues affecting their livelihood and welfare may well prove to be merely a rare interlude between the two far lengthier eras of past colonial subjection and future domination by Beijing.

Such cautious, deferential attitudes may have been more appropriate to the Hong Kong of the early postwar years than to the prosperity of the final pre-reversion years. The young, migrant Chinese who reached the territory to escape the confusions and conflicts of the 1940s and 1950s had little choice but to conform to the existing order. Their priorities were overwhelmingly economic and limited initially to quite modest goals. A generation later, however, Chinese society in Hong Kong had clearly begun to experience a massive improvement in living standards and the territory came to be seen as a land of opportunity where personal abilities and individual effort would receive their just rewards. It was an ethos that left success and failure very much up to the person in question, thereby relieving the colonial government of most responsibilities beyond maintaining a modicum of order and providing rudimentary educational and welfare services. At least until the MacLehose era the community looked inwards to its family units for providing much of the financial and human support that made possible the mobility and achievement that many clearly aspired to in what was, of course, a highly unequal set of communities. The life chances for the residents of Hong Kong were strongly influenced both by existing family income, which in turn often determined access to further education, and the less discussed issue of gender. It would have been hard to convince outsiders until recently that Hong Kong was an aspiring meritocracy. The power of inherited wealth has left even many of the largest corporations in the territory firmly in the control of their founding families, while large numbers of doctors and architects are themselves sons and daughters of parents drawn from similar professions. For all their many differences, both Anson Chan and Martin Lee share the good fortune of having been born into families with relatives who had been generals in the KMT armies.

Life chances for those without such advantageous backgrounds is seen to rest largely on educational attainment. The Hong Kong government's introduction of free and compulsory secondary education in 1979 accelerated the process of improving the provision of schooling in the territory. The entire subject of high school education is necessarily political in Hong Kong, reflecting the public's interest in education as the main vehicle for upward mobility in a competitive society with very considerable individual economic expectations. Once this important step had been implemented, attention inevitably began to focus on forms of higher education, to the extent that by 1994 it was estimated that over 25 per cent of the age groups of entrants to post-secondary education was enrolled in either degree or non-degree classes. Indeed, by the mid-1990s with the continuing expansion of existing universities and the creation of new ones, it was possible for Dean Cheng Kai-ming of the University of Hong Kong to argue that 'the supply of higher education has somewhat exceeded the demand'. Public criticism, however, of student language abilities in English and Chinese and a commonly held view that academic standards may have deteriorated guaranteed that there will be little complacency over the quality being provided.

Researchers have noted recently that Hong Kong society may possess a decidedly favourable image of itself as being more open and meritocratic than detailed investigation suggests. This, of course, may well be a failing common to other communities, but the lack of evidence to substantiate the allegedly high degree of social mobility apparently shared by many Hong Kong people could weaken what is, after all, one of the few common values in a still developing, uncertain city-state. Belief in this idea of equality of opportunity has provided an important ball of twine to bind heterogeneous groups from differing parts of China into an approximate whole.

Most of the community of Hong Kong has attempted to gain from what has been a lengthy and still continuing period of economic advance. The decades of substantial growth have clearly made possible the affluence of numerous newcomers and confirmed the broad vein of individualism that motivates many in the community. The attention to conspicuous consumption reflects (or helps mould) the ethos of contemporary Hong Kong. What remains in shorter supply, however, is any particularly pronounced sense of civic culture. The remarks of Derek Davies, made during the aftermath of the 1967 crisis, still held true until very recently and are likely to be the case once again following 1997:

in a free-booting industrial, commercial and non-political community such as Hong Kong the average citizen's only outlet is the prospect (or hope) of personal economic advancement. And the average Chinese citizen whose hopes of making good are growing faint sublimates such ambitions into a determination to see that his children are in a better position than he was at the beginning of his career.

Given that historically there have been very few political opportunities for the peoples of Hong Kong and that the provision of public goods was determined largely by the government, the options open to most residents were highly constrained and possibly will be again after 1997. The very strengths of the Chinese family structure in Hong Kong may have proved a weakness in not generating overmuch concern or involvement in the wider community.

Hong Kong continues to see its destiny and self-identity in economic terms. Governor Patten's speech-writers were quick to have their master announce at the commencement of his October 1995 policy statement that the first of the two 'bedrock principles' of the territory (the other was the rule of law) remains that 'we must first create the wealth before spending a share of it on improving our public services'. Patten insisted that

We must never lose sight of this fundamental economic reality, and we must accept its implications. There are no shortcuts, no soft options. Social progress is linked directly to economic progress. If we want better services, we must fund them by creating new wealth.

Such sentiments have been far easier for Chris Patten to make as governor of Hong Kong than during his former political career in Britain where the welfare state has traditionally played a more comprehensive role in the community than in Hong Kong. Public opinion throughout much of developed Asia has long regarded the growth of welfarism to be a major cause of Eurosclerosis.

The wide-ranging economic and financial freedoms enjoyed in contemporary Hong Kong are perhaps the most liberal in the world. There is little of the official hand that continues to guide Japan's 'directional state' or the government bureaucracy that still is attached to major portions of the Chinese economy. Hong Kong enjoys low individual and corporate taxation, capital gains can be retained and the presence of so many competitive financial institutions encourages the marketing of a host of services. This has made the territory a magnet for overseas investors and bankers, able to conduct business with the minimum of official supervision. Whether such opportunities to conduct their affairs will continue after 1997 is somewhat less certain; the press coverage of multi-millionaire and folk hero Li Ka-shing's recent establishment of a foreign-registered trust fund for parts of his financial holdings is indicative, however, of an unease that is increasingly felt but still rarely publicly acknowledged in business quarters.

The expansion of Chinese mainland firms within the territory has acted to counter this disquiet. These state-owned companies are clearly committed to collective decisions that will improve their investment portfolios and spur confidence in the crucial transition period. It has been calculated that there are approximately 2,000 PRC-funded firms operating in Hong Kong and some of the largest of these have invested impressive sums in the territory during the last few years. Hong Kong and Japanese journalists have reported that some of these entities are now under closer scrutiny from Beijing and that the familiar socialist strategy of placing commissars within state institutions may grow to ensure that party decisions are being upheld. One think-tank reckons that it is possible that mainland Chinese firms could be controlling one-third of Hong Kong's banking property and transport sectors by 1997. Whatever the approximate size (statistics are not easily obtainable), it can hardly be doubted that China is preparing to take a much large stake in the territory's economy. This will make it possible in the near future for the Chinese authorities to be in a position to reduce competition by, as appears to be the recent case in some purchases of valuable property sites, simply outbidding others in the same field. While it is possible that such firms as Citic Hong Kong and China Merchants' Holdings (100 per cent owned by the Ministry of Communications) may step in to buy the holdings of nervous Hong Kong residents in 1997 to prevent a financial rout, the greater danger is likely to be an overly strong Chinese state presence, if established trends continue.

In considering the territory's position after reversion the bulk of the population of Hong Kong has little choice but to stay on. It must be assumed that many of these individuals have accepted that, while life may well be different in some particulars, the same objectives of maintaining and possibly increasing one's standard of living and taking a rather cautious view of authority will persist. There are few alternatives. Those without second passports will have to survive as best they can, trusting that the administration of the SAR will continue within at least the broad tramlines of the pre-1997 government.

What it is impossible, of course, to accurately measure is the probability of interference and oblique suggestion from the north, through what the Japanese might term 'administrative guidance'. The premise that Beijing would remain cautious in pressing its views is conditional on there being limited change in the thinking of the PRC's leadership and the absence of what could be interpreted as provocative acts by elements within the newly established SAR. It would, for example, be asking for trouble if demonstrators, of whatever political ilk, were to foolishly institute gestures that no regime in Beijing could possibly tolerate. To take a simple but dangerous example, there would be immediate consequences if any elements in the newly established

SAR were to insult the PRC and its inner leadership by word or deed. The sight of protesters burning the Chinese flag and stamping on effigies of the great patriarch would surely have an instant impact on future political debate. Equally, if criticism of the CCP were to become widespread, it is highly probable that those held responsible would receive punishment through employment restrictions and an inability to return to Hong Kong, if they wished to leave for a temporary visit overseas.

The SAR, it can be predicted, will have more than sufficient domestic issues to handle in its initial months and will presumably work diligently to gain the fullest cooperation of the PRC. A mutual hesitancy to press the other partner too hard should therefore get the inauguration off to a reasonable start. Indeed, if this could not be achieved, the longer-term consequences would be dire. Without a considerable degree of good will on the part of both sides, the entire system of shared power would collapse before the great experiment had had a chance to prove itself. Hong Kong will have to accept that the territory's five-petalled bauhinia flower is set within an all-embracing sea of red on the new regional flag of the Hong Kong SAR. The territory must expect shortly to be tested as never before; it may well prove to be an uncomfortable passage.

# Appendix 1: Governors of Hong Kong since the Pacific war

| Governor | Appointed |
|---|---|
| Sir Mark Young | 10 September 1941 |
| Sir Alexander Grantham | 25 July 1947 |
| Sir Robert Black | 23 January 1958 |
| Sir David Trench | 14 April 1964 |
| Sir Murray MacLehose | 19 November 1971 |
| Sir Edward Youde | 20 May 1982 |
| Sir David Wilson | 9 April 1987 |
| Chris Patten | 9 July 1992 |

On 11 December 1996 Tung Chee-hwa (C.H. Tung) was elected the first chief executive of the SAR (see appendix 7).

# Appendix 2: Composition of LegCo, 1964–96

| Year | Ex officio | Appointed | Functional constituencies | Electoral college | Directly elected | Total |
|------|-----------|-----------|---------------------------|-------------------|------------------|-------|
| 1964 | 13 | 13 | 0 | 0 | 0 | 26 |
| 1976 | 23 | 23 | 0 | 0 | 0 | 46 |
| 1977 | 25 | 25 | 0 | 0 | 0 | 50 |
| 1980 | 27 | 27 | 0 | 0 | 0 | 54 |
| 1983 | 29 | 29 | 0 | 0 | 0 | 58 |
| 1985 | 11 | 22 | 12 | 12 | 0 | 57 |
| 1988 | 11 | 20 | 14 | 12 | 0 | 57 |
| 1991 | 4 | 18 | 21 | 0 | 18 | 61 |
| 1993 | 3 | 18 | 21 | 0 | 18 | 60 |
| 1995 | 0 | 0 | 30 | 10 | 20 | 60 |

# Appendix 3: Public expenditure

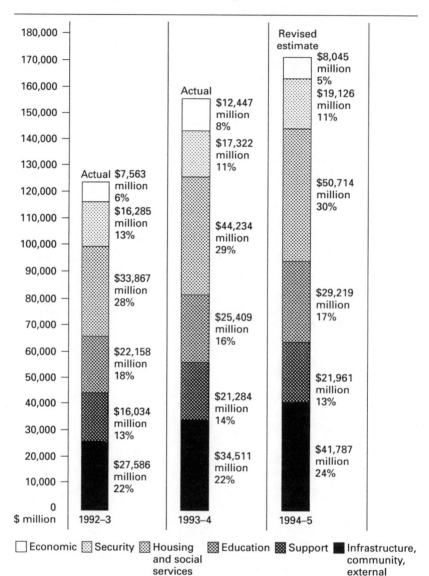

Public expenditure, by function, Hong Kong, 1995
Source: *Hong Kong Yearbook 1995* (Hong Kong), p. 477.

# Appendix 4: The Joint Declaration

JOINT DECLARATION OF THE GOVERNMENT OF THE
UNITED KINGDOM OF GREAT BRITAIN AND NORTHERN
IRELAND AND THE GOVERNMENT OF THE PEOPLE'S
REPUBLIC OF CHINA ON THE QUESTION OF HONG KONG

The Government of the United Kingdom of Great Britain and Northern Ireland
and the Government of the People's Republic of China have reviewed with
satisfaction the friendly relations existing between the two Governments and
peoples in recent years and agreed that a proper negotiated settlement of the
question of Hong Kong, which is left over from the past, is conducive to the
maintenance of the prosperity and stability of Hong Kong and to the further
strengthening and development of the relations between the two countries on a
new basis. To this end, they have, after talks between the delegations of the two
Governments, agreed to declare as follows:

1. The Government of the People's Republic of China declares that to recover
the Hong Kong area (including Hong Kong Island, Kowloon and the New
Territories, hereinafter referred to as Hong Kong) is the common aspiration of
the entire Chinese people, and that it has decided to resume the exercise of
sovereignty over Hong Kong with effect from 1 July 1997.

2. The Government of the United Kingdom declares that it will restore Hong
Kong to the People's Republic of China with effect from 1 July 1997.

3. The Government of the People's Republic of China declares that the basic
policies of the People's Republic of China regarding Hong Kong are as follows:
(1) Upholding national unity and territorial integrity and taking account of the
    history of Hong Kong and its realities, the People's Republic of China has
    decided to establish, in accordance with the provisions of Article 31 of the
    Constitution of the People's Republic of China, a Hong Kong Special
    Administrative Region upon resuming the exercise of sovereignty over
    Hong Kong.
(2) The Hong Kong Special Administrative Region will be directly under the
    authority of the Central People's Government of the People's Republic of
    China. The Hong Kong Special Administrative Region will enjoy a high
    degree of autonomy, except in foreign and defence affairs which are the
    responsibilities of the Central People's Government.
(3) The Hong Kong Special Administrative Region will be vested with

executive, legislative and independent judicial power, including that of final adjudication. The laws currently in force in Hong Kong will remain basically unchanged.

(4) The Government of the Hong Kong Special Administrative Region will be composed of local inhabitants. The chief executive will be appointed by the Central People's Government on the basis of the results of elections or consultations to be held locally. Principal officials will be nominated by the chief executive of the Hong Kong Special Administrative Region for appointment by the Central People's Government. Chinese and foreign nationals previously working in the public and police services in the government departments of Hong Kong may remain in employment. British and other foreign nationals may also be employed to serve as advisers or hold certain public posts in government departments of the Hong Kong Special Administrative Region.

(5) The current social and economic systems in Hong Kong will remain unchanged, and so will the lifestyle. Rights and freedoms, including those of the person, of speech, of the press, of assembly, of association, of travel, of movement, of correspondence, of strike, of choice of occupation, of academic research and of religious belief will be ensured by law in the Hong Kong Special Administrative Region. Private property, ownership of enterprises, legitimate right of inheritance and foreign investment will be protected by law.

(6) The Hong Kong Special Administrative Region will retain the status of a free port and a separate customs territory.

(7) The Hong Kong Special Administrative Region will retain the status of an international financial centre, and its markets for foreign exchange, gold, secrities and futures will continue. There will be free flow of capital. The Hong Kong dollar will continue to circulate and remain freely convertible.

(8) The Hong Kong Special Administrative Region will have independent finances. The Central People's Government will not levy taxes on the Hong Kong Special Administrative Region.

(9) The Hong Kong Special Administrative Region may establish mutually beneficial economic relations with the United Kingdom and other countries, whose economic interests in Hong Kong will be given due regard.

(10) Using the name of 'Hong Kong, China', the Hong Kong Special Administrative Region may on its own maintain and develop economic and cultural relations and conclude relevant agreements with states, regions and relevant international organisations.
The Government of the Hong Kong Special Administrative Region may on its own issue travel documents for entry into and exit from Hong Kong.

(11) The maintenance of public order in the Hong Kong Special Administrative Region will be the responsibility of the Government of the Hong Kong Special Administrative Region.

(12) The above-stated basic policies of the People's Republic of China regarding Hong Kong and the elaboration of them in Annex I to this Joint Declaration will be stipulated, in a Basic Law of the Hong Kong Special Administrative Region of the People's Republic of China, by the National People's

Congress of the People's Republic of China. and they will remain unchanged for 50 years.

4. The Government of the United Kingdom and the Government of the People's Republic of China declare that, during the transitional period between the date of the entry into force of this Joint Declaration and 30 June 1997, the Government of the United Kingdom will be responsible for the administration of Hong Kong with the object of maintaining and preserving its economic prosperity and social stability; and that the Government of the People's Republic of China will give its cooperation in this connection.

5. The Government of the United Kingdom and the Government of the People's Republic of China declare that, in order to ensure a smooth transfer of government in 1997, and with a view to the effective implementation of this Joint Declaration, a Sino–British Joint Liaison Group will be set up when this Joint Declaration enters into force; and that it will be established and will function in accordance with the provisions of Annex II to this Joint Declaration.

6. The Government of the United Kingdom and the Government of the People's Republic of China declare that land leases in Hong Kong and other related matters will be dealt with in accordance with the provisions of Annex III to this Joint Declaration.

7. The Government of the United Kingdom and the Government of the People's Republic of China agree to implement the preceding declarations and the Annexes to this Joint Declaration.

8. This Joint Declaration is subject to ratification and shall enter into force on the date of the exchange of instruments of ratification, which shall take place in Beijing before 30 June 1985. This Joint Declaration and its Annexes shall be equally binding.

Done in duplicate at Beijing on　　　　　　1984 in the English and Chinese languages, both texts being equally authentic.

| For the | For the |
|---|---|
| Government of the United Kingdom | Government of the |
| of Great Britain and Northern Ireland | People's Republic of China |

ANNEX I: ELABORATION BY THE GOVERNMENT OF THE PEOPLE'S REPUBLIC OF CHINA OF ITS BASIC POLICIES REGARDING HONG KONG

The Government of the People's Republic of China elaborates the basic policies of the People's Republic of China regarding Hong Kong as set out in paragraph 3 of the Joint Declaration of the Government of the United Kingdom of Great Britain and Northern Ireland and the Government of the People's Republic of China on the Question of Hong Kong as follows:

I

The Constitution of the People's Republic of China stipulates in Article 31 that 'the state may establish special administrative regions when necessary. The systems to be instituted in special administrative regions shall be prescribed by laws enacted by the National People's Congress in the light of the specific conditions.' In accordance with this Article, the People's Republic of China shall, upon the resumption of the exercise of sovereignty over Hong Kong on 1 July 1997, establish the Hong Kong Special Administrative Region of the People's Republic of China. The National People's Congress of the People's Republic of China shall enact and promulgate a Basic Law of the Hong Kong Special Administrative Region of the People's Republic of China (hereinafter referred to as the Basic Law) in accordance with the Constitution of the People's Republic of China, stipulating that after the establishment of the Hong Kong Special Administrative Region the socialist system and socialist policies shall not be practised in the Hong Kong Special Administrative Region and that Hong Kong's previous capitalist system and lifestyle shall remain unchanged for 50 years.

The Hong Kong Special Administrative Region shall be directly under the authority of the Central People's Government of the People's Republic of China and shall enjoy a high degree of autonomy. Except for foreign and defence affairs which are the responsibilities of the Central People's Government, the Hong Kong Special Administrative Region shall be vested with executive, legislative and independent judicial power, including that of final adjudication. The Central People's Government shall authorise the Hong Kong Special Administrative Region to conduct on its own those external affairs specified in Section XI of this Annex.

The government and legislature of the Hong Kong Special Administrative Region shall be composed of local inhabitants. The chief executive of the Hong Kong Special Administrative Region shall be selected by election or through consultations held locally and be appointed by the Central People's Government. Principal officials (equivalent to Secretaries) shall be nominated by the chief executive of the Hong Kong Special Administrative Region and appointed by the Central People's Government. The legislature of the Hong Kong Special Administrative Region shall be constituted by elections. The executive authorities shall abide by the law and shall be accountable to the legislature.

In addition to Chinese, English may also be used in organs of government and in the courts in the Hong Kong Special Administrative Region.

Apart from displaying the national flag and national emblem of the People's Republic of China, the Hong Kong Special Administrative Region may use a regional flag and emblem of its own.

II–XIV *not reproduced*

## ANNEX II: SINO-BRITISH JOINT LIAISON GROUP

1. In furtherance of their common aim and in order to ensure a smooth transfer of government in 1997, the Government of the United Kingdom and the Government of the People's Republic of China have agreed to continue their discussions in a friendly spirit and to develop the cooperative relationship which already exists between the two Governments over Hong Kong with a view to the effective implementation of the Joint Declaration.

2. In order to meet the requirements for liaison, consultation and the exchange of information, the two Governments have agreed to set up a Joint Liaison Group.

3. The functions of the Joint Liaison Group shall be:
   (a) to conduct consultations on the implementation of the Joint Declaration;
   (b) to discuss matters relating to the smooth transfer of government in 1997;
   (c) to exchange information and conduct consultations on such subjects as may be agreed by the two sides.
   Matters on which there is disagreement in the Joint Liaison Group shall be referred to the two Governments for solution through consultations.

4. Matters for consideration during the first half of the period between the establishment of the Joint Liaison Group and 1 July 1997 shall include:
   (a) action to be taken by the two Governments to enable the Hong Kong Special Administrative Region to maintain its economic relations as a separate customs territory, and in particular to ensure the maintenance of Hong Kong's participation in the General Agreement on Tariffs and Trade, the Multifibre Arrangement and other international arrangements; and
   (b) action to be taken by the two Governments to ensure the continued application of international rights and obligations affecting Hong Kong.

5. The two Governments have agreed that in the second half of the period between the establishment of the Joint Liaison Group and 1 July 1997 there will be need for closer cooperation, which will therefore be intensified during that period. Matters for consideration during this second period shall include:
   (a) procedures to be adopted for the smooth transition in 1997;
   (b) action to assist the Hong Kong Special Administrative Region to maintain and develop economic and cultural relations and conclude agreements on these matters with states, regions and relevant international organisations.

6. The Joint Liaison Group shall be an organ for liaison and not an organ of power. It shall play no part in the administration of Hong Kong or the Hong Kong Special Administrative Region. Nor shall it have any supervisory role over that administration. The members and supporting staff of the Joint Liaison Group shall only conduct activities within the scope of the functions of the Joint Liaison Group.

7. Each side shall designate a senior representative, who shall be of Ambassadorial rank, and four other members of the group. Each side may send up to 20 supporting staff.

8. The Joint Liaison Group shall be established on the entry into force of the Joint Declaration. From 1 July 1988 the Joint Liaison Group shall have its principal base in Hong Kong. The Joint Liaison Group shall continue its work until 1 January 2000.

9. The Joint Liaison Group shall meet in Beijing, London and Hong Kong. It shall meet at least once in each of the three locations in each year. The venue for each meeting shall be agreed between the two sides.

10. Members of the Joint Liaison Group shall enjoy diplomatic privileges and

immunities as appropriate when in the three locations. Proceedings of the Joint Liaison Group shall remain confidential unless otherwise agreed between the two sides.

11. The Joint Liaison Group may by agreement between the two sides decide to set up specialist subgroups to deal with particular subjects requiring expert assistance.

12. Meetings of the Joint Liaison Group and subgroups may be attended by experts other than the members of the Joint Liaison Group. Each side shall determine the composition of its delegation to particular meetings of the Joint Liaison Group or subgroup in accordance with the subjects to be discussed and the venue chosen.

13. The working procedures of the Joint Liaison Group shall be discussed and decided upon by the two sides within the guidelines laid down in this Annex.

### ANNEX III: LAND LEASES

The Government of the United Kingdom and the Government of the People's Republic of China have agreed that, with effect from the entry into force of the Joint Declaration, land leases in Hong Kong and other related matters shall be dealt with in accordance with the following provisions:

1. All leases of land granted or decided upon before the entry into force of the Joint Declaration and those granted thereafter in accordance with paragraph 2 or 3 of this Annex, and which extend beyond 30 June 1997, and all rights in relation to such leases shall continue to be recognised and protected under the law of the Hong Kong Special Administrative Region.

2. All leases of land granted by the British Hong Kong Government not containing a right of renewal that expire before 30 June 1997, except short term tenancies and leases for special purposes, may be extended if the lessee so wishes for a period expiring not later than 30 June 2047 without payment of an additional premium. An annual rent shall be charged from the date of extension equivalent to 3 per cent of the rateable value of the property at that date, adjusted in step with any changes in the rateable value thereafter. In the case of old schedule lots, village lots, small houses and similar rural holdings, where the property was on 30 June 1984 held by, or, in the case of small houses granted after that date, the property is granted to, a person descended through the male line from a person who was in 1898 a resident of an established village in Hong Kong, the rent shall remain unchanged so long as the property is held by that person or by one of his lawful successors in the male line. Where leases of land not having a right of renewal expire after 30 June 1997, they shall be dealt with in accordance with the relevant land laws and policies of the Hong Kong Special Administrative Region.

3. From the entry into force of the Joint Declaration until 30 June 1997, new leases of land may be granted by the British Hong Kong Government for terms expiring not later than 30 June 2047. Such leases shall be granted at a premium and nominal rental until 30 June 1997, after which date they shall not require

payment of an additional premium but an annual rent equivalent to 3 per cent of the rateable value of the property at that date, adjusted in step with changes in the rateable value thereafter, shall be charged.

4. The total amount of new land to be granted under paragraph 3 of this Annex shall be limited to 50 hectares a year (excluding land to be granted to the Hong Kong Housing Authority for public rental housing) from the entry into force of the Joint Declaration until 30 June 1997.

5. Modifications of the conditions specified in leases granted by the British Hong Kong Government may continue to be granted before 1 July 1997 at a premium equivalent to the difference between the value of the land under the previous conditions and its value under the modified conditions.

6. From the entry into force of the Joint Declaration until 30 June 1997, premium income obtained by the British Hong Kong Government from land transactions shall, after deduction of the average cost of land production, be shared equally between the British Hong Kong Government and the future Hong Kong Special Administrative Region Government. All the income obtained by the British Hong Kong Government, including the amount of the above mentioned deduction, shall be put into the Capital Works Reserve Fund for the financing of land development and public works in Hong Kong. The Hong Kong Special Administrative Region Government's share of the premium income shall be deposited in banks incorporated in Hong Kong and shall not be drawn on except for the financing of land development and public works in Hong Kong in accordance with the provisions of paragraph 7(d) of this Annex.

7. A Land Commission shall be established in Hong Kong immediately upon the entry into force of the Joint Declaration. The Land Commission shall be composed of an equal number of officials designated respectively by the Government of the United Kingdom and the Government of the People's Republic of China together with necessary supporting staff. The officials of the two sides shall be responsible to their respective governments. The Land Commission shall be dissolved on 30 June 1997. The terms of reference of the Land Commission shall be:

(a) to conduct consultations on the implementation of this Annex;

(b) to monitor observance of the limit specified in paragraph 4 of this Annex, the amount of land granted to the Hong Kong Housing Authority for public rental housing, and the division and use of premium income referred to in paragraph 6 of this Annex;

(c) to consider and decide on proposals from the British Hong Kong Government for increasing the limit referred to in paragraph 4 of this Annex;

(d) to examine proposals for drawing on the Hong Kong Special Administrative Region Government's share of premium income referred to in paragraph 6 of this Annex and to make recommendations to the Chinese side for decision.

Matters on which there is disagreement in the Land Commission shall be referred to the Government of the United Kingdom and the Government of the People's Republic of China for decision.

8. Specific details regarding the establishment of the Land Commission shall be finalised separately by the two sides through consultations.

Initialled by Britain and China, 26 September 1984.

Source: N. Miners, 1995. *The Government and Politics of Hong Kong* (Oxford).

# Appendix 5: The Basic Law

THE BASIC LAW OF THE HONG KONG SPECIAL
ADMINISTRATIVE REGION OF THE PEOPLE'S REPUBLIC
OF CHINA

*Adopted on 4 April 1990 by the VII National People's Congress of the People's
Republic of China at its Third Session.*

## Preamble

Hong Kong has been part of the territory of China since ancient times; it was
occupied by Britain after the Opium War in 1840. On 19 December 1984, the
Chinese and British Governments signed the Joint Declaration on the question
of Hong Kong, affirming that the Government of the People's Republic of China
will resume the exercise of sovereignty over Hong Kong with effect from 1 July
1997, thus fulfilling the long-cherished common aspiration of the Chinese
people for the recovery of Hong Kong.

Upholding national unity and territorial integrity, maintaining the prosperity
and stability of Hong King, and taking account of its history and realities, the
People's Republic of China has decided that upon China's resumption of the
exercise of sovereignty over Hong Kong, a Hong Kong Special Administrative
Region will be established in accordance with the provisions of Article 31 of the
Constitution of the People's Republic of China, and that under the principle of
'one country, two systems', the socialist system and policies will not be practised
in Hong Kong. The basic policies of the People's Republic of China regarding
Hong Kong have been elaborated by the Chinese Government in the
Sino–British Joint Declaration.

In accordance with the Constitution of the People's Republic of China, the
National People's Congress hereby enacts the Basic Law of the Hong Kong
Special Administrative Region of the People's Republic of China, prescribing the
systems to be practised in the Hong Kong Special Administrative Region, in
order to ensure the implementation of the basic policies of the People's Republic
of China regarding Hong Kong.

**CHAPTER I:** GENERAL PRINCIPLES

**Article 1** The Hong Kong Special Administrative Region is an inalienable part
of the People's Republic of China.

**Article 2** The National People's Congress authorizes the Hong Kong Special

Administrative Region to exercise a high degree of autonomy and enjoy executive, legislative and independent judicial power, including that of final adjudication, in accordance with the provisions of this Law.

**Article 3** The executive authorities and legislature of the Hong Kong Special Administrative Region shall be composed of permanent residents of Hong Kong in accordance with the relevant provisions of this Law.

**Article 4** The Hong Kong Special Administrative Region shall safeguard the rights and freedoms of the residents of the Hong Kong Special Administrative Region and of other persons in the Region in accordance with law.

**Article 5** The socialist system and policies shall not be practised in the Hong Kong Special Administrative Region, and the previous capitalist system and way of life shall remain unchanged for 50 years.

**Article 6** The Hong Kong Special Administrative Region shall protect the right of private ownership of property in accordance with law.

**Article 7** The land and natural resources within the Hong Kong Special Administrative Region shall be State property. The Government of the Hong Kong Special Administrative Region shall be responsible for their management, use and development and for their lease or grant to individuals, legal persons or organizations for use or development. The revenues derived therefrom shall be exclusively at the disposal of the government of the Region.

**Article 8** The laws previously in force in Hong Kong, that is, the common law, rules of equity, ordinances, subordinate legislation and customary law shall be maintained, except for any that contravene this Law, and subject to any amendment by the legislature of the Hong Kong Special Administrative Region.

**Article 9** In addition to the Chinese language, English may also be used as an official language by the executive authorities, legislature and judiciary of the Hong Kong Special Administrative Region.

**Article 10** Apart from displaying the national flag and national emblem of the People's Republic of China, the Hong Kong Special Administrative Region may also use a regional flag and regional emblem.

The regional flag of the Hong Kong Special Administrative Region is a red flag with a bauhinia highlighted by five star-tipped stamens.

The regional emblem of the Hong Kong Special Administrative Region is a bauhinia in the centre highlighted by five star-tipped stamens and encircled by the words 'Hong Kong Special Administrative Region of the People's Republic of China' in Chinese and 'HONG KONG' in English.

**Article 11** In accordance with Article 31 of the Constitution of the People's Republic of China, the systems and policies practised in the Hong Kong Special Administrative Region, including the social and economic systems, the system for safeguarding the fundamental rights and freedoms of its residents, the executive, legislative and judicial systems, and the relevant policies, shall be based on the provisions of this Law.

No law enacted by the legislature of the Hong Kong Special Administrative Region shall contravene this Law.

## CHAPTER II: RELATIONSHIP BETWEEN THE CENTRAL AUTHORITIES AND THE HONG KONG SPECIAL ADMINISTRATIVE REGION

**Article 12** The Hong Kong Special Administrative Region shall be a local administrative region of the People's Republic of China, which shall enjoy a high degree of autonomy and come directly under the Central People's Government.

**Article 13** The Central People's Government shall be responsible for the foreign affairs relating to the Hong Kong Special Administrative Region.

The Ministry of Foreign Affairs of the People's Republic of China shall establish an office in Hong Kong to deal with foreign affairs.

The Central People's Government authorizes the Hong Kong Special Administrative Region to conduct relevant external affairs on its own in accordance with this Law.

**Article 14** The Central People's Government shall be responsible for the defence of the Hong Kong Special Administrative Region.

The Government of the Hong Kong Special Administrative Region shall be responsible for the maintenance of public order in the Region.

Military forces stationed by the Central People's Government in the Hong Kong Special Administrative Region for defence shall not interfere in the local affairs of the Region. The Government of the Hong Kong Special Administrative Region may, when necessary, ask the Central People's Government for assistance from the garrison in the maintenance of public order and in disaster relief.

In addition to abiding by national laws, members of the garrison shall abide by the laws of the Hong Kong Special Administrative Region.

Expenditure for the garrison shall be borne by the Central People's Government.

**Article 15** The Central People's Government shall appoint the Chief Executive and the principal officials of the executive authorities of the Hong Kong Special Administrative Region in accordance with the provisions of Chapter IV of this Law.

**Article 16** The Hong Kong Special Administrative Region shall be vested with executive power. It shall, on its own, conduct the administrative affairs of the Region in accordance with the relevant provisions of this Law.

**Article 17** The Hong Kong Special Administrative Region shall be vested with legislative power.

Laws enacted by the legislature of the Hong Kong Special Administrative Region must be reported to the Standing Committee of the National People's Congress for the record. The reporting for record shall not affect the entry into force of such laws.

If the Standing Committee of the National People's Congress, after consulting the Committee for the Basic Law of the Hong Kong Special Administrative

Region under it, considers that any law enacted by the legislature of the Region is not in conformity with the provisions of this Law regarding affairs within the responsibility of the Central Authorities or regarding the relationship between the Central Authorities and the Region, the Standing Committee may return the law in question but shall not amend it. Any law returned by the Standing Committee of the National People's Congress shall immediately be invalidated. This invalidation shall not have retroactive effect, unless otherwise provided for in the laws of the Region.

**Article 18** The laws in force in the Hong Kong Special Administrative Region shall be this Law, the laws previously in force in Hong Kong as provided for in Article 8 of this Law, and the laws enacted by the legislature of the Region.

National laws shall not be applied in the Hong Kong Special Administrative Region except for those listed in Annex III to this Law. The laws listed therein shall be applied locally by way of promulgation or legislation by the Region.

The Standing Committee of the National People's Congress may add to or delete from the list of laws in Annex III after consulting its Committee for the Basic Law of the Hong Kong Special Administrative Region and the government of the Region. Laws listed in Annex III to this Law shall be confined to those relating to defence and foreign affairs as well as other matters outside the limits of the autonomy of the Region as specified by this Law.

In the event that the Standing Committee of the National People's Congress decides to declare a state of war or, by reason of turmoil within the Hong Kong Special Administrative Region which endangers national unity or security and is beyond the control of the government of the Region, decides that the Region is in a state of emergency, the Central People's Government may issue an order applying the relevant national laws in the Region.

**Article 19** The Hong Kong Special Administrative Region shall be vested with independent judicial power, including that of final adjudication.

The courts of the Hong Kong Special Administrative Region shall have jurisdiction over all cases in the Region, except that the restrictions on their jurisdiction imposed by the legal system and principles previously in force in Hong Kong shall be maintained.

The courts of the Hong Kong Special Administrative Region shall have no jurisdiction over acts of state such as defence and foreign affairs. The courts of the Region shall obtain a certificate from the Chief Executive on questions of fact concerning acts of state such as defence and foreign affairs whenever such questions arise in the adjudication of cases. This certificate shall be binding on the courts. Before issuing such a certificate, the Chief Executive shall obtain a certifying document from the Central People's Government.

**Article 20** The Hong Kong Special Administrative Region may enjoy other powers granted to it by the National People's Congress, the Standing Committee of the National People's Congress or the Central People's Government.

**Article 21** Chinese citizens who are residents of the Hong Kong Special Administrative Region shall be entitled to participate in the management of state affairs according to law.

In accordance with the assigned number of seats and the selection method specified by the National People's Congress, the Chinese citizens among the residents of the Hong Kong Special Administrative Region shall locally elect deputies of the Region to the National People's Congress to participate in the work of the highest organ of state power.

**Article 22** No department of the Central People's Government and no province, autonomous region, or municipality directly under the Central Government may interfere in the affairs which the Hong Kong Special Administrative Region administers on its own in accordance with this Law.

If there is a need for departments of the Central Government, or for provinces, autonomous regions, or municipalities directly under the Central Government to set up offices in the Hong Kong Special Administrative Region, they must obtain the consent of the government of the Region and the approval of the Central People's Government.

All offices set up in the Hong Kong Special Administrative Region by departments of the Central Government, or by provinces, autonomous regions, or municipalities directly under the Central Government, and the personnel of these offices shall abide by the laws of the Region.

For entry into the Hong Kong Special Administrative Region, people from other parts of China must apply for approval. Among them, the number of persons who enter the Region for the purpose of settlement shall be determined by the competent authorities of the Central People's Government after consulting the government of the Region.

The Hong Kong Special Administrative Region may establish an office in Beijing.

**Article 23** The Hong Kong Special Administrative Region shall enact laws on its own to prohibit any act of treason, secession, sedition, subversion against the Central People's Government, or theft of state secrets, to prohibit foreign political organizations or bodies from conducting political activities in the Region, and to prohibit political organizations or bodies of the Region from establishing ties with foreign political organizations or bodies.

**CHAPTER III:** FUNDAMENTAL RIGHTS AND DUTIES OF THE RESIDENTS

**Article 24** Residents of the Hong Kong Special Administrative Region ('Hong Kong residents') shall include permanent residents and non-permanent residents.

The permanent residents of the Hong Kong Special Administrative Region shall be:
(1) Chinese citizens born in Hong Kong before or after the establishment of the Hong Kong Special Administrative Region;
(2) Chinese citizens who have ordinarily resided in Hong Kong for a continuous period of not less than seven years before or after the establishment of the Hong Kong Special Administrative Region;
(3) Persons of Chinese nationality born outside Hong Kong of those residents listed in categories (1) and (2);
(4) Persons not of Chinese nationality who have entered Hong Kong with valid

travel documents, have ordinarily resided in Hong Kong for a continuous period of not less than seven years and have taken Hong Kong as their place of permanent residence before or after the establishment of the Hong Kong Special Administrative Region;

(5) Persons under 21 years of age born in Hong Kong of those residents listed in category (4) before or after the establishment of the Hong Kong Special Administrative Region; and

(6) Persons other than those residents listed in categories (1) to (5), who, before the establishment of the Hong Kong Special Administrative Region, had the right of abode in Hong Kong only.

The above-mentioned residents shall have the right of abode in the Hong Kong Special Administrative Region and shall be qualified to obtain, in accordance with the laws of the Region, permanent identity cards which state their right of abode.

The non-permanent residents of the Hong Kong Special Administrative Region shall be persons who are qualified to obtain Hong Kong identity cards in accordance with the laws of the Region but have no right of abode.

**Article 25**  All Hong Kong residents shall be equal before the law.

**Article 26**  Permanent residents of the Hong Kong Special Administrative Region shall have the right to vote and the right to stand for election in accordance with law.

**Article 27**  Hong Kong residents shall have freedom of speech, of the press and of publication; freedom of association, of assembly, of procession and of demonstration; and the right and freedom to form and join trade unions, and to strike.

**Article 28**  The freedom of the person of Hong Kong residents shall be inviolable.

No Hong Kong resident shall be subjected to arbitrary or unlawful arrest, detention or imprisonment. Arbitrary or unlawful search of the body of any resident or deprivation or restriction of the freedom of the person shall be prohibited. Torture of any resident or arbitrary or unlawful deprivation of the life of any resident shall be prohibited.

**Article 29**  The homes and other premises of Hong Kong residents shall be inviolable. Arbitrary or unlawful search of, or intrusion into, a resident's home or other premises shall be prohibited.

**Article 30**  The freedom and privacy of communication of Hong Kong residents shall be protected by law. No department or individual may, on any grounds, infringe upon the freedom and privacy of communication of residents except that the relevant authorities may inspect communication in accordance with legal procedures to meet the needs of public security or of investigation into criminal offences.

**Article 31**  Hong Kong residents shall have freedom of movement within the Hong Kong Special Administrative Region and freedom of emigration to other countries and regions. They shall have freedom to travel and to enter or leave the

Region. Unless restrained by law, holders of valid travel documents shall be free to leave the Region without special authorization.

**Article 32** Hong Kong residents shall have freedom of conscience.

Hong Kong residents shall have freedom of religious belief and freedom to preach and to conduct and participate in religious activities in public.

**Article 33** Hong Kong residents shall have freedom of choice of occupation.

**Article 34** Hong Kong residents shall have freedom to engage in academic research, literary and artistic creation, and other cultural activities.

**Article 35** Hong Kong residents shall have the right to confidential legal advice, access to the courts, choice of lawyers for timely protection of their lawful rights and interests or for representation in the courts, and to judicial remedies.

Hong Kong residents shall have the right to institute legal proceedings in the courts against the acts of the executive authorities and their personnel.

**Article 36** Hong Kong residents shall have the right to social welfare in accordance with law. The welfare benefits and retirement security of the labour force shall be protected by law.

**Article 37** The freedom of marriage of Hong Kong residents and their right to raise a family freely shall be protected by law.

**Article 38** Hong Kong residents shall enjoy the other rights and freedoms safeguarded by the laws of the Hong Kong Special Administrative Region.

**Article 39** The provisions of the International Covenant on Civil and Political Rights, the International Covenant on Economic, Social and Cultural Rights, and international labour conventions as applied to Hong Kong shall remain in force and shall be implemented through the laws of the Hong Kong Special Administrative Region.

The rights and freedoms enjoyed by Hong Kong residents shall not be restricted unless as prescribed by law. Such restrictions shall not contravene the provisions of the preceding paragraph of this Article.

**Article 40** The lawful traditional rights and interests of the indigenous inhabitants of the 'New Territories' shall be protected by the Hong Kong Special Administrative Region.

**Article 41** Persons in the Hong Kong Special Administrative Region other than Hong Kong residents shall, in accordance with law, enjoy the rights and freedoms of Hong Kong residents prescribed in this Chapter.

**Article 42** Hong Kong residents and other persons in Hong Kong shall have the obligation to abide by the laws in force in the Hong Kong Special Administrative Region.

**CHAPTER IV:** POLITICAL STRUCTURE

**Section 1: The Chief Executive**
**Article 43** The Chief Executive of the Hong Kong Special Administrative

Region shall be the head of the Hong Kong Special Administrative Region and shall represent the Region.

The Chief Executive of the Hong Kong Special Administrative Region shall be accountable to the Central People's Government and the Hong Kong Special Administrative Region in accordance with the provisions of this Law.

**Article 44** The Chief Executive of the Hong Kong Special Administrative Region shall be a Chinese citizen of not less than 40 years of age who is a permanent resident of the Region with no right of abode in any foreign country and has ordinarily resided in Hong Kong for a continuous period of not less than 20 years.

**Article 45** The Chief Executive of the Hong Kong Special Administrative Region shall be selected by election or through consultations held locally and be appointed by the Central People's Government.

The method for selecting the Chief Executive shall be specified in the light of the actual situation in the Hong Kong Special Administrative Region and in accordance with the principle of gradual and orderly progress. The ultimate aim is the selection of the Chief Executive by universal suffrage upon nomination by a broadly representative nominating committee in accordance with democratic procedures.

The specific method for selecting the Chief Executive is prescribed in Annex I: 'Method for the Selection of the Chief Executive of the Hong Kong Special Administrative Region'.

**Article 46** The term of office of the Chief Executive of the Hong Kong Special Administrative Region shall be five years. He or she may serve for not more than two consecutive terms.

**Article 47** The Chief Executive of the Hong Kong Special Administrative Region must be a person of integrity, dedicated to his or her duties.

The Chief Executive, on assuming office, shall declare his or her assets to the Chief Justice of the Court of Final Appeal of the Hong Kong Special Administrative Region. This declaration shall be put on record.

**Article 48** The Chief Executive of the Hong Kong Special Administrative Region shall exercise the following powers and functions:
  (1) To lead the government of the Region;
  (2) To be responsible for the implementation of this Law and other laws which, in accordance with this Law, apply in the Hong Kong Special Administrative Region;
  (3) To sign bills passed by the Legislative Council and to promulgate laws; To sign budgets passed by the Legislative Council and report the budgets and final accounts to the Central People's Government for the record;
  (4) To decide on government policies and to issue executive orders;
  (5) To nominate and to report to the Central People's Government for appointment the following principal officials: Secretaries and Deputy Secretaries of Departments, Directors of Bureaux, Commissioner Against Corruption, Director of Audit, Commissioner of Police, Director of Immigration and Commissioner of Customs and Excise; and to recommend

to the Central People's Government the removal of the above mentioned officials;

(6) To appoint or remove judges of the courts at all levels in accordance with legal procedures;

(7) To appoint or remove holders of public office in accordance with legal procedures;

(8) To implement the directives issued by the Central People's Government in respect of the relevant matters provided for in this Law;

(9) To conduct, on behalf of the Government of the Hong Kong Special Administrative Region, external affairs and other affairs as authorized by the Central Authorities;

(10) To approve the introduction of motions regarding revenues or expenditure to the Legislative Council;

(11) To decide, in the light of security and vital public interests, whether government officials or other personnel in charge of government affairs should testify or give evidence before the Legislative Council or its committees;

(12) To pardon persons convicted of criminal offences or commute their penalties; and

(13) To handle petitions and complaints.

**Article 49** If the Chief Executive of the Hong Kong Special Administrative Region considers that a bill passed by the Legislative Council is not compatible with the overall interests of the Region, he or she may return it to the Legislative Council within three months for reconsideration. If the Legislative Council passes the original bill again by not less than a two-thirds majority of all the members, the Chief Executive must sign and promulgate it within one month, or act in accordance with the provisions of Article 50 of this Law.

**Article 50** If the Chief Executive of the Hong Kong Special Administrative Region refuses to sign a bill passed the second time by the Legislative Council, or the Legislative Council refuses to pass a budget or any other important bill introduced by the government, and if consensus still cannot be reached after consultations, the Chief Executive may dissolve the Legislative Council.

The Chief Executive must consult the Executive Council before dissolving the Legislative Council. The Chief Executive may dissolve the Legislative Council only once in each term of his or her office.

**Article 51** If the Legislative Council of the Hong Kong Special Administrative Region refuses to pass the budget introduced by the government, the Chief Executive may apply to the Legislative Council for provisional appropriations. If appropriation of public funds cannot be approved because the Legislative Council has already been dissolved, the Chief Executive may, prior to the election of the new Legislative Council, approve provisional short-term appropriations according to the level of expenditure of the previous fiscal year.

**Article 52** The Chief Executive of the Hong Kong Special Administrative Region must resign under any of the following circumstances:

(1) When he or she loses the ability to discharge his or her duties as a result of serious illness or other reasons;

(2) When, after the Legislative Council is dissolved because he or she twice refuses to sign a bill passed by it, the new Legislative Council again passes by a two-thirds majority of all the members the original bill in dispute, but he or she still refuses to sign it; and

(3) When, after the Legislative Council is dissolved because it refuses to pass a budget or any other important bill, the new Legislative Council still refuses to pass the original bill in dispute.

**Article 53** If the Chief Executive of the Hong Kong Special Administrative Region is not able to discharge his or her duties for a short period, such duties shall temporarily be assumed by the Administrative Secretary, Financial Secretary or Secretary of Justice in this order of precedence.

In the event that the office of Chief Executive becomes vacant, a new Chief Executive shall be selected within six months in accordance with the provisions of Article 45 of this Law. During the period of vacancy, his or her duties shall be assumed according to the provisions of the preceding paragraph.

**Article 54** The Executive Council of the Hong Kong Special Administrative Region shall be an organ for assisting the Chief Executive in policy-making.

**Article 55** Members of the Executive Council of the Hong Kong Special Administrative Region shall be appointed by the Chief Executive from among the principal officials of the executive authorities, members of the Legislative Council and public figures. Their appointment or removal shall be decided by the Chief Executive. The term of office of members of the Executive Council shall not extend beyond the expiry of the term of office of the Chief Executive who appoints them.

Members of the Executive Council of the Hong Kong Special Administrative Region shall be Chinese citizens who are permanent residents of the Region with no right of abode in any foreign country.

The Chief Executive may, as he or she deems necessary, invite other persons concerned to sit in on meetings of the Council.

**Article 56** The Executive Council of the Hong Kong Special Administrative Region shall be presided over by the Chief Executive.

Except for the appointment, removal and disciplining of officials and the adoption of measures in emergencies, the Chief Executive shall consult the Executive Council before making important policy decisions, introducing bills to the Legislative Council, making subordinate legislation, or dissolving the Legislative Council.

If the Chief Executive does not accept a majority opinion of the Executive Council, he or she shall put the specific reasons on record.

**Article 57** A Commission Against Corruption shall be established in the Hong Kong Special Administrative Region. It shall function independently and be accountable to the Chief Executive.

**Article 58** A Commission of Audit shall be established in the Hong Kong Special Administrative Region. It shall function independently and be accountable to the Chief Executive.

**Section 2: The Executive Authorities**
**Article 59** The Government of the Hong Kong Special Administrative Region shall be the executive authorities of the Region.

**Article 60** The head of the Government of the Hong Kong Special Administrative Region shall be the Chief Executive of the Region.

A Department of Administration, a Department of Finance, a Department of Justice, and various bureaux, divisions and commissions shall be established in the Government of the Hong Kong Special Administrative Region.

**Article 61** The principal officials of the Hong Kong Special Administrative Region shall be Chinese citizens who are permanent residents of the Region with no right of abode in any foreign country and have ordinarily resided in Hong Kong for a continuous period of not less than 15 years.

**Article 62** The Government of the Hong Kong Special Administrative Region shall exercise the following powers and functions:
(1) To formulate and implement policies;
(2) To conduct administrative affairs;
(3) To conduct external affairs as authorized by the Central People's Government under this Law;
(4) To draw up and introduce budgets and final accounts;
(5) To draft and introduce bills, motions and subordinate legislation; and
(6) To designate officials to sit in on the meetings of the Legislative Council and to speak on behalf of the government.

**Article 63** The Department of Justice of the Hong Kong Special Administrative Region shall control criminal prosecutions, free from any interference.

**Article 64** The Government of the Hong Kong Special Administrative Region must abide by the law and be accountable to the Legislative Council of the Region: it shall implement laws passed by the Council and already in force; it shall present regular policy addresses to the Council; it shall answer questions raised by members of the Council; and it shall obtain approval from the Council for taxation and public expenditure.

**Article 65** The previous system of establishing advisory bodies by the executive authorities shall be maintained.

**Section 3: The Legislature**
**Article 66** The Legislative Council of the Hong Kong Special Administrative Region shall be the legislature of the Region.

**Article 67** The Legislative Council of the Hong Kong Special Administrative Region shall be composed of Chinese citizens who are permanent residents of the Region with no right of abode in any foreign country. However, permanent residents of the Region who are not of Chinese nationality or who have the right of abode in foreign countries may also be elected members of the Legislative Council of the Region, provided that the proportion of such members does not exceed 20 per cent of the total membership of the Council.

**Article 68** The Legislative Council of the Hong Kong Special Administrative Region shall be constituted by election.

The method for forming the Legislative Council shall be specified in the light of the actual situation in the Hong Kong Special Administrative Region and in accordance with the principle of gradual and orderly progress. The ultimate aim is the election of all the members of the Legislative Council by universal suffrage.

The specific method for forming the Legislative Council and its procedures for voting on bills and motions are prescribed in Annex II: 'Method for the Formation of the Legislative Council of the Hong Kong Special Administrative Region and Its Voting Procedures'.

**Article 69** The term of office of the Legislative Council of the Hong Kong Special Administrative Region shall be four years, except the first term which shall be two years.

**Article 70** If the Legislative Council of the Hong Kong Special Administrative Region is dissolved by the Chief Executive in accordance with the provisions of this Law, it must, within three months, be reconstituted by election in accordance with Article 68 of this Law.

**Article 71** The President of the Legislative Council of the Hong Kong Special Administrative Region shall be elected by and from among the members of the Legislative Council.

The President of the Legislative Council of the Hong Kong Special Administrative Region shall be a Chinese citizen of not less than 40 years of age. who is a permanent resident of the Region with no right of abode in any foreign country and has ordinarily resided in Hong Kong for a continuous period of not less than 20 years.

**Article 72** The President of the Legislative Council of the Hong Kong Special Administrative Region shall exercise the following powers and functions:
(1) To preside over meetings;
(2) To decide on the agenda, giving priority to government bills for inclusion in the agenda;
(3) To decide on the time of meetings;
(4) To call special sessions during the recess;
(5) To call emergency sessions on the request of the Chief Executive; and
(6) To exercise other powers and functions as prescribed in the rules of procedure of the Legislative Council.

**Article 73** The Legislative Council of the Hong Kong Special Administrative Region shall exercise the following powers and functions:
(1) To enact, amend or repeal laws in accordance with the provisions of this Law and legal procedures;
(2) To examine and approve budgets introduced by the government;
(3) To approve taxation and public expenditure;
(4) To receive and debate the policy addresses of the Chief Executive;
(5) To raise questions on the work of the government;
(6) To debate any issue concerning public interests;

(7) To endorse the appointment and removal of the judges of the Court of Final Appeal and the Chief Judge of the High Court;

(8) To receive and handle complaints from Hong Kong residents;

(9) If a motion initiated jointly by one-fourth of all the members of the Legislative Council charges the Chief Executive with serious breach of law or dereliction of duty and if he or she refuses to resign, the Council may, after passing a motion for investigation, give a mandate to the Chief Justice of the Court of Final Appeal to form and chair an independent investigation committee. The committee shall be responsible for carrying out the investigation and reporting its findings to the Council. If the committee considers the evidence sufficient to substantiate such charges, the Council may pass a motion of impeachment by a two-thirds majority of all its members and report it to the Central People's Government for decision; and

(10) To summon, as required when exercising the above-mentioned powers and functions, persons concerned to testify or give evidence.

**Article 74** Members of the Legislative Council of the Hong Kong Special Administrative Region may introduce bills in accordance with the provisions of this Law and legal procedures. Bills which do not relate to public expenditure or political structure or the operation of the government may be introduced individually or jointly by members of the Council. The written consent of the Chief Executive shall be required before bills relating to government policies are introduced.

**Article 75** The quorum for the meeting of the Legislative Council of the Hong Kong Special Administrative Region shall be not less than one half of all its members.

The rules of procedure of the Legislative Council shall be made by the Council on its own, provided that they do not contravene this Law.

**Article 76** A bill passed by the Legislative Council of the Hong Kong Special Administrative Region may take effect only after it is signed and promulgated by the Chief Executive.

**Article 77** Members of the Legislative Council of the Hong Kong Special Administrative Region shall be immune from legal action in respect of their statements at meetings of the Council.

**Article 78** Members of the Legislative Council of the Hong Kong Special Administrative Region shall not be subjected to arrest when attending or on their way to a meeting of the Council.

**Article 79** The President of the Legislative Council of the Hong Kong Special Administrative Region shall declare that a member of the Council is no longer qualified for the office under any of the following circumstances:

(1) When he or she loses the ability to discharge his or her duties as a result of serious illness or other reasons;

(2) When he or she, with no valid reason, is absent from meetings for three consecutive months without the consent of the President of the Legislative Council;

(3) When he or she loses or renounces his or her status as a permanent resident of the Region;

(4) When he or she accepts a government appointment and becomes a public servant;

(5) When he or she is bankrupt or fails to comply with a court order to repay debts;

(6) When he or she is convicted and sentenced to imprisonment for one month or more for a criminal offence committed within or outside the Region and is relieved of his or her duties by a motion passed by two-thirds of the members of the Legislative Council present; and

(7) When he or she is censured for misbehaviour or breach of oath by a vote of two-thirds of the members of the Legislative Council present.

## Section 4: The Judiciary

**Article 80** The courts of the Hong Kong Special Administrative Region at all levels shall be the judiciary of the Region, exercising the judicial power of the Region.

**Article 81** The Court of Final Appeal, the High Court, district courts, magistrates' courts and other special courts shall be established in the Hong Kong Special Administrative Region. The High Court shall comprise the Court of Appeal and the Court of First Instance.

The judicial system previously practised in Hong Kong shall be maintained except for those changes consequent upon the establishment of the Court of Final Appeal of the Hong Kong Special Administrative Region.

**Article 82** The power of final adjudication of the Hong Kong Special Administrative Region shall be vested in the Court of Final Appeal of the Region, which may as required invite judges from other common law jurisdictions to sit on the Court of Final Appeal.

**Article 83** The structure, powers and functions of the courts of the Hong Kong Special Administrative Region at all levels shall be prescribed by law.

**Article 84** The courts of the Hong Kong Special Administrative Region shall adjudicate cases in accordance with the laws applicable in the Region as prescribed in Article 18 of this Law and may refer to precedents of other common law jurisdictions.

**Article 85** The courts of the Hong Kong Special Administrative Region shall exercise judicial power independently, free from any interference. Members of the judiciary shall be immune from legal action in the performance of their judicial functions.

**Article 86** The principle of trial by jury previously practised in Hong Kong shall be maintained.

**Article 87** In criminal or civil proceedings in the Hong Kong Special Administrative Region, the principles previously applied in Hong Kong and the rights previously enjoyed by parties to proceedings shall be maintained.

Anyone who is lawfully arrested shall have the right to a fair trial by the judicial organs without delay and shall be presumed innocent until convicted by the judicial organs.

**Article 88** Judges of the courts of the Hong Kong Special Administrative Region shall be appointed by the Chief Executive on the recommendation of an independent commission composed of local judges, persons from the legal profession and eminent persons from other sectors.

**Article 89** A judge of a court of the Hong Kong Special Administrative Region may only be removed for inability to discharge his or her duties, or for misbehaviour, by the Chief Executive on the recommendation of a tribunal appointed by the Chief Justice of the Court of Final Appeal and consisting of not fewer than three local judges.

The Chief Justice of the Court of Final Appeal of the Hong Kong Special Administrative Region may be investigated only for inability to discharge his or her duties, or for misbehaviour, by a tribunal appointed by the Chief Executive and consisting of not fewer than five local judges and may be removed by the Chief Executive on the recommendation of the tribunal and in accordance with the procedures prescribed in this Law.

**Article 90** The Chief Justice of the Court of Final Appeal and the Chief Judge of the High Court of the Hong Kong Special Administrative Region shall be Chinese citizens who are permanent residents of the Region with no right of abode in any foreign country.

In the case of the appointment or removal of judges of the Court of Final Appeal and the Chief Judge of the High Court of the Hong Kong Special Administrative Region, the Chief Executive shall, in addition to following the procedures prescribed in Articles 88 and 89 of this Law, obtain the endorsement of the Legislative Council and report such appointment or removal to the Standing Committee of the National People's Congress for the record.

**Article 91** The Hong Kong Special Administrative Region shall maintain the previous system of appointment and removal of members of the judiciary other than judges.

**Article 92** Judges and other members of the judiciary of the Hong Kong Special Administrative Region shall be chosen on the basis of their judicial and professional qualities and may be recruited from other common law jurisdictions.

**Article 93** Judges and other members of the judiciary serving in Hong Kong before the establishment of the Hong Kong Special Administrative Region may all remain in employment and retain their seniority with pay, allowances, benefits and conditions of service no less favourable than before.

The Government of the Hong Kong Special Administrative Region shall pay to judges and other members of the judiciary who retire or leave the service in compliance with regulations, including those who have retired or left the service before the establishment of the Hong Kong Special Administrative Region, or to their dependants, all pensions, gratuities, allowances and benefits due to them on terms no less favourable than before, irrespective of their nationality or place of residence.

**Article 94** On the basis of the system previously operating in Hong Kong, the Government of the Hong Kong Special Administrative Region may make provisions for local lawyers and lawyers from outside Hong Kong to work and practise in the Region.

**Article 95** The Hong Kong Special Administrative Region may, through consultations and in accordance with law, maintain juridical relations with the judicial organs of other parts of the country, and they may render assistance to each other.

**Article 96** With the assistance or authorization of the Central People's Government, the Government of the Hong Kong Special Administrative Region may make appropriate arrangements with foreign states for reciprocal juridical assistance.

### Section 5: District Organizations
**Article 97** District organizations which are not organs of political power may be established in the Hong Kong Special Administrative Region, to be consulted by the government of the Region on district administration and other affairs, or to be responsible for providing services in such fields as culture, recreation and environmental sanitation.

**Article 98** The powers and functions of the district organizations and the method for their formation shall be prescribed by law.

### Section 6: Public Servants
**Article 99** Public servants serving in all government departments of the Hong Kong Special Administrative Region must be permanent residents of the Region, except where otherwise provided for in Article 101 of this Law regarding public servants of foreign nationalities and except for those below a certain rank as prescribed by law.

Public servants must be dedicated to their duties and be responsible to the Government of the Hong Kong Special Administrative Region.

**Article 100** Public servants serving in all Hong Kong government departments, including the police department, before the establishment of the Hong Kong Special Administrative Region, may all remain in employment and retain their seniority with pay, allowances, benefits and conditions of service no less favourable than before.

**Article 101** The Government of the Hong Kong Special Administrative Region may employ British and other foreign nationals previously serving in the public service in Hong Kong, or those holding permanent identity cards of the Region, to serve as public servants in government departments at all levels, but only Chinese citizens among permanent residents of the Region with no right of abode in any foreign country may fill the following posts: the Secretaries and Deputy Secretaries of Departments, Directors of Bureaux, Commissioner Against Corruption, Director of Audit, Commissioner of Police, Director of Immigration and Commissioner of Customs and Excise.

The Government of the Hong Kong Special Administrative Region may also employ British and other foreign nationals as advisers to government departments and, when required, may recruit qualified candidates from outside the Region to fill professional and technical posts in government departments. These foreign nationals shall be employed only in their individual capacities and shall be responsible to the government of the Region.

**Article 102** The Government of the Hong Kong Special Administrative Region shall pay to public servants who retire or who leave the service in compliance with regulations, including those who have retired or who have left the service in compliance with regulations before the establishment of the Hong Kong Special Administrative Region, or to their dependants, all pensions, gratuities, allowances and benefits due to them on terms no less favourable than before, irrespective of their nationality or place of residence.

**Article 103** The appointment and promotion of public servants shall be on the basis of their qualifications, experience and ability. Hong Kong's previous system of recruitment, employment, assessment, discipline, training and management for the public service, including special bodies for their appointment, pay and conditions of service, shall be maintained, except for any provisions for privileged treatment of foreign nationals.

**Article 104** When assuming office, the Chief Executive, principal officials, members of the Executive Council and of the Legislative Council, judges of the courts at all levels and other members of the judiciary in the Hong Kong Special Administrative Region must, in accordance with law, swear to uphold the Basic Law of the Hong Kong Special Administrative Region of the People's Republic of China and swear allegiance to the Hong Kong Special Administrative Region of the People's Republic of China.

CHAPTER V: ECONOMY

### Section 1: Public Finance, Monetary Affairs, Trade, Industry and Commerce

**Article 105** The Hong Kong Special Administrative Region shall, in accordance with law, protect the right of individuals and legal persons to the acquisition, use, disposal and inheritance of property and their right to compensation for lawful deprivation of their property.

Such compensation shall correspond to the real value of the property concerned at the time and shall be freely convertible and paid without undue delay.

The ownership of enterprises and the investments from outside the Region shall be protected by law.

**Article 106** The Hong Kong Special Administrative Region shall have independent finances.

The Hong Kong Special Administrative Region shall use its financial revenues exclusively for its own purposes, and they shall not be handed over to the Central People's Government.

The Central People's Government shall not levy taxes in the Hong Kong Special Administrative Region.

**Article 107** The Hong Kong Special Administrative Region shall follow the principle of keeping expenditure within the limits of revenues in drawing up its budget, and strive to achieve a fiscal balance, avoid deficits and keep the budget commensurate with the growth rate of its gross domestic product.

**Article 108** The Hong Kong Special Administrative Region shall practise an independent taxation system.

The Hong Kong Special Administrative Region shall, taking the low tax policy previously pursued in Hong Kong as reference, enact laws on its own concerning types of taxes, tax rates, tax reductions, allowances and exemptions, and other matters of taxation.

**Article 109** The Government of the Hong Kong Special Administrative Region shall provide an appropriate economic and legal environment for the maintenance of the status of Hong Kong as an international financial centre.

**Article 110** The monetary and financial systems of the Hong Kong Special Administrative Region shall be prescribed by law.

The Government of the Hong Kong Special Administrative Region shall, on its own, formulate monetary and financial policies, safeguard the free operation of financial business and financial markets, and regulate and supervise them in accordance with law.

**Article 111** The Hong Kong dollar, as the legal tender in the Hong Kong Special Administrative Region, shall continue to circulate.

The authority to issue Hong Kong currency shall be vested in the Government of the Hong Kong Special Administrative Region. The issue of Hong Kong currency must be backed by a 100 per cent reserve fund. The system regarding the issue of Hong Kong currency and the reserve fund system shall be prescribed by law.

The Government of the Hong Kong Special Administrative Region may authorize designated banks to issue or continue to issue Hong Kong currency under statutory authority, after satisfying itself that any issue of currency will be soundly based and that the arrangements for such issue are consistent with the object of maintaining the stability of the currency.

**Article 112** No foreign exchange control policies shall be applied in the Hong Kong Special Administrative Region. The Hong Kong dollar shall be freely convertible. Markets for foreign exchange, gold, securities, futures and the like shall continue .

The Government of the Hong Kong Special Administrative Region shall safeguard the free flow of capital within, into and out of the Region.

**Article 113** The Exchange Fund of the Hong Kong Special Administrative Region shall be managed and controlled by the government of the Region, primarily for regulating the exchange value of the Hong Kong dollar.

**Article 114** The Hong Kong Special Administrative Region shall maintain the status of a free port and shall not impose any tariff unless otherwise prescribed by law.

**Article 115** The Hong Kong Special Administrative Region shall pursue the policy of free trade and safeguard the free movement of goods, intangible assets and capital.

**Article 116** The Hong Kong Special Administrative Region shall be a separate customs territory.

The Hong Kong Special Administrative Region may, using the name 'Hong Kong, China', participate in relevant international organizations and international trade agreements (including preferential trade arrangements), such as the General Agreement on Tariffs and Trade and arrangements regarding international trade in textiles.

Export quotas, tariff preferences and other similar arrangements, which are obtained or made by the Hong Kong Special Administrative Region or which were obtained or made and remain valid, shall be enjoyed exclusively by the Region.

**Article 117** The Hong Kong Special Administrative Region may issue its own certificates of origin for products in accordance with prevailing rules of origin.

**Article 118** The Government of the Hong Kong Special Administrative Region shall provide an economic and legal environment for encouraging investments, technological progress and the development of new industries.

**Article 119** The Government of the Hong Kong Special Administrative Region shall formulate appropriate policies to promote and co-ordinate the development of various trades such as manufacturing, commerce, tourism, real estate. transport, public utilities, services, agriculture and fisheries, and pay regard to the protection of the environment.

**Section 2: Land Leases**
**Article 120** All leases of land granted, decided upon or renewed before the establishment of the Hong Kong Special Administrative Region which extend beyond 30 June 1997, and all rights in relation to such leases, shall continue to be recognized and protected under the law of the Region.

**Article 121** As regards all leases of land granted or renewed where the original leases contain no right of renewal, during the period from 27 May 1985 to 30 June 1997, which extend beyond 30 June 1997 and expire not later than 30 June 2047, the lessee is not required to pay an additional premium as from 1 July 1997, but an annual rent equivalent to 3 per cent of the rateable value of the property at that date, adjusted in step with any changes in the rateable value thereafter, shall be charged.

**Article 122** In the case or old schedule lots, village lots, small houses and similar rural holdings, where the property was on 30 June 1984 held by. or, in the case of small houses granted after that date, where the property is granted to, a lessee descended through the male line from a person who was in 1898 a resident of an established village in Hong Kong, the previous rent shall remain unchanged so long as the property is held by that lessee or by one of his lawful successors in the male line.

**Article 123** Where leases of land without a right of renewal expire after the establishment of the Hong Kong Special Administrative Region, they shall be dealt with in accordance with laws and policies formulated by the Region on its own.

### Section 3: Shipping
**Article 124** The Hong Kong Special Administrative Region shall maintain Hong Kong's previous systems of shipping management and shipping regulation, including the system for regulating conditions of seamen.

The Government of the Hong Kong Special Administrative Region shall, on its own, define its specific functions and responsibilities in respect of shipping.

**Article 125** The Hong Kong Special Administrative Region shall be authorized by the Central People's Government to continue to maintain a shipping register and issue related certificates under its legislation, using the name 'Hong Kong, China'.

**Article 126** With the exception of foreign warships, access for which requires the special permission of the Central People's Government, ships shall enjoy access to the ports of the Hong Kong Special Administrative Region in accordance with the laws of the Region.

**Article 127** Private shipping businesses and shipping-related businesses and private container terminals in the Hong Kong Special Administrative Region may continue to operate freely.

### Section 4: Civil Aviation
**Article 128** The Government of the Hong Kong Special Administrative Region shall provide conditions and take measures for the maintenance of the status of Hong Kong as a centre of international and regional aviation.

**Article 129** The Hong Kong Special Administrative Region shall continue the previous system of civil aviation management in Hong Kong and keep its own aircraft register in accordance with provisions laid down by the Central People's Government concerning nationality marks and registration marks of aircraft.

Access of foreign state aircraft to the Hong Kong Special Administrative Region shall require the special permission of the Central People's Government.

**Article 130** The Hong Kong Special Administrative Region shall be responsible on its own for matters of routine business and technical management of civil aviation, including the management of airports, the provision of air traffic services within the flight information region of the Hong Kong Special Administrative Region, and the discharge of other responsibilities allocated to it under the regional air navigation procedures of the International Civil Aviation Organization.

**Article 131** The Central People's Government shall, in consultation with the Government of the Hong Kong Special Administrative Region, make arrangements providing air services between the Region and other parts of the People's Republic of China for airlines incorporated in the Hong Kong Special Administrative Region and having their principal place of business in Hong Kong and other airlines of the People's Republic of China.

**Article 132** All air service agreements providing air services between other parts of the People's Republic of China and other states and regions with stops at the Hong Kong Special Administrative Region and air services between the Hong Kong Special Administrative Region and other states and regions with stops at other parts of the People's Republic of China shall be concluded by the Central People's Government.

In concluding the air service agreements referred to in the first paragraph of this Article, the Central People's Government shall take account of the special conditions and economic interests of the Hong Kong Special Administrative Region and consult the government of the Region.

Representatives of the Government of the Hong Kong Special Administrative Region may, as members of the delegations of the Government of the People's Republic of China, participate in air service consultations conducted by the Central People's Government with foreign governments concerning arrangements for such services referred to in the first paragraph of this Article.

**Article 133** Acting under specific authorizations from the Central People's Government, the Government of the Hong Kong Special Administrative Region may:
(1) renew or amend air service agreements and arrangements previously in force;
(2) negotiate and conclude new air service agreements providing routes for air lines incorporated in the Hong Kong Special Administrative Region and having their principal place of business in Hong Kong and providing rights for over-flights and technical stops; and
(3) negotiate and conclude provisional arrangements with foreign states or regions with which no air service agreements have been concluded.

All scheduled air services to, from or through Hong Kong, which do not operate to, from or through the mainland of China shall be regulated by the air service agreements or provisional arrangements referred to in this Article.

**Article 134** The Central People's Government shall give the Government of the Hong Kong Special Administrative Region the authority to:
(1) negotiate and conclude with other authorities all arrangements concerning the implementation of the air service agreements and provisional arrangements referred to in Article 133 of this Law;
(2) issue licences to airlines incorporated in the Hong Kong Special Administrative Region and having their principal place of business in Hong Kong;
(3) designate such airlines under the air service agreements and provisiona arrangements referred to in Article 133 of this Law; and
(4) issue permits to foreign airlines for services other than those to, from or through the mainland of China.

**Article 135** Airlines incorporated and having their principal place of business in

Hong Kong and businesses related to civil aviation functioning there prior to the establishment of the Hong Kong Special Administrative Region may continue to operate.

## CHAPTER VI: EDUCATION, SCIENCE, CULTURE, SPORTS, RELIGION, LABOUR AND SOCIAL SERVICES

**Article 136** On the basis of the previous educational system, the Government of the Hong Kong Special Administrative Region shall, on its own, formulate policies on the development and improvement of education, including policies regarding the educational system and its administration, the language of instruction, the allocation of funds, the examination system, the system of academic awards and the recognition of educational qualifications.

Community organizations and individuals may, in accordance with law, run educational undertakings of various kinds in the Hong Kong Special Administrative Region.

**Article 137** Educational institutions of all kinds may retain their autonomy and enjoy academic freedom. They may continue to recruit staff and use teaching materials from outside the Hong Kong Special Administrative Region. Schools run by religious organizations may continue to provide religious education, including courses in religion.

Students shall enjoy freedom of choice of educational institutions and freedom to pursue their education outside the Hong Kong Special Administrative Region.

**Article 138** The Government of the Hong Kong Special Administrative Region shall, on its own, formulate policies to develop Western and traditional Chinese medicine and to improve medical and health services. Community organizations and individuals may provide various medical and health services in accordance with law.

**Article 139** The Government of the Hong Kong Special Administrative Region shall, on its own, formulate policies on science and technology and protect by law achievements in scientific and technological research, patents, discoveries and inventions.

The Government of the Hong Kong Special Administrative Region shall, on its own, decide on the scientific and technological standards and specifications applicable in Hong Kong.

**Article 140** The Government of the Hong Kong Special Administrative Region shall, on its own, formulate policies on culture and protect by law the achievements and the lawful rights and interests of authors in their literary and artistic creation.

**Article 141** The Government of the Hong Kong Special Administrative Region shall not restrict the freedom of religious belief, interfere in the internal affairs of religious organizations or restrict religious activities which do not contravene the laws of the Region.

Religious organizations shall, in accordance with law, enjoy the rights to acquire, use, dispose of and inherit property and the right to receive financial assistance. Their previous property rights and interests shall be maintained and protected.

Religious organizations may, according to their previous practice, continue to run seminaries and other schools, hospitals and welfare institutions and to provide other social services.

Religious organizations and believers in the Hong Kong Special Administrative Region may maintain and develop their relations with religious organizations and believers elsewhere.

**Article 142** The Government of the Hong Kong Special Administrative Region shall, on the basis of maintaining the previous systems concerning the professions, formulate provisions on its own for assessing the qualifications for practice in the various professions.

Persons with professional qualifications or qualifications for professional practice obtained prior to the establishment of the Hong Kong Special Administrative Region may retain their previous qualifications in accordance with the relevant regulations and codes of practice.

The Government of the Hong Kong Special Administrative Region shall continue to recognize the professions and the professional organizations recognized prior to the establishment of the Region, and these organizations may, on their own, assess and confer professional qualifications.

The Government of the Hong Kong Special Administrative Region may, as required by developments in society and in consultation with the parties concerned, recognize new professions and professional organizations.

**Article 143** The Government of the Hong Kong Special Administrative Region shall, on its own, formulate policies on sports. Non-governmental sports organizations may continue to exist and develop in accordance with law.

**Article 144** The Government of the Hong Kong Special Administrative Region shall maintain the policy previously practised in Hong Kong in respect of subventions for non-governmental organizations in fields such as education, medicine and health, culture, art, recreation, sports, social welfare and social work. Staff members previously serving in subvented organizations in Hong Kong may remain in their employment in accordance with the previous system.

**Article 145** On the basis of the previous social welfare system, the Government of the Hong Kong Special Administrative Region shall, on its own, formulate policies on the development and improvement of this system in the light of the economic conditions and social needs.

**Article 146** Voluntary organizations providing social services in the Hong Kong Special Administrative Region may, on their own, decide their forms of service, provided that the law is not contravened.

**Article 147** The Hong Kong Special Administrative Region shall on its own formulate laws and policies relating to labour.

**Article 148** The relationship between non-governmental organizations in fields such as education, science, technology, culture, art, sports, the professions, medicine and health, labour, social welfare and social work as well as religious organizations in the Hong Kong Special Administrative Region and their counterparts on the mainland shall be based on the principles of non subordination, non-interference and mutual respect.

**Article 149** Non-governmental organizations in fields such as education, science, technology, culture, art, sports, the professions, medicine and health, labour, social welfare and social work as well as religious organizations in the Hong Kong Special Administrative Region may maintain and develop relations with their counterparts in foreign countries and regions and with relevant international organizations. They may, as required, use the name 'Hong Kong, China' in the relevant activities.

## CHAPTER VII: EXTERNAL AFFAIRS

**Article 150** Representatives of the Government of the Hong Kong Special Administrative Region may, as members of delegations of the Government of the People's Republic of China, participate in negotiations at the diplomatic level directly affecting the Region conducted by the Central People's Government.

**Article 151** The Hong Kong Special Administrative Region may on its own, using the name 'Hong Kong, China', maintain and develop relations and conclude and implement agreements with foreign states and regions and relevant international organizations in the appropriate fields, including the economic, trade, financial and monetary, shipping, communications, tourism, cultural and sports fields.

**Article 152** Representatives of the Government of the Hong Kong Special Administrative Region may, as members of delegations of the People's Republic of China, participate in international organizations or conferences in appropriate fields limited to states and affecting the Region, or may attend in such other capacity as may be permitted by the Central People's Government and the international organization or conference concerned, and may express their views, using the name 'Hong Kong, China'. The Hong Kong Special Administrative Region may, using the name 'Hong Kong, China', participate in international organizations and conferences not limited to states.

The Central People's Government shall take the necessary steps to ensure that the Hong Kong Special Administrative Region shall continue to retain its status in an appropriate capacity in those international organizations of which the People's Republic of China is a member and in which Hong Kong participates in one capacity or another.

The Central People's Government shall, where necessary, facilitate the continued participation of the Hong Kong Special Administrative Region in an appropriate capacity in those international organizations in which Hong Kong is a participant in one capacity or another, but of which the People's Republic of China is not a member.

**Article 153** The application to the Hong Kong Special Administrative Region of international agreements to which the People's Republic of China is or becomes a party shall be decided by the Central People's Government, in accordance with the circumstances and needs of the Region, and after seeking the views of the government of the Region.

International agreements to which the People's Republic of China is not a party but which are implemented in Hong Kong may continue to be implemented in the Hong Kong Special Administrative Region. The Central People's Government shall, as necessary, authorize or assist the government of the Region to make appropriate arrangements for the application to the Region of other relevant international agreements.

**Article 154** The Central People's Government shall authorize the Government of the Hong Kong Special Administrative Region to issue, in accordance with law, passports of the Hong Kong Special Administrative Region of the People's Republic of China to all Chinese citizens who hold permanent identity cards of the Region, and travel documents of the Hong Kong Special Administrative Region of the People's Republic of China to all other persons lawfully residing in the Region. The above passports and documents shall be valid for all states and regions and shall record the holder's right to return to the Region.

The Government of the Hong Kong Special Administrative Region may apply immigration controls on entry into, stay in and departure from the Region by persons from foreign states and regions.

**Article 155** The Central People's Government shall assist or authorize the Government of the Hong Kong Special Administrative Region to conclude visa abolition agreements with foreign states or regions.

**Article 156** The Hong Kong Special Administrative Region may, as necessary, establish official or semi-official economic and trade missions in foreign countries and shall report the establishment of such missions to the Central People's Government for the record.

**Article 157** The establishment of foreign consular and other official or semi-official missions in the Hong Kong Special Administrative Region shall require the approval of the Central People's Government.

Consular and other official missions established in Hong Kong by states which have formal diplomatic relations with the People's Republic of China may be maintained.

According to the circumstances of each case, consular and other official missions established in Hong Kong by states which have no formal diplomatic relations with the People's Republic of China may be permitted either to remain or be changed to semi-official missions.

States not recognized by the People's Republic of China may only establish non governmental institutions in the Region.

CHAPTER VIII: INTERPRETATION AND AMENDMENT OF
THE BASIC LAW

**Article 158** The power of interpretation of this Law shall be vested in the Standing Committee of the National People's Congress.

The Standing Committee of the National People's Congress shall authorize the courts of the Hong Kong Special Administrative Region to interpret on their own, in adjudicating cases, the provisions of this Law which are within the limits of the autonomy of the Region.

The courts of the Hong Kong Special Administrative Region may also interpret other provisions of this Law in adjudicating cases. However, if the courts of the Region, in adjudicating cases, need to interpret the provisions of this Law concerning affairs which are the responsibility of the Central People's Government, or concerning the relationship between the Central Authorities and the Region, and if such interpretation will affect the judgments on the cases, the courts of the Region shall, before making their final judgments which are not appealable, seek an interpretation of the relevant provisions from the Standing Committee of the National People's Congress through the Court of Final Appeal of the Region. When the Standing Committee makes an interpretation of the provisions concerned, the courts of the Region, in applying those provisions, shall follow the interpretation of the Standing Committee. However, judgments previously rendered shall not be affected.

The Standing Committee of the National People's Congress shall consult its Committee for the Basic Law of the Hong Kong Special Administrative Region before giving an interpretation of this Law.

**Article 159** The power of amendment of this Law shall be vested in the National People's Congress.

The power to propose bills for amendments to this Law shall be vested in the Standing Committee of the National People's Congress, the State Council and the Hong Kong Special Administrative Region. Amendment bills from the Hong Kong Special Administrative Region shall be submitted to the National People's Congress by the delegation of the Region to the National People's Congress after obtaining the consent of two-thirds of the deputies of the Region to the National People's Congress, two-thirds of all the members of the Legislative Council of the Region, and the Chief Executive of the Region.

Before a bill for amendment to this Law is put on the agenda of the National People's Congress, the Committee for the Basic Law of the Hong Kong Special Administrative Region shall study it and submit its views.

No amendment to this Law shall contravene the established basic policies of the People's Republic of China regarding Hong Kong.

CHAPTER IX: SUPPLEMENTARY PROVISIONS

**Article 160** Upon the establishment of the Hong Kong Special Administrative Region, the laws previously in force in Hong Kong shall be adopted as laws of the Region except for those which the Standing Committee of the National People's Congress declares to be in contravention of this Law. If any laws are later discovered to be in contravention of this Law, they shall be amended or cease to have force in accordance with the procedure as prescribed by this Law.

Documents, certificates, contracts, and rights and obligations valid under the laws previously in force in Hong Kong shall continue to be valid and be recognized and protected by the Hong Kong Special Administrative Region, provided that they do not contravene this Law.

## ANNEX I: METHOD FOR THE SELECTION OF THE CHIEF EXECUTIVE OF THE HONG KONG SPECIAL ADMINISTRATIVE REGION

1. The Chief Executive shall be elected by a broadly representative Election Committee in accordance with this Law and appointed by the Central People's Government.

2. The Election Committee shall be composed of 800 members from the following sectors:

| | |
|---|---|
| Industrial, commercial and financial sectors | 200 |
| The professions | 200 |
| Labour, social services, religious and other sectors | 200 |
| Members of the Legislative Council, representatives of district-based organizations, Hong Kong deputies to the National People's Congress, and representatives of Hong Kong members of the National Committee of the Chinese People's Political Consultative Conference | 200 |

The term of office of the Election Committee shall be five years.

3. The delimitation of the various sectors, the organizations in each sector eligible to return Election Committee members and the number of such members returned by each of these organizations shall be prescribed by an electoral law enacted by the Hong Kong Special Administrative Region in accordance with the principles of democracy and openness.

Corporate bodies in various sectors shall, on their own, elect members to the Election Committee, in accordance with the number of seats allocated and the election method as prescribed by the electoral law.

Members of the Election Committee shall vote in their individual capacities.

4. Candidates for the office of Chief Executive may be nominated jointly by not less than 100 members of the Election Committee. Each member may nominate only one candidate.

5. The Election Committee shall, on the basis of the list of nominees, elect the Chief Executive designate by secret ballot on a one-person-one-vote basis. The specific election method shall be prescribed by the electoral law.

6. The first Chief Executive shall be selected in accordance with the 'Decision of the National People's Congress on the Method for the Formation of the First Government and the First Legislative Council of the Hong Kong Special Administrative Region'.

7. If there is a need to amend the method for selecting the Chief Executives for the terms subsequent to the year 2007, such amendments must be made with the endorsement of a two-thirds majority of all the members of the Legislative Council and the consent of the Chief Executive, and they shall be reported to the Standing Committee of the National People's Congress for approval.

## ANNEX II: METHOD FOR THE FORMATION OF THE LEGISLATIVE COUNCIL OF THE HONG KONG SPECIAL ADMINISTRATIVE REGION AND ITS VOTING PROCEDURES

### I. Method for the formation of the Legislative Council

1. The Legislative Council of the Hong Kong Special Administrative Region shall be composed of 60 members in each term. In the first term, the Legislative Council shall be formed in accordance with the 'Decision of the National People's Congress on the Method for the Formation of the First Government and the First Legislative Council of the Hong Kong Special Administrative Region'. The composition of the Legislative Council in the second and third terms shall be as follows:

Second term
| | |
|---|---|
| Members returned by functional constituencies | 30 |
| Members returned by the Election Committee | 6 |
| Members returned by geographical constituencies through direct elections | 24 |

Third term
| | |
|---|---|
| Members returned by functional constituencies | 30 |
| Members returned by geographical constituencies through direct elections | 30 |

2. Except in the case of the first Legislative Council, the above-mentioned Election Committee refers to the one provided for in Annex I of this Law. The division of geographical constituencies and the voting method for direct elections therein; the delimitation of functional sectors and corporate bodies, their seat allocation and election methods; and the method for electing members of the Legislative Council by the Election Committee shall be specified by an electoral law introduced by the Government of the Hong Kong Special Administrative Region and passed by the Legislative Council.

### II. Procedures for voting on bills and motions in the Legislative Council

Unless otherwise provided for in this Law, the Legislative Council shall adopt the following procedures for voting on bills and motions:

The passage of bills introduced by the government shall require at least a simple majority vote of the members of the Legislative Council present.

The passage of motions, bills or amendments to government bills introduced by individual members of the Legislative Council shall require a simple majority vote of each of the two groups of members present: members returned by functional constituencies and those returned by geographical constituencies through direct elections and by the Election Committee.

### III. Method for the formation of the Legislative Council and its voting procedures subsequent to the year 2007

With regard to the method for forming the Legislative Council of the Hong Kong Special Administrative Region and its procedures for voting on bills and motions after 2007, if there is a need to amend the provisions of this Annex, such amendments must be made with the endorsement of a two-thirds majority of all the members of the Council and the consent of the Chief Executive, and they shall be reported to the Standing Committee of the National People's Congress for the record.

## ANNEX III: NATIONAL LAWS TO BE APPLIED IN THE HONG KONG SPECIAL ADMINISTRATIVE REGION

The following national laws shall be applied locally with effect from 1 July 1997 by way of promulgation or legislation by the Hong Kong Special Administrative Region:

1. Resolution on the Capital, Calendar, National Anthem and National Flag of the People's Republic of China

2. Resolution on the National Day of the People's Republic of China

3. Order on the National Emblem of the People's Republic of China Proclaimed by the Central People's Government

4. Declaration of the Government of the People's Republic of China on the Territorial Sea

5. Nationality Law of the People's Republic of China

6. Regulations of the People's Republic of China Concerning Diplomatic Privileges and Immunities

## DECISION OF THE NATIONAL PEOPLE'S CONGRESS ON THE METHOD FOR THE FORMATION OF THE FIRST GOVERNMENT AND THE FIRST LEGISLATIVE COUNCIL OF THE HONG KONG SPECIAL ADMINISTRATIVE REGION

*Adopted at the Third Session of the VII National People's Congress on 4 April 1990*

1. The first Government and the first Legislative Council of the Hong Kong Special Administrative Region shall be formed in accordance with the principles of state sovereignty and smooth transition.

2. Within the year 1996, the National People's Congress shall establish a Preparatory Committee for the Hong Kong Special Administrative Region, which shall be responsible for preparing the establishment of the Region and shall prescribe the specific method for forming the first Government and the first Legislative Council in accordance with this Decision. The Preparatory Committee shall be composed of mainland members and of Hong Kong members who shall constitute not less than 50 per cent of its membership. Its chairman and members shall be appointed by the Standing Committee of the National People's Congress.

3. The Preparatory Committee for the Hong Kong Special Administrative Region shall be responsible for preparing the establishment of the Selection

Committee for the First Government of the Hong Kong Special Administrative Region (the 'Selection Committee').

The Selection Committee shall be composed entirely of permanent residents of Hong Kong and must be broadly representative. It shall include Hong Kong deputies to the National People's Congress, representatives of Hong Kong members of the National Committee of the Chinese People's Political Consultative Conference, persons with practical experience who have served in Hong Kong's executive, legislative and advisory organs prior to the establishment of the Hong Kong Special Administrative Region, and persons representative of various strata and sectors of society.

The Selection Committee shall be composed of 400 members in the following proportions:

| | |
|---|---|
| Industrial, commercial and financial sectors | 25 per cent |
| The professions | |
| Labour, grassroots, religious and other sectors | 25 per cent |
| Former political figures, Hong Kong deputies to the National People's Congress, and representatives of Hong Kong members of the National Committee of the Chinese People's Political Consultative Conference | 25 per cent |

4. The Selection Committee shall recommend the candidate for the first Chief Executive through local consultations or through nomination and election after consultations, and report the recommended candidate to the Central People's Government for appointment. The term of office of the first Chief Executive shall be the same as the regular term.

5. The Chief Executive of the Hong Kong Special Administrative Region shall be responsible for preparing the formation of the first Government of the Region in accordance with this Law.

6. The first Legislative Council of the Hong Kong Special Administrative Region shall be composed of 60 members, with 20 members returned by geographical constituencies through direct elections, 10 members returned by an election committee, and 30 members returned by functional constituencies. If the composition of the last Hong Kong Legislative Council before the establishment of the Hong Kong Special Administrative Region is in conformity with the relevant provisions of this Decision and the Basic Law of the Hong Kong Special Administrative Region, those of its members who uphold the Basic Law of the Hong Kong Special Administrative Region of the People's Republic of China and pledge allegiance to the Hong Kong Special Administrative Region of the People's Republic of China, and who meet the requirements set forth in the Basic Law of the Region may, upon confirmation by the Preparatory Committee, become members of the first Legislative Council of the Region.

The term of office of members of the first Legislative Council of the Hong Kong Special Administrative Region shall be two years.

Source: People's Republic of China, 1992. *The Basic Law of the Hong Kong Special Administrative Region of the People's Republic of China* (Hong Kong).

# Appendix 6: The die is cast

## What WILL CHANGE

- **Business:** Mainland companies will increase their share of the local economy
- **Military:** Chinese gunboats will be docked in the harbour and PLA troops stationed in the business district
- **Media:** Local and foreign journals will be monitored closely
- **Politics:** The current elected legislature will be dismantled and replaced by a provisional legislature
- **Language:** Chinese will become more and more common in the courts and civil service

## What WON'T CHANGE

- **Financial status:** Hong Kong will still play a pivotal role as a global financial centre
- **Monetary policy:** Beijing says it won't de-link the Hong Kong currency from the US dollar
- **Borders:** The Hong Kong–China crossing at Shenzhen will remain tightly controlled
- **Entry:** The number of Chinese allowed to enter Hong Kong will continue to be restricted
- **Second-class status:** Major decisions relating to foreign affairs and defence will be taken over Hong Kong's head – but in Beijing rather than London

## What's UP FOR GRABS

- **Law:** Courts could lose their independence
- **Order:** Crime and corruption could skyrocket
- **Taxes:** Rates could shoot up
- **Favouritism:** Government contracts could veer towards mainland firms
- **Freedoms:** Consular protection could be denied to Hong Kong Chinese holding foreign passports
- **Politics:** The pace of democratization towards a fully elected legislature and elected chief executive is undecided
- **Education:** School curriculum could be changed; textbooks are already being revised

Hong Kong won't be quite the same after the 1997 handover
Source: *Far Eastern Economic Review*, 7 December 1995.

# Appendix 7: The first chief executive of the SAR

On 11 December 1996 Tung Chee-hwa (C.H. Tung) was elected the first chief executive of the Special Administrative Region of Hong Kong. Following the overwhelming vote of a hand-picked 400-member Chinese selection committee, Tung began preparations for assuming office on 1 July 1997 by visiting Governor Patten and then flying to Beijing to meet his future overlords.

Tung, who comfortably defeated two rival candidates, argued that his election was unprecedented in Hong Kong's history. With this stage-managed endorsement Tung, the most conservative, pro-business and closest to Beijing of the contestants, could now claim to have a mandate of sorts to oversee the transition era.

He started by reassuring the territory that Anson Chan, the present chief secretary, would remain in her post after the transfer of sovereignty. His insistence, however, on maintaining the Chinese-sponsored Provision Legislature has disappointed many in the territory. It follows that Chris Patten's elected LegCo will be dissolved immediately after the SAR is inaugurated and that the 60-member Provisional Legislature (boycotted and subject to challenge from Hong Kong's Democratic Party) will remain in power for a year pending fresh elections. Anxiety is also widespread over clear restrictions on freedom of speech, assembly and demonstrations that will now follow, as ordered by the PRC, once Tung and his tame Provisional Legislature takes over. Official British protests at these limitations on human rights were dismissed as 'totally unreasonable' by the Chinese foreign ministry. Not surprisingly, Governor Patten could only claim to be 'cautiously optimistic' over the future of his ward. News of the death of China's paramount leader Deng Xiaoping on 19 February was received calmly in the territory, but it would take some time before the new leadership in Beijing under President Jiang Zemin could consolidate its hold on power. It was not felt likely that major shifts in established policies for Hong Kong would alter in the short-term, although much, as always, would depend on circumstances beyond the territory's control. Massive international attention on the territory was now both recognition indeed of the rise of Hong Kong and concern for its fate after 1997.

# Select bibliography

This merely lists a few of the books on Hong Kong that I have found helpful. Most are in paperback. General works on Britain, the People's Republic of China and the Asian–Pacific region have been excluded.

Birch, Alan, 1991. *The Colony that Never Was* (Hong Kong)

Cheng, Joseph Y.S. and Lo, Sonny S.H. (eds.), 1995. *From Colony to SAR* (Hong Kong)

Cheng, Tong-yung, 1982. *The Economy of Hong Kong* (Hong Kong)

China, People's Republic of, 1992. *The Basic Law of the Hong Kong Special Administrative Region of the People's Republic of China* (Hong Kong)

Cottrell, Robert, 1993. *The End of Hong Kong* (London)

Cradock, Percy, 1994. *Experiences of China* (London)

Davis, Michael C., 1989. *Constitutional Confrontation in Hong Kong* (Basingstoke)

Deng Xiaoping, 1993. *On the Question of Hong Kong* (Hong Kong)

Dwyer, D.J. (ed.), 1971. *Asian Urbanization: A Hong Kong Casebook* (Hong Kong)

Endacott, G.B., 1965. *A History of Hong Kong* (Hong Kong)

Faure, David (ed.), 1995. *History of Hong Kong* (Hong Kong)

Freris, Andrew F., 1991. *The Financial Markets of Hong Kong* (London)

Grantham, Sir Alexander, 1965. *Via Ports* (Hong Kong)

Harris, Peter,1988. *Hong Kong: A Study in Bureaucracy and Politics* (Hong Kong)

Hayes, James, 1983. *The Rural Communities of Hong Kong* (Hong Kong)

Hong Kong, Chinese University, annual. *The Other Hong Kong Report* (Hong Kong)

Hong Kong, Government, annual. *Hong Kong Yearbook* (Hong Kong)

King, Frank H.H., 1987–91. *The History of the Hongkong and Shanghai Banking Corporation,* 4 vols. (Cambridge)

Lau Siu-kai, 1991. *Society and Politics in Hong Kong* (Hong Kong)

Leung, Benjamin K.P. and Wong, Teresa Y.C. (eds.), 1994. *25 Years of Social and Economic Development in Hong Kong* (Hong Kong)

Lo, T. Wing, 1993. *Corruption and Politics in Hong Kong and China* (Buckingham)

Miners, Norman, 1995. *The Government and Politics of Hong Kong* (Hong Kong)

Mo, Timothy, 1978. *The Monkey King* (London)

Roberti, Mark, 1994. *The Fall of Hong Kong* (New York)

Roberts, Elfed Vaughan *et al.* (eds.), (1992).*Historical Dictionary of Hong Kong and Macao* (Metuchen, NJ)

Scott, Ian, 1989. *Political Change and the Crisis of Legitimacy in Hong Kong* (London)

Shambaugh, David (ed.), 1995. *Greater China: The Next Superpower?* (Oxford)

Thatcher, Margaret, 1993. *The Downing Street Years* (London)

Tsai, Jung-Fang, 1993. *Hong Kong in Chinese History: Community and Social Unrest in the British Colony, 1842–1913* (New York)

Tsang, Steve Yui-Sang, 1988. *Democracy Shelved: Great Britain, China and Attempts at Constitutional Reform in Hong Kong, 1945–1952* (Hong Kong)

Wacks, Raymond (ed.), 1989. *Future of the Law in Hong Kong* (Hong Kong)

Walden, John, 1987. *Excellency, Your Gap is Growing* (Hong Kong)

Wang, Enbao, 1995. *Hong Kong, 1997* (Boulder, CO)

Wang, Gungwu and Wong Siu-lun (eds.), 1995. *Hong Kong's Transition* (Hong Kong)

Welsh, Frank, 1993. *A History of Hong Kong* (London)

Wesley-Smith, Peter, 1989. *An Introduction to the Hong Kong Legal System* (Hong Kong)

# Index